D0421811

LOVING EDIE

Also by Meredith May

The Honey Bus

LOVING EDIE

HOW A DOG AFRAID OF EVERYTHING TAUGHT ME TO BE BRAVE

MEREDITH MAY

PARK ROW BOOKS

PARK
ROW™
BOOKS™

Recycling programs
for this product may
not exist in your area.

ISBN-13: 978-0-7783-1202-4

Loving Edie: How a Dog Afraid of Everything Taught Me to Be Brave

Copyright © 2022 by Meredith May

All rights reserved. No part of this book may be used or reproduced in any manner whatsoever without written permission except in the case of brief quotations embodied in critical articles and reviews.

This publication contains opinions and ideas of the author. It is intended for informational and educational purposes only. The reader should seek the services of a competent professional for expert assistance or professional advice. Reference to any organization, publication or website does not constitute or imply an endorsement by the author or the publisher. The author and the publisher specifically disclaim any and all liability arising directly or indirectly from the use or application of any information contained in this publication.

Park Row Books
22 Adelaide St. West, 41st Floor
Toronto, Ontario M5H 4E3, Canada
ParkRowBooks.com
BookClubbish.com

Printed in U.S.A.

For Jenn

Disclaimer

Some names of the people who appear in this book have been changed to protect identities.

CONTENTS

Dogs have a way of finding the people who need them, filling an emptiness we don't even know we have.

—Thom Jones, "Saying Goodbye to Shelby" (2003)

PROLOGUE

Fear makes me feel alive. They call my kind of people adrenaline chasers, those who flirt with danger for the exquisite, specific euphoria that comes from relying on your wits to survive.

I first felt this rush at four years old. Grandpa was visiting from California, and when he asked my mother if he could take me to the beach near our home in Rhode Island, she gave her permission but with one caveat.

"She doesn't know how to swim," she warned Grandpa. "So don't let her go in the water."

Grandpa and I stood on the shore, he in Levi's cutoffs and me in my bathing suit, watching the waves roll toward us and crash into fizzy foam. The waves were small, rising only to his waist, but that meant they were at my shoulders. He looked at me and wriggled his eyebrows. I smiled back. We counted to three and ran full force toward the water.

Following Grandpa's movements, I dove headfirst into the wave break and immediately got spun around and slammed into the sand. I came up sputtering and disoriented, and he put me on his knee, and explained how to look into the distance at the incoming waves, to read their rhythm and anticipate their arrival. Then he taught me to wait until I felt the tug of the undertow, to turn my back and get in position, then lift my feet and ride the swell all the way in. He demonstrated, holding me by the waist and letting a wave propel us to shore. Bodysurfing felt like flying.

Conquering the sea made me feel invincible and started me on a lifelong quest for heart-pumping exhilaration. By age seven I was on a diving team, somersaulting off the three-meter board with that young person's trust that nothing could ever hurt me. I grew into the teenager who adored scary movies, whose idea of a good time involved either skydiving, white-water rafting, or bungee jumping. It comes as no surprise that I landed in a career with inherent danger. I became a newspaper journalist, the one who runs toward the wildfire, the war zone, the protest, to bear witness.

For half a century, fear has been my life coach, motivating me to squeeze every drop out of each day. And all this time, I've yet to break a bone or scare myself beyond my limit. Fear has never betrayed me.

Until it did. Until my fearlessness was consumed by one tiny, helpless golden retriever puppy who was *very, very, very* scared.

1

Just Right

From my airplane window I can see the San Francisco morning commute at its usual standstill, but from this high up it's almost beautiful, the headlights outlining the knot of overpasses like one massive, twinkling, macramé.

As long as the plane stays in the air, we're still on vacation, I think to myself, clinging to the last tendrils of New Zealand before real life clomps back in. Next to me my wife is sleeping, her head tipped back with her mouth slightly open, and she's making that little exhale-puff-snore thing she does. We've been in the air for thirteen hours, and she's been out for approximately twelve of them. I've never seen her this restful.

Jenn, the taker-of-middle-seats; Jenn, the eater of any meal placed before her; Jenn the giver of coats when I forget mine. After five years of marriage, she has yet to raise her voice to me. I can't claim the same restraint, yet somehow, she forgives each and every one of my hissy fits, using verbal judo to talk me down before we ever make it to an actual argument. My agreeable wife, when asked what she wanted to do for her fiftieth birthday, said she didn't want to make a fuss over it. When pressed, she suggested a simple dinner, maybe the wood-fired roasted chicken at Zuni Café, where we had our first date. I suggested we fly to the other side of the world, shut off our phones, and disappear for a month.

Okay, she'd said.

We arrived in Auckland in early November 2018 with the sketchiest of itineraries, rented a twenty-five-foot motor home meant for six, and drove from the top of the country to the southernmost tip, counting more sheep than people. I chauffeured so Jenn could lean out the passenger window to snap photos of said sheep with her film camera. Our whim dictated our route, and we relied on an app that connects travelers with Kiwis who allow camper vans to park on their farms. We marveled at how *nice* everybody was—making us meals and lending their bicycles, showing us how to bottle-feed their lambs, and driving us to caves not found in tourist guides to see glowworms for free.

With each day, our urban shield of stranger distrust thinned a bit more. New Zealand reminded us that there are still places where people don't have to compete for everything— for apartments, for parking spaces, for school admissions, for angel investors, for tables in restaurants. With enough room to breathe in New Zealand, people had the serenity to be authentically kind.

Jenn awakes with a snort and her eyes flick open. Still in the fug of sleep, she quickly scans her surroundings, unsure of where she is.

"We're descending," I say, slipping my hand into hers and giving it a squeeze. She looks at the pulsating city below and the worry lines reappear on her forehead. I can tell she's thinking about work—most likely the stack of crime reports piling up on her desk at the police station. Lately there's been a rash of girl packs rushing luxury boutiques in Union Square, fleeing with whatever designer clothes they can snatch in seconds. Jenn feels bad for the shop owners who can't defend themselves against the raids, but also for the girls, some as young as eleven, who will exchange their futures for a Louis Vuitton purse. It's a crime she never could have imagined investigating when she joined the force twenty-three years ago. The city has hardened since she was a wide-eyed recruit.

"Quick...tell me your favorite part of the trip," I say to distract her. "First thing that comes to mind."

"Eating meat pies in the RV at night," she says.

An invisible sunbeam enters my heart. She didn't say snorkeling in a pod of wild dolphins in the open ocean, or tasting manuka honey straight from a beekeeper's hive, not even kayaking through fjords dripping with waterfalls. No—eating dinner squeezed into the motor home dinette, with me. She chose our relationship ritual that's most precious to her: every night we shake the day off, sit down to a hot meal, and talk.

As a cop wife, I can't ever fully understand what traumas she absorbs at work as Lieutenant Jackson, but what I do know is that first responders need a soft place to land at the end of the day. I know this because during the first year of our marriage, Jenn asked me to read a book she brought home from a conference on policing and mental health. It was written for spouses, and for the first time I started to understand why my wife can't make simple decisions at home like what to eat for dinner or what to watch on Netflix. After a full day of split-second, high-stress decision-making, her brain needs to recharge. I learned that firefighters, emergency room workers, and police who absorb constant stress on the job have a better chance of surviving their careers, emotionally and physically, if they have routine at home.

I finished the book, downloaded the *New York Times* cooking app, and instituted our family of two ritual: every day at 4:00 p.m. I lift my fingers off the keyboard, put on an apron, tune the stereo to the local jazz station, and start slinging pots and pans. No matter what goes down during the day, Jenn knows she'll come home to the aroma of dinner, a saxophone softly grooving, and her wife in an ironic '50s apron pouring her a glass of wine. Even when we were in New Zealand with adventure as our goal, it was the unbroken routine of home that she loved the most.

"Yeah, me too," I say.

"Oh, come on, you were going to say the dolphins."

"Okay, yeah, I was," I say, laughing at what a beautiful disaster that outing turned out to be. The seas were so rough that half the tourists on the boat, including me and Jenn, were heaving into plastic buckets. Even so, somersaulting and squealing underwater with a curious pod of dusky dolphins was my recurring dream come to life, one of those shimmery moments when another species allowed me a fleeting glimpse into their world. I was not going to let a little seasickness get in my way. Poor Jenn couldn't uncurl herself from a fetal position to get in the water. But she endured the ill-fated voyage because she knew how much it meant to me.

The plane's landing gear engages with a whine, and we touch down with a few screeching hops until the reverse

thrusters slow us to a stop. The pilot comes on the overhead
speaker to tell us all the gates are occupied so we're going to
sit on the tarmac for a bit. I feel hairline fissures crack through
my tranquility. I'm dreading the quiet that's waiting for us at
home. The awful silence of a home without a dog.

It's been almost a year since we had to put down my twelve-
year-old golden retriever, Stella, and every morning when I
wake, I still look toward the corner where she used to sleep,
not fully remembering that she's gone. Although Jenn and
I have talked casually about getting a puppy at some point,
whenever I bring it up, Jenn deflects. She says she's still in
mourning. Or that she wants to enjoy our freedom just a little
bit longer. She tells me to slow down a bit, and wait until we
are really, truly ready to take care of another dog.

So I wait. But I feel wrong without a dog by my side. In my
grandpa's house in Carmel Valley where I grew up, there was
always a terrier or dachshund trailing Grandpa's heels. When
I left for Mills College in Oakland, my doglessness was re-
solved by my crew coach's cattle dog, a stray that swam up to
her motorboat in the predawn dark during practice, attracted
to the safety lights on our rowing shells. She pulled the dog
out of the water and named it Briones on the spot, after the
8.5-square-mile reservoir where we trained. Briones never left
her side, riding shotgun in the coaching launch during every
practice. Briones was the perfect stand-in for all the rowers
who missed their family dogs, and dutifully took on the role
of team mascot, attending all our regattas and group dinners.

After graduation I lived in various illegally converted base-
ment apartments with roommates, the cheapest rent I could
find in the Bay Area on my starting newspaper reporter's sal-
ary. Not an ideal living situation for a dog, so I had to devise

creative ways to get my dog fix. I spent a lot of time at my colleague Kendra's, the only woman on the newspaper photo staff, who, at six feet tall, stood her ground literally and figuratively among her coworkers. She could shoot a photo, and shoot the shit, with the best of them. From the very first time we were sent on an assignment to document a spate of drive-by cow shootings in a rural part of the Bay Area, I knew we'd be friends. She had moxie, striding right up to wary cattle ranchers for interviews and photos. I was fascinated by this bold woman who put her art at the top of her personal pyramid scale and surrounded herself with creatives. She rented a large home with a handful of artists—graphic designers, performers, and musicians—who loved throwing dance parties so they could dress up in colorful wigs and glittery costumes. Kendra lived inside an art incubator, where she and her roommates spent their free time building art installations for the annual summer Burning Man Festival in the Nevada desert. I was drawn to Kendra's house, where it was like taking a crash course in how to be cool. I listened to bootleg tapes of San Francisco's hottest underground house DJs, and received lessons in the proper way to apply body paint.

I befriended all the dogs that lived there, too, but my secret favorite was Neal, a tall, narrow-shouldered, red-haired golden retriever and extreme snuggler. Before leaving Kendra's house, I always made sure to take a quick power nap on the bed with Neal, in his favorite position with his forehead in my armpit and an arm and leg over me as I lay on my back. When I stroked his fur, it felt like he was wearing a silk kimono.

When I was finally able to afford shared rent on a home with a backyard in the East Bay, Kendra called. She said she knew of a four-year-old golden retriever that had been abandoned in a divorce and needed a home. Because of my fondness for Neal, she immediately thought of me. I, too, had been abandoned by divorce, and left in the care of my grandparents just before my fifth birthday. Of course I would save this discarded soul.

A van showed up outside my home, and a woman opened the back doors and pulled out a grossly obese dog by a rope around its neck and handed Layla over. I would later learn that the poor thing was left alone in a backyard, and a neighbor felt so bad she'd toss over entire loaves of bread for Layla to eat. After diet and exercise, Layla returned to a healthy seventy-two pounds and became my hiking buddy. She lived to eleven, and her parting gift to me was the certainty that life is better with a dog in it. Within three months of her passing, I went to a golden retriever breeder and picked out Stella when she was eight weeks old.

Now I have the same urge to run out and get a new puppy again. I've spent the last nineteen years with a golden retriever by my side, and now, without one, I feel like I'm missing a limb.

Jenn isn't so sure. Stella was the first dog Jenn had ever lived with, part of a package deal when I moved into her home. Although my dog and my wife had just five years of cohabitation, they had a special connection, often disappearing together on long walks to have private conversations about who knows what. I know not to pry. While she learned to love my dog, Jenn isn't sure she wants to raise a puppy. But I'm trying to be patient. Jenn has her reasons, and I'm hoping she'll come around in her own time.

Stella was such an easy dog to love—she could walk without a leash on bustling San Francisco sidewalks without ever leaving our sides, stopping at the intersections to wait for the command to cross. Stella came running when called, sat politely before people to greet them, and waited for us to wake before getting out of her own bed. She rarely barked, didn't hop on furniture, and would ignore a piece of bacon on the floor until given permission to approach. She loved swimming in the ocean, chasing tennis balls, going to the vet, and knew no other setting than euphoric. She believed people were put on earth to adore her and walked with a cockiness in her stride like a little Mayor-of-Everywhere, introducing herself to every dog or human she encountered, confident she'd secure their vote. She often woke herself up from a pleasant dream with the sound of her own happy tail madly thumping the wooden floor. Just being with Stella made the world less prickly.

After her eleventh birthday, she began to stumble on the hardwood floors. We bought booties with rubber soles that steadied her for about a year, until we had to add yoga mats around the house to give her even more traction. Then the inevitable day came when Stella couldn't muster the energy to walk, and we had to carry her into the pet hospital. We were ushered into a private room, where we sat on the carpet and draped our dog across our laps as the vet gave her the injections that stopped her heart. I sang into Stella's ear until her breath stopped, and when it did, I felt something fuse between Jenn and me, like our hearts scarred over the same wound. Stella began her life as my dog, but over the years she had worked her way into Jenn's life, too.

Which I think surprised her a little bit. When I first scrolled through Jenn's profile on Match.com in 2009, she had checked cat under the question *Are you a dog or cat person?* I was worried that we might not get along because "cat person" can be code for dog dislike. At the time I was living with Stella in the bottom flat of a two-story Victorian in Noe Valley owned by my friends Barbara and Mag. They lived upstairs, and our homes were connected by an outdoor spiral staircase that overlooked a terraced garden with fountains. Barbara had a Cardigan Welsh corgi named Toby, whose black-and-white markings made it look like he was wearing an itty-bitty tuxedo, and Mag owned Phoebe, a scraggly, salt-and-pepper bow-legged hound of ancient, but undetermined age with the Greyest of Poupon breed names: Petit Basset Griffon Vendéen. The apartments had identical dog doors, and our pets had their own visitation schedules, coming and going between the two flats at will, stealing dog toys and slippers that we returned in a rope-pull dumbwaiter that traveled between our units. The dogs were a joyful whirlwind underfoot that stirred up the chi in our homes. If a Match.com date couldn't handle sharing my living space with dogs swirling about, it would be a deal breaker.

But when Jenn showed up on my doorstep wearing a porkpie hat and a bow tie, carrying flowers for me and a stuffed pig with Velcro pull-apart limbs for Stella, she aced both our tests. The three of us quickly fell into a routine, walking different routes on the steep inclines of our neighborhood, but always ending up at Spike's Coffee in the Castro, where Stella was greeted by a klatch of regulars, each with a dog under their café table and treats in their pockets. We took Stella with us on beach picnics, to the weekend roller disco in Golden Gate Park, and to our favorite French restaurant, which allowed dogs on its outdoor patio.

That pull-apart pig was the only stuffed toy Stella didn't eventually disembowel. She had a special fondness for it, forever clutching one of its limbs in her mouth like a talisman, even dragging it into her bed at night. Stella seemed to have a premonition about Jenn, as if she knew Jenn was *the one*. It took me about a year to see what Stella sensed immediately. Compared to the high adrenaline artists and athletes I'd been dating, Jenn was so consistent and kind she almost bored me. I'd always gravitated toward aloof women who made me work to earn their love because that's what I knew best, having spent my childhood trying to entice my depressed mother to pay attention to me. These lovers were capricious with their affection, but the game of trying to get it felt as achingly familiar as an addiction.

Stella cuddled various appendages of that pull-apart pig as she patiently waited for me to come around. It finally happened, nearly a year later, when Jenn took me on a date to a chocolate bar. By then I'd discovered Jenn was an unapologetic dessert person, which was difficult for me because I avoided most sugary things in a nonstop effort to stay trim. But after telling me in so many different ways that she found me beautiful, I was starting to develop a kinder body image. Plus Jenn had a Groupon.

The chocolate bar was a small hole-in-the-wall, with room for no more than a long white counter and eight stools. The chocolatier poured Mayan drinking chocolate with chili into diminutive espresso cups and slid them before us. Jenn took a sip and unconsciously started bouncing on her stool in kid-like pleasure, which I found kind of adorable. We chatted about our weekend plans, and I asked about her upcoming half-marathon through Golden Gate Park. Jenn ran with an all-women's team named The Iguanas, which was the laidback counterpart to the San Francisco women's team for serious athletes, The Impalas.

"I'm not going for a record. I just like the run itself."

It was hard for my rower's brain to grasp the concept of competition-free sport. I swiveled to face this placid woman and inquired, "Why race if it's not to win?"

"I consider myself lucky just to be walking."

I put my cup down. I sensed she wanted to tell me something serious, something private.

Jenn remembers the wind that day. She had spent the morning painting in her kindergarten class and when school let out, walked toward her bus stop as usual. She was in the crosswalk when a gust blew her artwork out of her hands. She ran after it.

The next thing she remembers is waking up in a hospital with a nun in a wide black habit peering down at her. Jenn had suffered a hairline fracture to her skull, and her legs were bandaged, held aloft by pulleys and wires suspended from the ceiling. She'd later learn that when the car hit her, it didn't stop right away, and her legs had been pulled around the rear axle. Jenn had remained unconscious for several hours after the accident, and doctors initially told Jenn's mother that they didn't expect Jenn to survive. But she did. Jenn remained with her legs in traction for a month, until she was put in a body cast that covered her from the waist down. When the cast was removed several months later, doctors told her mother they weren't sure if Jenn would ever walk normally again. Her family could not afford physical therapy.

"I remember lying on the sofa, staring at the coffee table. And I got the idea that if I held on, maybe I could walk around it. It hurt like hell, but I tried a little bit every day until finally I could do it. I just kept going around and around, clutching that table."

Jenn became a miracle to me in that moment. I fell in love with her in that chocolate bar, awestruck by the resilience she'd had to develop at five, and how it carried her through to adulthood, when she's not only walking, but running marathons. Jenn was no longer boring to me. Suddenly her quiet strength was more exciting than any flashy romance with a sometimes girlfriend.

Three years after that chocolate tasting, Stella and I moved our things into Jenn's house, including the pull-apart pig. A year later, in 2013, I had a platinum wedding band secretly made for Jenn with a diamond and three blue sapphires—police colors—embedded in it. I invited our friends Maile and Eddy to a Valentine's Day dinner and told them I was going to propose during dessert. They sat across from us and hid their cameras on their laps under the table. I had a beautiful speech prepared, but my nerves and the wine conspired to steal the script. Jenn was mid–crème brûlée when I clumsily handed her the velvet box and sputtered out something about wanting to get married and spend the rest of my life with her.

"Whaaaaat?" Jenn said, crinkling her nose. "It's not even legal."

Not the response I was hoping for. Technically, she was correct. A scattering of states allowed same-sex marriage, but California wasn't one of them, still embroiled in legal debate after opponents in 2008 forced the state to stop issuing marriage licenses to gay couples only five months after it began. But momentum was building for marriage equality once again.

"It's going to happen any minute, so we'll be ready when it does," I said, feeling the air seeping out of my romantic gesture. I heard the shutters on Eddy's and Maile's cameras slowing down, as they backed off, sensing a potentially awkward moment that we might not want documented.

Then Jenn started giggling. She covered her face with her palms to hide her laughter. She wasn't used to being the center of attention, and was embarrassed by my public declaration of love, and undoubtedly, by being put on the spot. It only occurred to me then that it probably wasn't the smartest move to set up an ambush for a wedding proposal. I didn't even give her an opportunity to say no. She lifted her head and looked at the three of us with a bemused smile, then said, "Pssssssssssshhhh. Okay!"

Turns out she wasn't just being polite, because she didn't retract her answer once we got home or in the weeks afterward. And turns out we were on the right side of history. A little more than a month after my clumsy marriage proposal, California began allowing couples like us to marry. We had a simple ceremony, with about forty people gathered in the mayor's balcony inside San Francisco city hall with my rowing teammate Ken presiding in a Utilikilt and brocaded vest that accentuated his muscles. Afterward we had lunch on Forbes Island at Fisherman's Wharf, an actual floating island with sand and palm trees above the water and a restaurant below the surface decorated to look like the inside of a nineteenth-century sailing ship. Fish swam by the portholes at our dining tables as we sipped champagne.

We'd been married almost four years when Stella died. Unencumbered for the first time, we found ourselves with the freedom to do things like fly off to New Zealand, but that didn't make up for coming home to a house that was too dang quiet. Stella, despite the hair on the couch and the muddy

paw prints on the floor, made us get off that couch and interact with the world outside. Stella was our social glue, the
extrovert who drew people to her, and by default, to us. We
never would have met so many people if not for Stella walking
up to them first. Kids wanted to pet her. Millennials wanted
to take selfies with her. Her gregariousness landed her in a
dog book, an athletic-wear catalog, on greeting cards, in the
San Francisco Chronicle and several neighborhood newspapers.

Now I feel invisible without her. I find myself looking wist-
fully at other people walking their dogs, wishing for those
days back when I organized my schedule around a daily dog
walk. And when I see a puppy, I lose all self-control. I walk
right up to the owners, not even ashamed to interrupt them,
asking to pet, and even hold, their pup. The longer Jenn makes
me wait, the more I inch toward crazy dog lady.

During one of our conversations about puppies, Jenn suggested getting an older dog at a shelter, one that would already be potty-trained and require less work. But I argued
for a puppy that would bond with both of us from the start.
Also, shelter dogs are a risk, I warned. They are often suffering from emotional trauma from abandonment or abuse,
or from being caged in a chaotic shelter…or all of the above.
I conceded that puppies *were* a lot of work, but promised we
could handle it, especially with me writing from home. I was
golden-fluent, I argued, and assured Jenn I'd teach her what
to do with a puppy.

"I'll keep thinking about it," she'd said.

She was still thinking about it when we took a walk a few
weeks later at Fort Funston, a thirty-five-acre park a few
minutes from our house where we used to take Stella several
times a week. If dogs had a Disneyland, this would be it. A

decommissioned military bunker on the windswept sand-
stone cliffs overlooking the Pacific, it's now national open
space, where hundreds of dogs romp off-leash over dunes,
through the waves, and along forested trails that are outfit-
ted with dog water stations. As Central Park is to nannies,
Fort Funston is to professional dog walkers. It's the premiere
dog spot in a city where dogs outnumber children. Not that
there's anything wrong with that. That's just how we roll in
San Francisco, pushing our pampered pups in strollers to day
care or water aerobics or acupuncture treatments. The city is
loaded with dual-income, childless-by-choice, middle-aged
couples like Jenn and me who strengthen our relationships
by co-parenting dogs in this most unnatural of animal environments. And we all descend on Fort Funston, where we
gather to let our dogs feel what it's like to run free.

And here we are in the canine mecca minus the canine,
which is a little bit like showing up to a pool party without
a bathing suit. All we can do is watch the action as we walk
unnoticed past groups of dog owners clustered together discussing their pets. This is the first time we've come to Fort
Funston without Stella, and the difference is startling. I feel
like a lonely ghost.

"Stella's dune," says Jenn, stopping before a hill of sand
that for some reason had been Stella's chosen spot, a speck of
land she defended from all canine comers. Jenn had taken a
zillion photos of Stella lying in wait behind a clump of dark
green ice plant at the top of the dune. When an unsuspect-
ing dog walked by, Stella would spring out of her hiding spot
and chase the dog back down to the walking path, then reverse course and entice the dog to chase her back up. Looking at the empty hill of sand, I still see Jenn in a ball cap

sitting cross-legged on top, her morning coffee in one hand and Stella spraying sand between her hind legs as she madly digs a hole next to her. When it came time to decide where to spread Stella's ashes, we didn't even have to think about it.

Jenn is facing the ocean, lost in thought.

"This is too sad," she says.

"Yeah, let's turn back."

We're almost to the parking lot when I see a man approaching with a golden retriever puppy on a leash. As we get closer, I see the puppy looks so much like baby Stella that my breath catches in my throat. Her coat is the same shade of buttercream, and her smile stretches ear to ear. She's already heeling on a leash, and she is plucky and confident, greeting us with play bows. I drop to my knees and she bounces right over to me and into my lap. She smells like sugar cookies, and I want to steal her so badly I can feel tears coming.

"What's her name?" I ask, not taking my eyes off her, not even looking up at the owner.

"Stevie Nicks."

Stevie Nicks. The first singer who gave voice to my teenage angst, sending the earliest blips of sexual electricity through my veins. The one I wore out a stereo needle for. The only star that ever made me Beatles-scream at a concert. *That* Stevie.

As I am apt to do because it makes life more interesting, I choose to see it as a sign. Obviously, Stella is reaching out from the afterlife to give us her blessing. It's time for a new puppy. I keep the poor guy standing there for a good fifteen minutes as I interrogate him for Stevie's origin story. By the time we part, I have the breeder's name and cell phone number. And another lucky sign—the breeder lives just fifteen minutes away.

Back in the car, I tap a few times on my phone, pull up puppy Stevie Nicks's Instagram page and scroll through. There's Stevie running through the surf. Stevie posing on a robin's-egg-blue midcentury modern couch for a design magazine. Stevie wrestling with three dog friends. She's so damned cute I can't stand it.

"Yes, yes, very cute," Jenn says, taking a quick glance while trying to keep her eyes on the road.

Over the next few weeks, Jenn remained noncommittal. I was beginning to suspect that maybe her reluctance had deeper roots. The dogs of Jenn's childhood in rural Humboldt County were left outside to fend for themselves, strays that her stepfather liked to bully and intimidate when he was in one of his moods. As a girl she trained herself not to get attached to pets because inevitably her stepfather would get rid of them, always under vague circumstances. She'd bring stray cats home but when her stepfather would eventually tire of them, he'd either force Jenn to relinquish them to a shelter or shoot the animals in front of her and make her bury them.

When Jenn was in fifth grade, her mom brought home Rosie, a ten-week-old black Lab mix plucked from a box of free puppies in the grocery store parking lot. When Rosie's antics irritated Jenn's stepfather, he threatened to kill the dog. A few days later, Jenn was walking home from the bus stop when she heard whimpering and found Rosie curled up in a ravine, suffering from some type of internal injury. Jenn carried Rosie home, but her parents couldn't afford a vet and the puppy died that night. Jenn and her mother never believed her stepfather's story that a raptor must have gotten Rosie. Jenn refused to give her stepfather the pleasure of seeing her cry. Instead, she cauterized her feelings and swore off dogs for life.

My wife told me these stories in bits and pieces over the years, each time stopping herself after only a few paragraphs, unable to continue. Puppies triggered a sort of post-traumatic stress in her, forcing her to remember the unhappy childhood she'd spent her entire adult life trying to forget. I understood that she needed to protect herself, but it made me sad that my wife had been cheated out of one of the purest forms of friendship there is. The unwavering loyalty of a dog is what I'd always counted on to beat back the lingering loneliness from my own childhood. The way a dog looks at you, as if you are their world, is a balm that can't be explained, only experienced, and I wanted that for my wife, badly. If she could feel the solidity of a dog's devotion, maybe it would help her heal, too.

So, as a last-ditch effort, I resorted to a campaign of cuteness that was just this side of dirty poker. Each night, before we fell asleep, I showed her YouTube videos of frolicking golden puppies. Puppies learning to swim, puppies boxing with kittens, puppies gobbling birthday cakes. All set to chirpy cartoon music.

Then, a week before we left for New Zealand, Jenn casually asked me a question over dinner.

"How 'bout Edith?"

The name was nerdy perfect. I called the breeder the next day.

"He says he's pretty sure he'll have female pups in a couple months!" I squealed.

"I know, I was listening," said Jenn, giving me the look that says, *Slow down. What do you know about this guy?* "Let's do some more research when we get back from New Zealand."

She didn't say no.

Now we're bathed in the harsh glare of fluorescent lights in airport customs, in a queue that's snaking back on itself so many times we're penned inside a people maze, unable to see the beginning or end. On one side of the throng is an expedited line for airline personnel, and weary passengers are giving side-eye to the pilots and flight attendants as they whisk past with their black-leather rolling briefcases. Right behind us, a little boy is having a meltdown because his parents won't let him tug on the belted dividers separating the lines. He sinks to the floor in protest, his shrieks sailing over the white noise of waiting.

Then an idea unfurls before me. Technically, we are "back from New Zealand."

"Honey," I whisper, "do you think we should check in with the breeder to see if he has any puppies?"

Jenn presses her lips together like she's trying to weigh her words. Her look says, *I know I should stop you.* Jenn is a planner, a thinker, a worst-case-scenario preparer. But I also know that sometimes she finds my spontaneity irresistible. I'm hoping that if I catch her while the travel euphoria is still in her system, this will be one of those times.

"Uh…" she says, stalling for time.

I hold my finger over my phone. "Let's just find out?"

"Right," says Jenn, knowing full well that I'm working her. But she nods her head yes.

The breeder answers, and says he has three female golden retrievers left from a litter of ten. But he also has several people coming to see them in three hours.

"We'll be there in two," I tell him.

Jenn checks her watch and then the stagnation ahead of us.

"I don't think we'll make it," she says.

"We might," I counter.

We get home, toss our suitcases in the living room, hit the ATM, and speed to the breeder's address. By now my adrenaline is pumping just as much from the race as it is for a new puppy. My athlete brain switches on, turning our quest into a do-or-die competition to make sure no one gets to our puppy before we do.

"You're the first ones," the breeder says, waving us into his garage, where three eight-week-old golden retrievers are sitting in a large metal kennel on a folding table, watching us come toward them. The smallest one cowers in one corner—presumably the runt. One stands on hind legs and rocks the cage to get out. But the third puppy, she looks at us with what I could swear is mock indifference and rolls over to expose her belly. She isn't too shy, isn't too excited—she's just right.

"That one," we say in unison, pointing at the same pup.

I ask a few questions about her vaccinations, and the breeder gives me her medical records showing she's had her first round of shots, plus a physical exam. He walks us to the backyard to see the mother, and I quickly glance through the cyclone fence at a golden retriever that's playing with another dog, a lab mix of some sort. I nod my head in approval, eager to get this transaction over with before the other prospective buyers show up. When he asks if we have any questions or concerns, I tell him I've had a lot of experience with goldens, so I'm good, thanks. He gives us a dog crate, a bag of puppy kibble, a rope toy and a squeaky pink fish, takes our family portrait, and we're out the door in thirty minutes.

Edith nestles her nose in the hollow above my collarbone on the ride home. Our new puppy smells like warm bread, and I can feel her heartbeat beneath her skin. I notice that she isn't whimpering like most puppies do when separated from their litter. Yes, I tell myself, we chose wisely. Our dog is already showing early signs of confidence.

"Did we just really do this?" I say. I'm so jet-lagged, a small part of me thinks I'm still in the air, dreaming.

Jenn smiles and reaches over to scratch Edie's ear. "Meredith, I know you. There was no way we were going to walk out of there without a puppy."

Edie looks up at me with eyes so wide I can see my reflection in them. She's imprinting, right now. Inhaling our scent. Learning the sound of our voices, of her own name. But she's already mastered her first trick. She's won my wife over in a matter of minutes.

"Edie May-Jackson," I drawl, sending us into a spasm of giggles. Her name sounds right Southern; so out of place in San Francisco, where people like to give their dogs much more twee names such as Tesla or Kombucha.

"Miss Edie May-Jackson…if you're nasty," quips Jenn.

"Gimme a beat!" I shout, rocking my shoulders side to side like Janet Jackson. If we had real children, we'd be absolutely mortifying them right now. But instead we sing off-key to Edith, who is guaranteed to never, ever, roll her eyes at us.

I roll the names Edith and Edie over and over on my tongue. Edith has an Edwardian feel that amuses me, but the nickname Edie has a charm to it that seems more fitting for a puppy. I go back and forth, trying them both on, unable to choose. We weren't thinking of any particular person when we chose the name Edith; we just have a soft spot for vintage names. It occurs to me now that there are some magnificent Ediths out there: Piaf, Head, Wharton, Bouvier.

"And Bunker!" Jenn adds.

As we drive into the unknown of our new family, it dawns on us that every famous Edith we can think of had been notoriously, stubbornly, eccentric. Chanteuse, couturier, '70s sitcom wife, writer, or downfallen socialite: every Edith was an iconoclast—a rebellious, lovably quirky, freethinker who was damned and determined to do things *her* way.

I wonder if this puppy will refuse to be a wallflower, just like her namesakes. Will she be feisty, or charming, or a little of both? Who will she become, and who will we become because of her? Whatever she turns out to be, Edie will always mark the "before" and "after" point in our relationship, the moment when Jenn and I stopped being two separate individuals with distinct histories and became a couple embarking on a shared future. Taking Edie home represents a promise more tangible than saying, "I do" in front of a room full of our favorite people. It means both of us can imagine a decade or more into the future, and see our family of three still in it.

In my mind I conceptualize this as two sticks representing Jenn and me, surrounded by a square that is our house. Edie enters the box as a third stick, and we all fuse into a triangle.

2

Puppy Love

While I wait with Edie in the car, Jenn rushes indoors to puppy-proof the house. We hadn't expected to get a puppy the same day we returned from being out of the country for a month, so we weren't exactly prepared. Jenn assembles the dog crate in the dining room, covers it with a blanket to make it more den-like, then encircles it with an unfolding wire playpen that I'd kept since Stella was a puppy. She puts a bowl of water inside the enclosure, then tosses in the pink squeaky fish and rope toy from the breeder. Jenn checks that our seventeen-year-old cat, Lulu, is still in her favorite spot where our cat sitter last reported seeing her, burrowed under the covers at the foot of our bed.

The front door swings open and Jenn leans her head out. "Ready!"

I cradle Edie over the threshold and gently set her down

in the corral. She stands stock-still, her four-inch tail pointing to the ceiling. Her baby fur stands up like a bristle brush,
every hair electrified by late-afternoon sun that filters through
her coat, making it look like we can see her aura. We watch,
hushed, waiting for her to do something. She glances at the
two lousy toys and looks up at us with shiny black eyes that
appear beseeching, as if to say, *This is all you've got?* Somehow, this tiny thing has called our bluff. I get the sense she's
fully aware she's drawn the short straw, and now she's stuck
with two humans who obviously didn't properly prepare for
her arrival.

I rummage through the kitchen for makeshift playthings
and unearth a small round Tupperware container about the
size of a biscuit, and the turkey baster. I set them on the floor
and Edie stares at them, unimpressed. Then I remember the
stash I'd kept hidden from Jenn during my puppy campaign.
I open a cupboard, push aside the cleaning supplies, and dig
out the plush lamb with the Kewpie doll–eyelashes. I add
the stuffed toy to the entertainment options and gingerly,
Edie walks over to sniff it. She nudges it with her nose, then
gently takes one leg in her mouth and drags it backward into
the crate, where she spoons it and watches us from the safety
of the darkened cave. It's the one object in this strange new
place that looks most like her.

Jenn and I coo in unison, falling in love in stereo. Jenn
drops to her belly in front of the crate and takes cell phone
photos of Edie. Our new puppy curls into a tighter ball, not
sure about all of this. She yawns and I see she has a black spot
about the size of a jellybean at the back of her tongue. We
probably should give her space so she can rest, but we can't
stop admiring her, so enthralled are we. Everything about

her is so mini, so adorable. The bulge of her little pink belly. Her teensy black claws. The crimped hair on her ears. I'm almost afraid to hug her because I might accidentally squeeze her to death.

"Do you think Edie should have her own Instagram page?" I whisper. I'm already designing it in my mind—#ediepants. Edie's first bath. Edie asleep in our arms. Edie somersaulting with other puppies. Edie harassing our crabby cat. Monthly anniversary portraits so her followers can mark her growth.

Jenn already thinks I spend too much time fiddling with social media. As a police lieutenant who is married to a journalist, she has to constantly remind me not to put our shared life on blast. Privacy is part of her job; a matter of personal safety when her day-to-day requires enforcing laws that some would rather not follow. And then she chose to marry me, whose journalistic instinct is to document and share everything. This is the ironic yin-yang of our pairing, but in a way, it balances us. I've trained her to trust people more, and she's trained me to have some boundaries. I keep my online presence to just me, unless she gives me permission to include her in a post. Jenn does have a Facebook and Instagram account, but she rarely uses them. She sees them more as investigative tools—scrolling to keep an eye on what her friends, and her wife, are doing.

But a dog with its own Instagram account? That makes less than zero sense to my wife, who shakes her head no when I bring it up.

"You're right. That's a bit much," I say, while at that very moment posting Edie and her lamb on my personal Instagram page. It's a crime not to share such cuteness, in my humble opinion.

That night we move Edie's crate to our bedroom. As soon as we fall asleep, she starts whimpering. It's the unmistakable cry of a little one for its mother, and it's so mournful it feels like someone is poking needles into the bruised part of my heart. I feel Edie's longing wrap itself around my own lonely childhood and shake it back awake.

"I know, baby, I know," I say, stroking her velvety ears. I pick Edie up and hold her head under my chin. I make soft clucking noises as I rock side to side, and she presses her wet nose into my neck. "I got you, little one. I'm going to take care of you now."

Her cries subside a bit, but she's still trembling. I open a sound effects app on my phone, find audio of a heartbeat, and place it atop Edie's crate so she can hear the *thumpa-thumpa*. I sit next to her crate and pet her until we both calm down enough for sleep.

By the end of the first week, our routine has been vaporized by the body rhythms of our new ten-pound animated teddy bear. Eat, poop, play, sleep—rinse, wash, repeat—every three hours. We go through a Costco-size supply of paper towels wiping after her, documenting where and when she goes number one or number two in a potty-training journal we keep on the kitchen counter. She gets an A for pooping almost entirely outside; yet Urination 101 is more of a C-.

None of this fazes Jenn, who takes it upon herself to get up several times during the night to carry Edie down three sets of stairs to the backyard to pee. When I offer to take a turn, she waves me off, and it makes me smile to imagine the two of them out there in the moonlight, becoming accustomed to one another. Whatever uncertainty Jenn had about adding more responsibility to our relationship seems to have vanished, replaced by a latent maternal instinct that surprises both of us. A new book appears on her nightstand: *The Art of Raising a Puppy*, the international bestseller written by the Christian monks who designed a compassion-based program to breed, raise, and train German shepherds at the New Skete Monastery in New York. It's the go-to classic for new dog owners, the canine equivalent of *What to Expect When You're Expecting*. I'm delighted she found it on her own, that she diligently reads a chapter every night, pausing often to read me the parts she finds particularly germane.

"You know, there's a lot in here about how you should research the health and personality traits of the mother and father before you choose a puppy," she says one night, taking off her glasses and scrutinizing me.

"Bah," I say, with a dismissive flick of my wrist. "That's if you want a show dog or something. I didn't know squat about Layla or Stella's lineage, and they both turned out just fine."

Jenn raises an eyebrow at me, then turns back to her book. She isn't buying it.

"What matters more is how you raise them," I try again.

"Oh-kaay," she says.

I don't feel like I've won my argument, so I can't go back to reading my book until I do.

"Look at her," I say, pointing at Edie, who is sleeping on her back, all four paws held aloft and twitching in a dream. "Is she not perfect?"

Jenn smiles and I tell her how much I love that she's worrying. It's an FBI clue that she's already smitten. I ask her to trust me, to trust that I might know a thing or two about raising golden retrievers.

"Okay," she says, this time with sincerity.

By week two, our orbits have tightened around this little being, the nucleus of our surrogate family and the closest approximation we'll ever have to raising an actual baby. Eager to do everything right, we spare no creature comfort for our creature. We forgo Christmas presents and instead buy gifts for Edie. We get three dog beds—one for each floor, a collapsible canvas travel crate, a toy box overflowing with stuffed animals, chew bones, and treat-dispensing dog puzzles that claim to enhance cognitive development. We scrutinize dog food ingredients, rejecting anything nonorganic or with too many words we can't pronounce. Standing before a wall of dog harnesses at the pet store, we pass over anything pink, floral or sparkly, and choose camouflage because that way no one will put any gender assumptions on our dog. We are becoming *Best in Show* dog parents, the very people we used to make fun of, but the purpose and cohesion Edie brings to our lives is just too powerful to resist. The joint responsibility for a vulnerable being is unearthing a need to nurture something, while giving us glimpses of the not-so-unfit mothers we might have been.

It shocks us how much we enjoy this. Neither of us thought of ourselves as the mothering type. We didn't have children because we weren't that happy as children ourselves, both of us bewildered by divorces that sent our fathers away and broke our mothers' spirits. As survivors of tumultuous childhoods, our most precious possession is our independence. It's probably what drew us together—a shared apprehension of families, and an uncertainty that we possessed the skills to be good mothers ourselves.

The similarities in our childhoods came out in bits and pieces over our first years together in a slow, careful conver-

sation on a topic both of us had learned to downplay for polite company, especially for people we were attracted to. We'd
learned the hard way that the weight of our heavy pasts could
scare off people who rightfully didn't want to help carry our
burdens. But there was something about the way Jenn listened to the stories I shared without offering shiny platitudes
about resilience or trying to normalize my mother's neglect
in a well-meaning yet naive attempt to make me feel better.
There was a respectful knowing in her eyes that made me
trust that I could tell her everything.

She listened with all of her being as I explained how I lost
both parents just before my fifth birthday—one to geogra-
phy and one to mental illness. We were living in Newport,
Rhode Island, where my father was stationed with the Navy
and my mother was a disgruntled housewife. The worst time
of day was the afternoons when Dad would come home. Mom
had been saving up her list of complaints—that he didn't pay
enough attention to her, that he didn't make enough money,
that he never changed a diaper or dusted a surface. The one-
way fighting started before dinner, through the meal, and
long into the night as my mother raged at my sullen father,
punctuating her arguments by throwing dishware and ripping curtains from their rods. On her worst days, my father
would later tell me, she'd wait until he fell asleep and then
hit him in the head.

I learned to tread lightly around my mother, lest I become
the object of her fury. I kept my back against the wall in her
presence, and steered my three-year-old brother, Matthew,
out of the room when she came near. It was after one of their
epic fights, when the heavy wooden pepper mill went flying
across the dinner table, that my father had finally had enough.

"I want a divorce," were his final words to her.

Not long after, Dad drove us to the airport. Mom, mascara slicking down her cheeks, walked my brother and me onto an airplane. Five hours later we landed in California, where we moved into my mother's childhood bedroom in my grandparents' tiny red house in Carmel Valley. I squeezed into a bed with my mother and Matthew slept in a cot at our feet. Not only did my mother separate from my father, she divorced herself from us, relinquishing parenthood to my grandparents as she crawled under the covers and fell into a downward spiral from which she never returned. For the next decade, she measured the length of a day in cigarettes, the weeks in Agatha Christie murder mysteries, the months in cobwebs spun across the ceiling. She forbade us from the room except to sleep and took all her meals in bed, delivered by Granny.

My father was never mentioned again. I thought we were just visiting, and he'd come for us soon. When he did show up six months later, it was only to deliver Mom's Volvo that he'd driven across the country. I stood in my grandparents' driveway and screamed at his back as he walked away from our house that day, begging him not to leave me. I can still remember how my throat felt like it was tearing inside as I watched him go, and how I had to relive the moment over and over in my dreams. It would be two years before I saw my father again, when he sent a plane ticket for a weeklong visit. Every summer after that for the next decade Dad flew Matthew and me for brief visits. But it was hard to maintain a connection in between those trips with the animosity between our families. I would later learn he got hung up on when he tried to call, and his letters were torn up before I ever saw them.

Although I had a distant relationship with my father, it was closer than the one I had with the parent I lived with. Mom curled her body around mine in bed nightly, yet when daylight came, she wordlessly peeled herself away. My mother was not the type to read to us or bake us cookies or to come to our classroom and help kids glue macaroni and glitter on construction paper. Her children didn't rank on her hierarchy of needs, unless we could bring her an aspirin, or a sandwich, or body heat. The only time I felt like somebody's child was when Mom and I slept. It was only then that she reached for me.

As quasi-orphans, my brother and I gravitated toward our stepgrandfather, an eccentric mountain man who kept more than one hundred beehives tucked into the remote canyons along the Big Sur coast. He also kept a run-down World War II military bus marooned in the backyard that he'd gutted and retrofitted into a honey factory. Grandpa took my brother and me under his wing, bringing us to his Big Sur bee yards, where he opened his hives to show us how honeybees are loyal, hardworking, and selfless—the exact opposite of a dysfunctional family. Grandpa made us his beekeeping apprentices, giving us a purpose and giving him a way to impart the life lessons we weren't getting at home by telling us stories about how bees work together to solve problems.

We were too little to understand adult concepts like generosity and benevolence, so instead Grandpa opened his hives to show us how nurse bees take care of the young, how scout bees dance to share the location of flower sources, and how the bond between the queen and her worker bee daughters is the lifeline of a colony. He taught us that each hive has just one queen mother, and she is the only bee that can lay eggs.

But she can't feed herself, or keep warm at night, so relies on her daughters to feed her and cuddle around her at night for body warmth. Watching the bees caress and feed their queen, I immediately understood what I was seeing—an unbreakable mother-daughter bond.

It wasn't until I turned forty and started beekeeping as an adult that I truly understood what my grandfather had done for my brother and me. In 2011, I had decided it was time to get my own bees, because Grandpa was too frail to continue lifting his hive boxes, which can get up to fifty pounds when they are full of honey. When he reluctantly retired after seventy years, he seemed lost, like a cowboy without his horse. I didn't have a place in San Francisco to put a beehive, but I caught wind that one of my editors was lobbying for permission to put beehives on the roof of the *San Francisco Chronicle*, where I was working as a reporter. I offered to help and wound up becoming one of the two staff beekeepers in charge, and parlayed it into writing a monthly column about urban rooftop beekeeping.

But my ulterior motive was to apprentice under Grandpa again. In the four more years we had together before he died, we talked by phone more frequently than we'd ever had, as I sought his advice on how to build the hives and where to position them, what pollinator plants to add to the rooftop garden, how to feed the bees and monitor them for mites and viruses. I drove to see him regularly, and we spent hours in the honey bus and on his back porch watching the bees fly in and out of his last hive, talking about our lives and our lives with bees. Each time I got ready to head back to the city, he'd give me another piece of his beekeeping gear. He prepared me to carry his legacy, slowly gifting me his turn-of-the-century beekeeping books, his bee suits, and the redwood jig he made for stringing wooden honeycomb frames with wire.

He prepared me for the day the bees arrived at the *San Francisco Chronicle*. A crowd of coworkers had gathered to photograph me transferring the bees from their travel cage to the empty hives. The moment I held bees again, their scent, their sound, their vibration in my palms felt so familiar—*so personal*—that I was overcome with a feeling of protection and safety. I broke down sobbing at the memory of being surrounded by a cloud of honeybees, of feeling my Grandpa's calm presence around me. That's when I understood why I had an unusual connection to these stinging insects, because of everything Grandpa had taught us in his silent understated way, when we were children. By slipping bee parables into his beekeeping lessons, he had taught us that everything we needed to know about love and family was contained within the social structure of a bee colony. He took us outdoors, away from the insular problems inside our house, and showed us that the world is big and full of wonder, giving us reason to hope that we would make our way to a happier future.

By contrast, living indoors with a depressed mother, I vicariously absorbed the unspoken lesson that to give life is to lose your own. The dynamics inside my home gave me a worldview that was very different from my elementary school girlfriends who spent a lot of time discussing which boy they were going to marry, and how many babies they were going to have. Watching my mother steep in regret made me uncertain about marriage and motherhood because I knew neither was guaranteed. I wasn't sure what I wanted to be when I grew up; all I could say for certain was that I wanted to be the opposite of my mother. Independent and happy. I remember sitting in a circle of girls in the sandbox one recess, as they one by one announced the names they'd chosen for their future children. I felt my stomach solidify into a river rock as I prayed the bell would interrupt us.

"I'm not sure," I mumbled, when the audience turned to me. Heads tilted slightly, as if they were cocking their ears to hear me more clearly. Not sure of the names? Not sure of what?

"Allaire," I blurted. Anything to redirect their gaze. It was my middle name, after my father's grandma. Pronounced *ah-lair*. It's French, and my mother, who didn't speak the language, had me believe that it meant free like the wind.

The girls scrunched up their foreheads. All-what? What did she say? Who names their kid Air?

It was no use. After that, I began spending my recess in the classroom reading to avoid the playground family planning sessions.

My reluctance to discuss matrimony was no doubt reinforced by listening to my mother and grandmother repeatedly rail against their first husbands, blaming them not only for their divorces but for everything that had gone wrong in their lives since. I don't know how my grandfather sat quietly while they played their wounded soundtrack on repeat: *Men aren't worth a pot to piss in; no offense, Franklin. Men only want to marry their mothers; no offense, Franklin.* Grandpa was Granny's second husband, and their one rarified exception to the pointlessness of men.

Granny's first husband, whose name she had permanently replaced with "good-ole-what's-his-face," was on his way to World War II when they hastily married. She was nineteen. He returned from Normandy with a mean streak, which he took out on Mom, whipping her with a thin tree branch while telling her she'd never amount to anything. The abuse lasted seventeen years, as Granny made excuses and covered the bruises, until finally she summoned the courage to leave him. But the marks he left behind were another kind of permanent—they made my mother incapable of expressing or receiving love and my Granny so full of remorse that when we showed up on her doorstep, she enabled my mother to slip away into a second childhood. She doted on my mother seeking forgiveness, which only reinforced my mother's weakness, and thus our abandonment.

When I began dating boys in high school, my mother called me into the bedroom for her one and only parenting talk.

"Don't throw yourself away over some boy," she'd said, propped up on her pillows and barely visible through a fog of cigarette smoke. "Get a job before you get married."

I didn't have the heart to tell her that no teenagers I knew were getting married. She hadn't seen the outside world in so long, she probably didn't know times had changed.

"Don't get me wrong," she continued, not waiting for an answer. "I wanted both you kids, but just think if I'd never met your father, I could have really done something with my life."

When I asked her what that something was, she turned toward the drawn curtains with a faraway look, as if she were actually looking out the window.

"I could have been a famous Civil War historian."

I pitied my mother, but as long as her life remained someone else's fault, she never had to crawl out from under her dark cloud. I'd long since learned to turn away from the sting of her unspoken comments—that she'd be happier if my brother and

I hadn't been born—but still they tattooed themselves on my skin in invisible ink. When my friends began having babies in their twenties and thirties and I still didn't feel compelled, I wondered. Was my aversion to giving birth a sensibility I'd inherited from my mother's DNA, or was it learned from watching her languish in regret? Nature or nurture, it didn't really matter; I worried that the only type of mother I knew how to be was an aloof one. Knowing what it feels like to be an unwanted child, I didn't dare risk making another child feel that. I don't think it's a coincidence that my brother also chose not to have a baby. I suspect he fears something similar.

Jenn did not recoil from my story, as all the others had. She, too, had to raise herself, and so knew that people like us don't want sympathy, what we want is to feel less weird. We want a companion who can finish our sentences and laugh at our dark jokes because they've also spent a lifetime dodging questions about their families. We want to compare our histories with someone who can truly relate, whose firsthand experiences of loss and adult solo Thanksgivings normalize ours. We want, for just a moment, to feel uncensored in the presence of another human.

Whether overtly or subconsciously, Jenn and I strove to build adulthoods that were the opposite of our childhoods. Jenn's home lacked structure, so she became a police officer, a source of mild shame for her marijuana-growing, Humboldt kin. My mother dropped out of society, so I dove into it headfirst, becoming a journalist so I could travel and meet as many fascinating people as I could. Mom lacked the energy to move a muscle, so I got up at 4:30 a.m. for thirty-plus years to train with a competitive rowing team. It felt really good to slam that oar into the water, over and over and over again.

Coming from families held hostage by secrets and fear, both of us grew up counting the days until we could escape. Both of us left for good at seventeen, taking some clothes, books, and keepsakes from our rooms and abandoning the rest. That's when we became adults, and to this day our adult freedom is our most precious possession. Had we felt the stability of family beneath our feet, I think we would have at least considered having children and creating our own families. But it's like our biological clocks lost a spring somewhere along the way. They never started ticking in our twenties and thirties. We were both too busy trying to parent ourselves.

Now we are in our fifties and doting over Edie as if she were our flesh and blood. We are late-bloomer parents, but trying our best to make up for lost time by giving Edie her happiest life possible. After her first fitful night, Edie's nighttime cries are not as despondent. They are little whistles, signals to let her out of her crate because she needs a bathroom break. I'm a heavy sleeper, and Jenn is always on half-alert, ready to leap out of bed at the slightest sound that might signal an intruder. So she hears Edie first, and I usually wake up when she flicks the covers off to get up.

"What's the matter, Noonie? Gotta go outside?" whispers Jenn, using the inexplicable nickname she landed on for Edith.

Jenn is being considerate, trying to not wake me. I hear Edie's telltale exhale as she bends into her "downward dog" wakeup stretch, rump in the air with forearms extended outside the crate door.

I smile in my fake-sleep as I listen to them tiptoe out, captivated by the way life waits until we are absolutely ready, then gives us a do-over.

3

Puppy Antisocial

Vaccinating a puppy seems way more drawn-out than I remember. The immunization list sounds like the cast of an Italian opera: Lepto, Parvo, Bordetella, Influenza. Our weekly date night is long gone, replaced by watching British baking shows in the veterinarian's lobby, waiting for yet another injection to ward off all manner of creepy-crawlies that can take down a dog: distemper, hepatitis, giardia, rabies, hookworms, roundworms, whipworms.

Edie is good-natured and sits still for each needle, so delighted is she to be touched all over by a stranger with a pocketful of cookies. At three months old, she weighs just eleven pounds, and her trusting soul must account for at least half of that. I'm downright delighted when she licks the vet's chin as he injects her, thrilled to see that Edie is so relaxed in a situation so many dogs find terrifying. It makes me feel that we must be doing something right as puppy parents if this little pip-squeak is already mimicking the way Stella used to sashay into the vet's lobby with the sass of a drag queen, speaking through her posture: "I'm *heeeeeere* people, now get in line to adore me!"

Until Edie completes her initial round of shots, she'll be on house arrest, paws forbidden to touch the ground outside lest she picks up a virus. But this poses a conundrum. Her brain is developing fast right now, and according to the pile of puppy books we consult, three to sixteen weeks of age is the brief window of time when puppies need to be exposed to as many people and dogs as possible so they learn proper social skills to navigate both the human and canine worlds. Not only that, they also need to be introduced to new sites and smells and environments, everything from the beach to the busy Home Depot parking lot, so they learn what's safe. The whole purpose of early socialization is to help the puppy develop a database of what's normal, to prepare them for the life you want them to live.

Puppies learn how to play appropriately from other puppies. It's how they learn to soften their play bites, to take breaks and relax in between tumble sessions, and to read and respond appropriately to canine body language—giving more when it's wanted and backing off when it's not. Skipping this step, the books warn, could lead to a dog that doesn't learn how to moderate its arousal level, a bully that roughhouses too much and ignores other puppies' boundaries. Conversely, it could lead to a fearful dog that cowers or bites because it hasn't learned what normal puppy play behavior looks like.

Early exposure to people also helps keep fear and aggression in check. Experts advise introducing puppies to more than a dozen new people a week. Which also sounds like a full-time job, so I'm wondering how people who work outside the home are expected to accomplish this. And by "new people" the authors mean not just your personal friends who tend to come from the same generation and culture. If we want to raise a well-adjusted canine citizen, Edie needs to meet strangers from San Francisco's diverse polyglot. We need to get Edie comfortable around seniors, young children, people in uniforms, people who speak different languages, wheelchair users, hipsters with handlebar mustaches.

Back when I was socializing Stella, the emphasis was on quantity, and the standard advice was to introduce puppies to two hundred different people and expose them to fifty distinct places by the time they were six months old. My solution was to stand outside Peet's Coffee in my Oakland neighborhood every Sunday morning for a month. There's no better bait than a puppy; Stella was fawned over and handled by hundreds of customers.

These days, the focus has shifted more toward quality, not quota. It's not so much about the number of contacts, but whether those contacts are beneficial to the puppy. Is the puppy happy and relaxed about the interaction, so that she's forming a positive association with people? Or are you making her uncomfortable by letting a stranger reach for her without her consent? We wouldn't hand our newborn baby to a stranger on the street, but we do it with our puppies without a second thought. The art in all this is being able to read the puppy's body language to know whether they are enjoying what you're making them do.

So we put the word out to our friends that Edie is ready for her first visitors, and the response is so huge that we have to start booking appointments to ensure she can still get her multiple daily naps in. First in line is my brother and sister-in-law, professional photographers toting high-powered cameras to capture Edie's first baby pictures. They arrive in the afternoon when the light is golden and drive us to Ocean Beach where there's a bizarre foot-high slick of seafoam at the water's edge. Edie still hasn't finished her shots and it's not the best beach day, cold and a little windy, but I risk it and go along with my brother because I love him fiercely and obey his photographer command to crouch down in the foam with Edie. And sure enough, his shot is money—a windswept Edie sitting between my legs staring directly at the camera, and me in a slightly ridiculous wool hat with a big bow on one side and hazard-cone orange rain boots, both of us stage-lit by the sunlight reflecting off a receding wave. But what makes the image weirdly wonderful are those *Twilight Zone* blobs of shampoo foam on the sand encircling us.

Maile and Eddy are next up with their new pug-mix puppies, Pancho and Pepper, that they rescued through a nonprofit agency that helps the unhoused find homes for the pets they can no longer care for. They are Edie's first puppy visitors, and she is out of her mind with excitement when she sees these snorting gremlins with the goldfish eyes wiggle into the room. She springs straight in the air like a baby goat, then takes off running so they'll chase her. Pepper is tentative, but Pancho streaks after Edie, and they tussle in a tumbleweed of fur over the linoleum in the kitchen, grunting and growling as they wage their imaginary battle. Then, an invisible wind sends them back toward the living room, and no matter how we try, we can't get a photo that isn't a blur. Just as I'd suspected, Edie loves to play.

Next comes Mag and Barbara with Stella's former housemates, Phoebe the basset and Toby the corgi. The dogs are older now, and less receptive to Edie's play invitations, but the déjà vu of seeing a golden round out the old canine trio is powerful. We watch, hushed, as Edie, Phoebe, and Toby inspect one another for scents. It feels so right, like putting the last puzzle piece in place, to have a golden retriever complete our gang of six once more.

After a few weeks of indoor play with our social circle, I strike out looking for more variety for Edie. I put her into an oversize straw farmers' market bag, sling the bag over my shoulder and head for Java Beach, an old-school neighborhood coffee shop bustling with every kind of San Franciscan you can imagine. It draws retired Irish cops, surfers still in their wet suits, parents and kids on their way to the zoo across the street, construction workers, panhandlers, and tech gig workers hunkered over laptops. Well-behaved dogs are also allowed inside.

"Oh. My. God. STOP IT!" says the woman behind the espresso machine when she sees Edie peeping out from my bag. She abandons her line of to-go cups waiting to be filled to meet Edie. The cashier and the guy toasting bagels take five and gather around me, too.

"Can I?" she says, reaching to pull Edie out, and of course I consent, having been that person who can't help herself around puppies not that long ago. She nuzzles noses with Edie, closing her eyes in delight. "Oh, don't you just love puppy breath?"

I'm not really sure what puppy breath is, but so many people have said the same thing to me that I just nod in agreement. Personally, I think Edie's breath is a little eau de quahog.

"Thank you, I needed that," she says, and I think I see her wipe a tear on her shirtsleeve as she returns to pulling shots.

The bagel guy reaches for Edie next. He cradles her like a

baby in his tattooed forearms, and wiggles his fingers above her as she bats at them with her paws. Edie is a glowing orb of furry light, a warm fuzzy that has brought the swirling café to a standstill as a crowd gathers to admire her. Babies squeal and clap from their strollers as their parents point at Edie. The tech workers come out from behind their laptops and snap selfies with Edie. Seniors pet my puppy and slip into stories about the dogs of their youth.

So far, her body language seems to be saying, "Yes, please." She's liquid in bagel guy's arms, not squirming in the slightest. Watching her love so indiscriminately, I wonder if Edie understands that I'm her person. Can a dog be *too* confident? When this puppy is allowed to walk outside, I'm afraid she may just wander off with the first person who winks at her. Reaching for her again, I bask in her glow, savoring this fleeting moment of puppydom, when all the world showers my baby girl with love, and by extension, a few drops land on me.

Jenn never had the chance to feel a pure, uncomplicated puppy love like this with Rosie. Had she been allowed to have a canine best friend in childhood, I think she wouldn't have suffered as much loneliness as a little girl, growing up isolated from her friends on sixty-five acres in rural northern California, and isolated within her own family by a stepfather who begrudgingly acknowledged her.

Born in the Summer of Love to two Southern California beach teenagers, Jenn's upbringing was shaky from the start. When Jenn's mother discovered she was pregnant on her nineteenth birthday, her parents gave her three options: go to Mexico City for an abortion, go to a home for unwed mothers in Texas and give the baby up for adoption, or get married. The high school sweethearts argued about whether they were ready to become parents, but they were in love, so they chose marriage. The ceremony was held inside a Baptist Church before a preacher who was also the father of the groom. When the bridesmaids walked down the aisle on a length of butcher paper that was used in place of a carpet runner the florist forgot to bring, Jenn's mother winced with each crunching step, certain it was a bad omen.

The couple lived in Baptist church–owned apartments and homes, relying on family financial support for the next three years, until Jenn's preacher grandfather was sent to prison for some type of fraud that was never quite fully explained to Jenn's mother. She wanted nothing to do with it, and didn't ask for details. She wanted to get as far away from that side of the family as possible.

Jenn's parents decided it was a good time to strike out on their own, and on Groundhog Day 1972, they drove twelve hours north so Jenn's father could study zoology at Humboldt State University. But instant maturity didn't materialize with a change of scenery. The lure of college social life won the tugging match against the responsibility of a family, and one day Jenn's dad asked her mother if he could date a pretty girl in his biology class, but still stay married. The answer was short, and swift. They got a divorce, and Jenn's father moved out.

He came by only sporadically to visit Jenn after that. Each time he showed up to take her somewhere, her insides would twirl in excitement, but then something always happened that left her feeling deflated. She remembers him dropping her off at the movie theater when she was five to watch Marx Brothers matinees alone, or eating grilled cheese sandwiches in a restaurant with his girlfriend-at-the-time while he slipped away to do whatever it was he found more pressing. By the time she'd turn six, he'd be gone for good, moving away from Humboldt without leaving a forwarding address.

On her own for the first time, Jenn's mother scrambled to provide for Jenn. She got a job in the environmental education office of the Humboldt County public school system, and signed herself up for general education courses at the local junior college. Weekends and summers, she picked up occasional bartending shifts at Walt's Friendly Tavern in Blue Lake. Jenn remembers this period playing cards with babysitters, or drinking a never-ending glass of apple juice and listening to Otis Redding and Jim Croce on the bar's jukebox while her mom poured beers.

One day Jenn's mom spotted a six-foot-four guy with long blond hair stride into her US history class wearing a fringed leather jacket. Turns out he was a free spirit who shared her love of Mother Earth and distrust of The Man. They both admired the back-to-the-land movement that was taking hold of their generation in the wake of the assassinations of Martin Luther King Jr. and JFK, sparking an exodus of disillusioned young people out of mainstream America to live free on rural communes and homesteads. He strummed Dylan songs for Jenn's mother on his guitar, and wooed her with his plans to build a log cabin on some raw land and live off-the-grid, tapping natural springs for water, the sun for power, and the earth for a vegetable garden. He had everything figured out. What little money they'd need would come from the royalties on the folk albums he was going to record. She was smitten with this real-life mountain man, ready to follow him out of the rat race and into paradise.

But first, he moved himself into her duplex apartment without being invited. Jenn's mother came home from work to find him in the living room, with a story about getting kicked out of his place after a dispute with the landlord. She was irked, but he lobbed his problem back at her, telling her he had nowhere else to go. She relented, but only if he'd pay half the rent. Suddenly Jenn was living with a stranger who made himself comfortable on the couch with his guitar and a six-pack, practicing his folk songs, day after day after day.

When Jenn's mother became pregnant again, she no longer believed in the institution of marriage, but her boyfriend's parents did. They pressured her to change her mind, reminding her that they'd given the couple a sizable down payment to purchase sixty-five acres of land in rural Humboldt. She submitted to social and financial pressure, and the boyfriend became a fiancé.

Jenn was asked by her mother to wear a dress for the wedding, which for an eight-year-old tomboy was a horrifying proposition. Jenn preferred her hair short and roamed around in overalls, always with a sheriff's badge affixed to the bib and a popgun in the side-leg hammer loop. She pushed back, insisting she wear a suit. They argued about it, but in the end, Jenn stood in the less expensive compromise of tan velour pants and matching vest to watch her mother exchange vows. Jenn, who to this day still wears men's clothes because they fit her better, has always been self-assured in her androgyny and 100 percent certain of herself. My wife didn't then, nor does now, give a flying fig if other people find her gender hard to place.

Jenn's new stepfather was charismatic, with big dreams but no specific plans to achieve greatness. He found working for someone else oppressive, so he didn't. He kept himself busy working on his folk album. On the days his music was flowing, he was gregarious and funny. When the muse didn't appear, he stormed the house, shouting and punching the walls looking for it. On his worst days, he accused Jenn's mother of infidelity, pounding on the bathroom door as she hid inside. The next day he'd be overflowing with apologies. His behavior became increasingly erratic, and worsened when he'd been drinking. One day he'd cook and serve dinner with a smile, the next he'd fumble into the house late at night and urinate into the bookcase. Jenn withdrew into the shadows, careful not to poke the bear that was now living with her.

Jenn's mother gave birth to a baby girl, and when the baby was eighteen months old the family moved to their sixty-five acres of raw land in the mountains of Humboldt, an isolated area accessible only by four-wheel drive, without running water or electricity. Her parents were finally going to start living their pastoral dream. Her stepfather drew plans for a two-story cabin he intended to build for the family.

Meanwhile, they slept in green Sears & Roebuck tents and hauled buckets of water from a generous neighbor's spring. Their tents were flimsy, and flooded when it rained. What her parents sold to Jenn as a summer camping adventure quickly lost its luster as their temporary living arrangement stretched into late fall. Still, no cabin. Jenn's clothes smelled and her hair was tangled. The kids at school pointed this out, mercilessly.

Jenn remembers one day her mother and stepfather disappeared from the campsite. She was inside her tent and didn't know they had decided to go on a hike, leaving her baby sister in an upturned camper shell that did double-duty as an outdoor playpen. When Jenn realized her parents were missing and she was alone with the toddler, she panicked, worried her parents might be dead or, like her father, never coming back. She had no idea how to take care of a baby.

"I just stood there and screamed," Jenn said. "One word, over and over."

That word was *Mom*.

It could have been an hour, an afternoon, all day; Jenn can't remember how long they were gone. But when they returned to her frantic tears, her stepfather scolded her for not being more mature.

"What's wrong with you?" her stepfather bellowed. When she couldn't answer the question, he filled in the blanks. Too weak, maybe, or too selfish, to babysit and help the family, he spat.

Jenn was already an outsider at school, and increasingly becoming one at home, too.

After five months of camping, the family finally broke down their tents and moved into the bones of their future home. The framing was up, covered with plywood and tar paper, and the plywood floors were in. The interior walls were still a skeletal maze of two-by-fours. Her stepfather had stapled flimsy plastic sheeting over the window openings, blocking the view. But instead of hustling to finish as winter approached, the pace of construction crawled, then stalled into a perpetual project that kept getting kicked into the future. They hung blankets from the rafters to combat the cold, and slept huddled together in sleeping bags next to a tin woodstove. A second baby girl was born. Still, there was no recording contract. There were more mouths to feed, and more financial stress. The mountain of beer bottles in the meadow was growing higher by the day. For the next five years, they lived in a simulacrum of a home that froze in winter and baked in summer.

Her stepfather tried to make money the way many do in Humboldt and planted marijuana plants. But even that was a bust. One time he propagated all male plants; another time he put the crop in the attic to dry and it molded over winter. It would be her mother who would save the family by waitressing and working as a part-time speech therapy aide in the public schools.

As her stepfather's musical dreams faded, his temper became more unpredictable and his punishments increasingly cruel. He turned the compound into what I can only imagine felt like a labor camp for Jenn, making her dig fire lines with a hoe, clear brush, and crawl under the cabin to clear out beer bottles. He got inspired to build a rabbit hutch, after hearing from a neighbor that rabbit manure made marijuana plants grow. This time his crop was successful, but Jenn's chore list grew. She was tasked with cleaning the hutches, and chasing down the rabbits when they escaped. At harvest time, she spent entire days clipping marijuana leaves from the buds to prepare them for sale. Her stepfather was great at making to-do lists, then making other people do the to-dos.

Once, he put Jenn and her mother to work stacking split logs he planned to sell for firewood. He drove the whole family to a clearing below the unfinished cabin. He left the babies in the station wagon with the back door open, and began chopping while Jenn and her mother carried the wood to the top of the hill. Jenn's youngest half sister, still in diapers, crawled out of the car while no one was watching and tottered in her bare feet over to a smoldering slash pile. She saw the gray powdery ash and decided to run barefoot through the soft-looking material. When the toddler's screams pierced the sky, everyone dropped what was in their hands and came running. Jenn remembers seeing bubbles on the soles of her sister's feet as her mother wrapped them in ice. Her parents hustled the babies to the station wagon and roared down the

mountain for the hospital, leaving Jenn behind with her stepfather's parting words shimmering in the dust:

"You were supposed to keep an eye on her."

Jenn believed she was to blame. The accident confirmed a
core belief: that she lacked what it took to care for children.
She *was* clumsy and stupid. Someone as inept as she couldn't
be trusted with a baby. Her kid sister would survive and collect
a few scars, but Jenn would feel responsible until she reached
adulthood, when she was finally old enough to understand
that children aren't capable of protecting other children.

Like me, Jenn did not fit in at school. When so much is
going on at home, it's hard to make friends: to laugh with
abandon, to dance, to be that fun friend that classmates want
to be around. We hear our classmates talking about family
vacations or Father's Day dinners and we retreat to a quiet
corner, not wanting to hear the rest.

When Jenn was in middle school, her father resurfaced. He
was at his parents' homestead in Arkansas where he was living
with a new wife and her two young children. Jenn's grandma
called and wanted to know if she would like to visit him. It
had been six years since she'd last seen her dad.

Her yes was instant, and she got on the next plane at the
tiny airport in Arcata. She fantasized the whole way about a
storybook reunion, and he must have been doing the same. As
if making up for all the things he'd missed teaching her, he
whisked her from one activity to the next. He took her in a skiff
to the middle of the family pond and taught her how to reel in
sunfish, he showed her how to shoot a .22-caliber rifle, and he
opened his beehives and let her pull out wax comb dripping
with honey. He shared the paints that he'd used in his college
art classes, and patiently taught her pointillism technique. She

created a dragon made up of tiny paint dots, then added an owl wing to it, studying the real owl wing he kept on a shelf.

It seemed like the start of something, but it would turn out to be the final send-off. After Jenn came home from Arkansas, they tried to stay in contact through letters, but never got beyond surface pleasantries about the weather and repetitive how-are-you questions. By the time Jenn was following in her father's footsteps at Humboldt State, the letters had petered out. She'd accepted by then what she knew deep in her gut: retroactive father-daughter relationships rarely work out.

With Jenn away at college, her mother became a bigger target for her stepfather's rage. Their fights were so upsetting that Jenn stopped coming home for holidays and encouraged her mother to end the relationship. Ultimately, after many fits and starts, her mother secured a divorce—which included, as a precaution, a lifetime restraining order. Although he had never threatened her life directly, Jenn's mother wasn't sure he wouldn't. Jenn and her mother would find a way back to one another, but those dark years would inform every decision Jenn would make about who she wanted to be. A mother definitely wasn't one of them.

But I know she could have been a great mom. I see it in the way she cradles her cat, Lulu, in her arms every night when she sleeps. How she hops out of bed every time Edie whimpers. How, when Edie outgrew her penny-sized dog tag embossed with a capital letter *E*, Jenn replaced it with a larger one and then slipped the tiny tag onto her key chain. I notice these small signs that my wife has an enormous amount of love to give. But I keep these observations to myself, letting Jenn fall for Edie on her own time.

When Edie's received enough vaccinations, she is cleared

to join a puppy social at the SPCA. I don't remember puppy play groups being a thing when I had Stella a dozen years ago, but apparently they're standard procedure now in puppy parenting. I go online to book her a spot in a play group, without considering that San Francisco's population has gone up nearly 20 percent in the last dozen years. There are 135,000 more people living within the seven-by-seven-mile city limits now, and all of them must have dogs, because the SPCA schedule is booked a month in advance.

No problem, I'll just widen my search. I try Berkeley, Oakland, San Mateo, Marin. Classes are full everywhere. I now know what my friends with kids are talking about when they start searching for a summer camp spot a year ahead of time. With each dead end my fingers tap a little more frantically, as I worry that Edie is going to be left out, pushed to the side by the swifter, smarter, more responsible dog owners who knew to start this process earlier. I refresh the page over and over, hoping for a different result each time, as if her development all depends on this one make-or-break moment. In a last ditch effort, I try to game the system by putting Edith's name on the waiting lists at six different SPCA locations, hoping someone will cancel, somewhere.

After a week goes by with no response, I start calling around, and the old-fashioned telephone comes through for me. The San Francisco SPCA had a cancellation right before I called. I grab it.

In the days leading up to play group, I can hardly contain my excitement. I remind Jenn an annoying number of times to bring her camera to shoot stills *and* video so we can capture Edie's first party. Given how joy explodes out of her pores whenever Pancho and Pepper visit, I can't wait to see her reaction when she's presented with a room full of puppies.

The San Francisco SPCA rises out of the city's industrial garment district like a $29-million-dollar lotus flower; a 60,000-square-foot, light-filled remodel of a former Hamm's brewery, with modern sculptures and faux indoor trees, and climate-controlled cat and dog apartments instead of cages. Its 97 percent adoption rate is among the highest in the nation, and potential pet owners are carefully screened. There's an on-site animal hospital, and a small army of volunteers who exercise and groom the animals around the clock.

When it opened, the SPCA was celebrated with glitzy galas and in press releases as a feat of urban renewal for a neighborhood of former textile warehouses and sewing factories struggling to remake itself. As Jenn and I make our way there, we drive past chain stores that now occupy cinderblock warehouses painted in dull colors with metal fire escapes and opaque chicken-wire glass windows. We pass auto body shops encircled by weathered and listing fences, and as the traffic inches slowly down the narrow streets we catch glimpses down the alleys of pop-up tent cities where the city's houseless nomads have staked their claims. Finally, we reach the gleaming SPCA, relishing the rare San Francisco luxury of being able to park in a spacious guest parking lot behind the building. I'm downright giddy, chirping at Edie about the adventure that awaits her. I swing open the back door, clip her leash to her harness and she just sits there, eyeing me warily.

"C'mon, wanna go play with your friends?"

Edie apparently still wants to think about it. She nudges her nose out the door and takes a whiff, then pulls her head back into the Prius. She seems conflicted.

"Wanna cookie?" Jenn says, waving a biscuit just outside the car door.

Edie leaps to the pavement, snapping the cookie out of Jenn's hand in midair.

I have to wonder if Edie is working us. Is she truly conflicted, or has she figured out that all she has to do is ignore our first command so that we'll bribe her with an encouragement cookie?

"Oh, look who's ready now," I say.

We cross the parking lot, heading toward a typical midmorning San Francisco street teeming with honking cars, double-parked Uber drivers, and ferret-thin bike messengers slaloming through it all. It's only a two-block walk to the SPCA's front door, but we'll have to maneuver around a half dozen rumbling delivery trucks backed into loading bays, their cabs blocking the sidewalk, forcing pedestrians to detour into the busy street.

Edie takes a few steps, then sits down. I feel a tug on the leash and look back to see what the holdup is. Edie's forearms are rigid, and she's leaning back with all her body weight, every muscle in her body resisting forward motion.

Maybe she needs a moment to get her bearings. For whatever reason, she's not quite ready to go, so I'll just give her a minute. Joggers, delivery people pushing dollies, and owners coming and going from the SPCA with their pets navigate around our standoff, as Edie and I obstruct foot traffic, staring at one another with the leash taut between us. I'm not about to give in to Edie's protest, not after all the struggle to get her a coveted spot in class. I'm happy to wait her out.

"C'mon, Edie! This is going to be fun!" I try, giving the leash a little tug. I don't know how it's possible that such a tiny thing suddenly feels like an industrial-size sack of flour.

I tug again, a little harder this time. Edie's toenails screech against the sidewalk, as she doubles down on her grievance.

"Don't pull her!" Jenn says, wresting the leash out of my hand. Now the three of us are having a real family tug-of-war for all the world to see. I suddenly feel horrible—how did I become a puppy-yanker? I walk back to Edie and crouch next to her.

"Hey baby girl, what's wrong?"

Her eyes are so wide I can see the whites around her pupils. I scratch her chest and her muscles are rigid beneath my fingers. I caress her back and tummy. Edie's entire body feels like it's made out of wood. Our puppy is terrified.

"This street is way too busy for her," I say.

I slide one arm under Edie's armpits, and the other under her bum, and carry her with her back pressed against my chest, her four paws bouncing with each step of mine, the rest of the way to the SPCA. We step into a long hallway already crisscrossed with leashes as puppies get an early start on play, yipping impatiently, which only causes their owners to bark back at their charges, demanding better manners. I sit down in a plastic chair closest to the door away from the ruckus and place Edie on my lap, while Jenn needles her way through the crowd to get to the check-in desk.

I can feel Edie trembling, and I whisper to her that she's a good girl, and that she's okay, and cluck softly to her like I did when we first brought her home, hoping the familiar sound of reassurance will settle her nerves. Edie won't acknowledge me, instead she is on sentry alert, swiveling her head to survey all the little explosions of puppy joy happening all around us. Edie's speeding heartbeat seems to amplify my own, as worry creeps in. I've never seen a puppy recoil from other puppies. That just goes against the law of the universe. I tell myself that Edie just needs a minute to recover from all the loud noises we encountered on the sidewalk. Once she's in the center of a puppy pile, she'll snap out of it.

Jenn appears and takes the empty seat next to me.

"How's she doing?"

"Still dubious."

"Cookie?" Jenn offers again, but Edie ignores her.

"Huh, that's a first," Jenn says, dropping the cookie back into the fanny pack.

Just then, three women in matching SPCA polo shirts, khaki pants, and lanyards emerge from a door in the hallway and lay out the rules. They will separate the dogs by size and assign them to three separate play areas inside a huge gymnasium. Each section will have no more than six puppies, and an SPCA trainer will be on hand to help guide play and show owners how to interrupt their pets for periodic time-outs. They ask newcomers for a show of hands. Then they ask if anyone has a dog with special needs, or a dog who might be fearful. I sit there, silent, even though I'm the only owner whose puppy refuses to leave her lap.

We are directed to take Edie into the partition where the largest breed puppies will play—the Labs, standard poodles, German shepherds, and another golden who is tugging on his leash to get closer to Edie. The trainer instructs us to kneel next to our dogs and keep one hand on the clip of the leash. On three, we release our hounds. As if pulled by a magnet, the puppies come together into a knot of legs and tails, their barking echoing off the concrete walls. I don't see Edie. I look closer, and can't find her in the scrum. I look behind me and there she is, bolting in the opposite direction with her ears back, toward the farthest corner of the room.

When Jenn and I catch up to her, she's panting and pacing

in the corner like a caged panther, looking for a way out. She's wedged herself so far into the corner that her nose is touching the wall. She's sniffing frantically, trying to find the door we came through.

As Jenn reattaches the leash to Edie's collar, I turn in a circle, looking for help, for someone, anyone, to tell me what's wrong with our puppy. My mind unspools as it tries to make sense of what my eyes can't believe. Edie, who we so carefully socialized, Edie the nonstop frolicker, the sparring partner of Pancho, the chewer of shoelaces, and harasser of Lulu, is running in terror from her peers. This is so unexpected, so nonsensical, my brain seizes up and I don't know what to do. I stand there feeling paralyzed, looking at Edie as if she's somebody else's dog.

"Shhhhh, it's okay, Noonie," Jenn says, massaging her fingers into Edie's coat, trying to soothe her.

Edie pulls her nose out of the corner for a quick glance over her shoulder to acknowledge us, then snaps her head back. She yawns dramatically, opening her mouth wide like a crocodile, then snapping it shut and shaking her head violently at the finish.

"That's a sign of stress," says an SPCA trainer, who I hadn't noticed come up behind us.

"What's happening?" I practically beg for an answer.

The trainer asks if this is Edie's first puppy play group, and I nod. She explains that the noise and activity can overwhelm some dogs at first, and directs us to move Edie into the adjacent pen with the medium-sized breeds. As soon as she says it, I feel like she's just handed me my test back with a big, red *F* written on the top. And that's just not who I am. It throws me off to be the person who needs extra help in the classroom, and it embarrasses me. I was always a teacher's pet, the second-grader enlisted to help tutor the kindergarteners, the precocious girl who skipped third grade and graduated from high school a year early. I don't go *backward*. As we're lifting Edie over the partition to the next pen over, I am overcome with shame. I don't like needing help, and I don't want SPCA pity. I want answers. What's wrong with Edie?

The trainer in the new pen has her eyes on us, having watched the whole scenario go down before we stepped in. We set Edie down amid a group of midsize terriers and cattle dogs, but to Edie's mind, size doesn't matter. Before we can even unclip her, she's tugging Jenn back in the direction of the door. The trainer jogs over to us and politely suggests we move Edie into the toy dog section.

This is Edie's final shot. This last play area is for teacup breeds—Chihuahuas and Pomeranians so small they can run under Edie's belly without touching a hair on her coat. Edie surveys the new scene, chooses a wall farthest from the dogs, and sits in front of it, the only wallflower in the pack. She hangs her head, and refuses to make eye contact with anyone.

"Well, at least she's not running away," Jenn offers.

Edie looks so forlorn; I can't stand it. When I sit on the floor and put her in my lap to comfort her, another SPCA trainer comes over to chastise me for rewarding Edie for being antisocial. I stand up and gently nudge Edie toward the micropuppies, but the woman abruptly corrects me again, explaining that I am supposed to be Edie's safety zone, and never to push her away from me. I want to scream.

"Which is it, then?" I demand, not even trying to mask my irritation.

I feel Jenn clasp my elbow and guide me away from the woman with the SPCA lanyard.

"She's only trying to help," Jenn says. My wife has adopted an extra soothing tone, and it pisses me off that she's using her professional crisis intervention skills on me.

"Help! She's giving me completely mixed messages! If I'm not supposed to comfort Edie, or encourage her to play, what am I supposed to do?"

"Those are probably the extremes," Jenn says. "I'm sure the answer is somewhere in between."

"Well, it would be nice if she could tell us what it is."

"Breathe, Meredith. This is the San Francisco SPCA. They know what they're doing. Let me go talk to her."

With Edie shivering by my side, I watch Jenn and the trainer talking, wishing I had my wife's decorum. She's absolutely unflappable. I'll never forget the time a man showed up when I was having a garage sale outside Mag and Barbara's house, screaming that he lived in my flat and that everything I was selling belonged to him. His rage was terrifying, and he was obviously high on something, but Jenn was the only person he'd listen to. She somehow got him to sit down on the sidewalk and take deep breaths. In less than five minutes, two police cruisers, a fire engine, and an ambulance materialized with lights and sirens wailing, answering the call she'd surreptitiously placed while talking him down.

Jenn and the SPCA woman are waving me and Edie over. The trainer directs us to one of the plastic kiddie swimming pools set out for puppy exploring and tells us to throw treats in to get Edie to focus on something besides the other dogs. We toss pieces of her kibble into the empty pool and the woman frowns. We were supposed to bring "high-value" treats, like the organic duck jerky she has in a canvas pouch strapped to her waist. Edie sniffs, leans over the edge and stretches her neck as far as it will go, but despite all the SPCA woman's coaxing, Edie won't set one toenail inside that plastic pool. Instead, a Chihuahua puppy no bigger than a chipmunk leaps in and steals Edie's food.

I'm exasperated and flattened that we have a cowardly dog, and I'm not taking it well. I want this woman to know that we aren't clueless; that this is my *THIRD* golden; that we've done everything by the book to ensure Edie's health and wellness. Edie can't be acting this way because we failed to socialize her, so that leaves just one possibility—there's something off about Edie. We've reached the end of the line at this puppy social, and she's done nothing but be antisocial. Now, it's me who's panicking. I'm deeply worried about Edie.

The organizer suggests a time-out and gives us permission to take our panting puppy to the staff kitchen for some water. But when we get there, Edie won't even look at the bowl we place before her. Long strings of drool sway from either side of her muzzle—yet another sign of stress. "Let's cut bait," Jenn says. "This obviously isn't working out."

My voice is hitching as I try to stifle a cry. If there's something wrong with Edie's brain, I can't fix that. I wouldn't even know where to begin.

"Hey, hey, there's no need to cry, it's okay," Jenn says, now sidled with two meltdowns.

"It's not, Jenn. This is not okay."

"It's just too much stimulation. We can try again when she's a little older."

"But it shouldn't be too much stimulation. Did you see how many puppies her age were thrilled to be stimulated?"

"She'll grow out of it. Just give it time. C'mon, let's get her out of here."

Jenn tries to get me to talk more in the car, but I'm morose. I'm not used to failure, yet I'm somehow failing this dog. Edie's timidity is beyond baffling, and it's an emotion I've never understood or had patience for. Jenn and I got through our childhoods by confronting fear, not succumbing to it. Stress is our frenemy—we thrive on it, we are familiar with it, and while we don't always enjoy it, we know that we will eventually outwit it. But now we've taken in a fragile little puppy who is wired exactly the opposite of us. And how do you reassure another species without words that they are safe? I'm confronted with a problem I have no idea how to begin to solve.

"Something's wrong with Edie," I finally say.

Jenn is taken aback. "Don't say that! Don't let her hear you say that. If you give that energy, it'll become true. It's just puppy fear. Trust me, she'll grow out of it."

Trust me? Me who has never had a dog? I think this, and thankfully I do not say it.

Jenn means well, but she is naive. She is reassuring me based on what she assumes is true, not on the real experience of raising a dog. All I know is that when I took Stella to her first obedience class, she befriended every puppy in the room within minutes. I remember she even held up class a few times because she wouldn't stop playing, forcing me to fetch her from under a piano in the corner where she liked to tussle with her classmates.

Jenn never knew Stella as a puppy, so she can't see what I see, and that is Stella at the same age as Edie, bounding through the world with trust and abandon—a yellow goofball bursting with confidence and mischief.

Something about this just doesn't feel right.

4

Puppy School

We are the first ones here. The parking lot outside the American Legion Hall in San Carlos has only a handful of cars. They're clustered near a blue door that's propped open by a sand-filled coffee can sprouting a stubble of cigarette butts.

"You sure this is it?" Jenn asks, looking around for a sign indicating where the puppy training class is. A Steve Miller song is thumping behind the blue door, punctuated by muffled laughter and the distinct sound of clinking beer bottles. I'd canceled all our coveted spots in the SPCA play groups and enrolled Edie in a six-week puppy training program, but somehow we're standing outside a bar.

"Let's give it a few more minutes," I say, warily eyeing the daylight downshift to dusk.

Just then, a woman with leathery skin and feathered hair peeks out from behind the door. She's wearing the warm, spontaneous grin of someone who's spent the better part of a day on a barstool. When her gaze lands on Edie, she hops in place with the unbridled glee of a game show winner.

"Guys! Guys!" she shouts into the bar. "It's seven o'clock!"

A half dozen people teeter into the parking lot to ogle our puppy. They skip the hellos as they close in around Edie, trying to coax her to come closer. One man goes down on a knee and clicks his tongue at Edie like he's calling a horse.

"C'mere, baby—" *cluck-cluck-cluck* "—come on, now, it's okay."

From Edie's point of view, they must look like zombies, murmuring unintelligibly as they surround her with out-stretched arms. I feel Jenn's body stiffen in response, and her apprehension must travel down the leash and straight into Edie because our puppy does an about-face, tugging the leash toward our car.

"Is there a puppy class near here?" I say, as Jenn picks Edie up and holds her protectively.

"Right there, honey," a woman says, lifting a pink acrylic nail from her pint glass to point to an identical unmarked blue door a few feet away. Several car doors open behind us and we turn to see more people arriving with puppies. The bar crowd shifts its focus to the other puppies as Jenn bounces Edie softly like a mother with her child, trying to settle her while we watch a chocolate Lab, a terrier, another golden, and some type of miniature purse dog respond enthusiastically to the welcoming committee. Edie is wriggling to get out of Jenn's arms, still campaigning to return to the back seat of the car.

"Maybe she isn't ready for this," Jenn says.

Edie *has* to be ready for this. She's four months old, the same age as all the other puppies waiting for class to start. If we keep coddling Edie every time she gets scared, all we'll be doing is rewarding and reinforcing her timidity. Then she'll never grow a backbone. But I say none of this to Jenn, because I don't want Jenn to know how increasingly concerned I've become about Edie. I had promised Jenn that I could handle raising a puppy, and so now I'm handling it with tough love. The only thing that matters to me right now is getting Edie over her fear quickly before it becomes a permanent trait.

"We came all this way, let's just see how she does," I say.

Jenn shrugs her shoulders, her way of letting me know she disagrees, but not enough to make an issue of it. And here we come to our first parenting crossroads. To Jenn, it's just puppy school, and she doesn't see what the big deal is if we wait a month or so and sign up for the next one. But Jenn doesn't have a puppy baseline. Edie should be growing more confident, not less, as time goes on. She should be more Stella-like. What we need is an expert, not more time. Also, I'm not about to give up now, after carefully choosing *this* particular class, and *this* particular instructor, and then slogging through ninety minutes of commuter traffic to get here.

I enrolled Edie in the same SIRIUS Dog and Puppy Training School that Stella had attended, because it worked. Stella's excellent manners proved that dogs can be trained without using intimidation or punishment, which was a revolutionary concept when SIRIUS started in the Bay Area in the early 1980s as one of the nation's earliest off-leash socialization and training programs specifically for puppies. Dr. Ian Dunbar, the founder, advocated a training method based on rewards to shape behavior, rather than the "hit-'em-with-a-rolled-up-newspaper" punishment approach. He eventually started The Center for Applied Animal Behavior in Berkeley, and his humane approach went mainstream, having successfully argued against the need for corporal punishment, choke collars, shock devices, or verbal abuse to extract a dog's compliance. Stella never forgot what she learned in SIRIUS puppy class, mastering in twelve weeks how to sit, lie down, stay, go to bed, leave it, drop it, come when called, and walk calmly on a leash. All of it served her the rest of her life, keeping her safe and making strangers feel safe around her. Jenn always thought Stella was born with a good disposition, but now she's about to find out that it was carefully crafted by cookies.

It would've been so much easier to enroll Edie in the Dunbar-method class five miles from our house. But I wanted to make sure we chose an experienced instructor who would know what to do if Edie had another meltdown. I spent an entire day studying the résumés of every SIRIUS trainer at all seventeen Bay Area locations, and settled on Sara.

Sara's résumé blew me away. She has a PhD in Psychology/Animal Behavior from Rutgers University with a specialty in animal communication and animal/environmental interrelationships. She is certified to teach dog training by the Certification Council for Professional Dog Trainers, her profession's leading standardized credentialing program in North America. To earn her "Certified Professional Dog Training—Knowledge Assessed" credential, she had to study current behavioral science and pass an extensive test on ethology, canine learning theory, dog training technique, animal husbandry, and classroom teaching skills.

I also liked that she once worked in the Behavior and Training Department at San Francisco Animal Care and Control, the city-run animal shelter. Sara's job was to assess the behavior of stray and surrendered dogs to figure out which ones were adoptable. She taught handling skills to volunteer dog walkers and counseled people who adopted pets. She also volunteered at the Peninsula Humane Society, where she helped socialize shelter puppies and answered people's dog behavior questions on the help line.

I don't believe I could have found anyone more qualified to help us unravel the knot that is Edie.

Our unwitting savior is ready for us, in a crisp oxford shirt and jeans, tennis shoes, and a fanny pack worn in front stuffed with tiny cubes of cheese. On the table behind her is an array of other tasty morsels dogs might like if the go-to cheese is rebuffed, as well as rolls of paper towels, floor cleaner in a spray bottle, and plastic dog waste bags. Sara is petite, with dark spring curls and a high, reedy voice that she amplifies with a clip-on microphone that projects through a small speaker she wears on a strap slung across her chest. Her whole demeanor is no-nonsense, from the way she eyes the five puppies and their handlers as we enter the room, looking for clues to what sorts of issues are going to come up in this particular class.

I give myself an imaginary high five for picking the right woman for the job. What I notice about her is her focus on the welfare of the animals. She's not nervous, she's not trying to please us; she's too busy reading the unspoken dynamics between people and their pets as we walk in. I wonder what she thinks about Jenn and me, the only ones carrying our puppy into the room because Edie refuses to go willingly.

Sara opens the class by sharing her approach to training, which aligns with Dunbar's positive reinforcement methodology. The command "No!" has limited usefulness, she says, because it doesn't tell our puppies what we want them to do. We will learn instead to communicate with our puppies by using treats, verbal cues, hand signals, and praise to reinforce the behaviors we want to see.

She has us start at the beginning—teaching our puppies to enjoy being handled. Sara asks us to sit with our puppies in our laps and feed them treats for letting us touch their ears, paws, mouth, tail. We transform ourselves into human Pez dispensers, feeding bits of hotdog to Edie, reinforcing the notion that good things happen when we touch her. What we are doing is classical Pavlovian conditioning, creating a positive association by teaching Edie to link our touch with a yummy treat.

Edie aces the first assignment, and we are allowed to progress to the next step—rewarding her for doing something when we ask. If Edie looks at us when we say her name, she gets a cookie. If she takes steps toward us when we say "Come!" while walking backward, bingo! Cookie! The professional term for rewarding specific behavior is "operant conditioning." In this case, we are rewarding Edie for her first baby steps toward becoming a dog that comes running the instant you call her.

To our surprise, Edie starts to calm down during class. She's highly treat motivated, and it's easy to get her to follow us. When Sara says time is up, I can't believe an hour has gone by already. Or that Edie lasted the entire time.

The following week, Edie allows herself to be walked into puppy class. The agenda for the second class is to teach Edie to sit. Following the Dunbar method, there will be no pushing Edie's rump down. Instead, we will be using verbal cues and hand signals. Jenn and I recycle the hand sign I used with Stella, which is the right hand index finger pointing up in the "#1" sign. I offer to skip this exercise, because I've already trained two dogs how to sit, and this will be Jenn's first time.

First, Jenn lures Edie into a seated position with a treat. She begins by saying "sit" and showing Edie the treat in her hand, then raising the cookie in front of Edie's nose. The idea is to get Edie's eyes to follow the cookie, which makes her rear naturally hit the ground. The moment she's seated, *jackpot!* She gets the treat. Next, Sara instructs Jenn to remove the lure, and verbally ask Edie to sit while raising our hand signal. Eventually, Edie will learn to associate the #1 sign with the reward. The goal is to get our dog to sit when she hears the word or sees us lift a finger.

But we shouldn't feed Edie the treat out of our signaling hand, Sara says, pausing to make sure we all understand this very important point. In dog training, it's vital to keep the signaling and feeding hands separate. That way, puppies learn to focus on the signal first, and the reward second. They learn to fulfill what you want, to get what they want. If we mess this part up, we could inadvertently shape Edie into a dog that refuses to obey unless she gets paid upfront.

I take a seat on a folding chair against the wall, while Jenn walks to the middle of the room where she and Edie get into position, standing facing one another.

"Sit," Jenn says, pointing to the ground.

What is that? That's not even one of the hand signals.

Sara asks Jenn if that's the signal we're already using at home.

"Yes?" Jenn says, looking to me for confirmation.

"No!" I call from the sidelines. "Sit is pointing up."

"Oh, right," Jenn says.

"Sit," my wife says, matter-of-factly. This time she points correctly but there's no authority in her voice. Her command lands like a stone dropped into a pond. Edie wanders toward the chocolate Lab.

Sara walks over and gently suggests we try getting our puppy's attention in a distracting environment with more energy and a higher voice. She demonstrates, calling Edie in an animated puppet-show voice, and we watch, spellbound, as our preoccupied puppy lifts her head to track the funny sound, and then jogs to Sara to sit at her feet for a bit of cheese. It's the first time Edie has tasted the miracle of dairy, and her whole body vibrates with pleasure.

"Maybe we shoulda brought cheese," Jenn says.

We brought a plastic baggie with bits of hotdog, which now that I think about it, is full of junk meat and could possibly make Edie sick. The other dog owners brought chicken, dehydrated beef liver, or organic treats designed specifically for training. It's the second time we've messed up the high-value treat thing, and we really need to step it up. I wander over to the table where Sara has set out an array of edible puppy enticements, and take note of what she uses.

"Take whatever you need," she offers.

Jenn gets ready to give it another go. Edie is turned away from Jenn, inhaling a scent on the linoleum.

"Sit!" Jenn chirps to the back of Edie's head, finger aloft.

Oh, dear Lord.

"Honey, you need to get her eye contact first," I correct her again. "She can't see your hand."

It's all I can do to keep from interrupting Jenn to show her how to do it. Jenn offers Edie a bit of cheese to distract her from the floor. Edie gobbles the treat, then looks expectantly for more. Jenn takes another morsel from her pocket and holds her index finger up.

"Sit!"

This time Edie sits. Our puppy quickly figures out that if she keeps her eyes on the prize, her butt will touch the floor and a cookie will land in her mouth. I watch Jenn lure Edie more than a dozen times, before I realize Jenn didn't understand the part about removing the lure and moving on to just the hand signal. It's important to get rid of the lure as soon as possible, because luring too much could create a dog that will ignore your commands, refusing to do anything without seeing the treat first.

"Honey, hide the treat in your other hand!"

"What?"

"Your free hand!"

"Which hand?"

Now I need to take over. I walk over to Jenn and hold out my palm.

"Let me show you," I say. Jenn drops a treat in my left hand, I make a fist around it and hide it behind my back.

"Sit," I say, pointing to the ceiling with my right index finger. Edie lowers her tushie to the ground, and I bring my left fist around, unclasp my fingers, and present Edie with the reward.

"Like that."

Jenn tries again, but still gets it wrong, feeding Edie out of her signaling hand.

"Jenn, seriously!"

"What? What'd I do?"

My exasperation takes over and now we're arguing in front of Edie, and our dog looks from one of us to the other, unsure what to do. I'm like that Little League parent who screams at the umpire, interrupting the game, and worse I'm only confusing our poor dog.

Jenn and I don't argue. That's not to say I don't try, but she has mastered how to massage my outbursts into calm, adult conversations. And we certainly never raise our voices in public. But this time, Jenn is staring me down. She yanks the leash from my hand and booms, "I got this!"

I'm stunned, and stare at Jenn as if I've never seen her before. This must be her police voice, two octaves lower than I've ever heard. It's scary and I immediately back down. I hear someone clearing their throat behind us.

"She doesn't know who to follow," Sara says diplomatically. "Perhaps it would work better if you each took turns teaching her."

That's when I realize I need a time-out, and slink back to my chair. I have a meditative think and come up with this wisdom: I have become extremely anxious about Edie's anxiousness. This puppy is defying everything I thought I knew about raising goldens, making me doubt myself and the promises I made to Jenn. I'm worried Jenn is starting to doubt me, too. I've lost my dog mojo and I desperately want it back, and quickly, before we run out of time to fix this dog. Edie is nearly sixteen weeks old, marking the cutoff on the short window of time to rid her of her fears before they become part of her adult personality. In my impatience I can't even give Jenn the benefit of the doubt that she will learn the dog commands and hand signals correctly. I am a canine helicopter mom!

I close my eyes and hum the chorus to "Let It Be" so softly that no one can hear me. I punctuate each lyric with a long exhale before moving on to the next verse. By the time I finish my calming Beatles breathing exercises, Sara announces it's time for free play. She selects two puppies at a time to romp off-leash in the center of the room, and points at Edie and Teddy, the chocolate Lab. My heart flutters. Will Edie recoil in front of the whole class? Or will she make us proud? My inner Little League parent rockets back to the surface: *C'mon, baby, keep your eye on the ball! Elbows up! Bend your knees! You can DO this!*

"Okay, go play!" Sara chimes, her voice bursting with intentional exuberance.

Teddy gallops toward Edie and offers a play bow at her feet. Edie considers this, then takes a few tentative steps closer and gently bats him on the shoulder with her right paw. It's on. Teddy springs into the air, and Edie tackles him. Teddy squirms free and returns the favor, pouncing on Edie, who pedals her hind feet into his belly. He tugs on her ears, then she wriggles away so he can chase her. Using a language only they can hear, they abruptly reverse course so Edie can take a turn as the chaser. Sara lets it go for a couple minutes, then instructs us and Teddy's owner to say "Gotcha!" as we grab their collars and offer a treat to stop their play session. Stopping a pleasurable experience such as playing is a huge bummer for puppies, but if they get a consolation cookie, they will learn that it's not the end of the world. It teaches them to still come to you, even when they'd rather keep playing. Cookies prevent puppies from forming the opinion that their owners are buzzkills who should be ignored.

"Was that fun, Edie?" says Jenn, lifting her up and carrying her back to the wall where we wait for the other puppies to have their turn. We are both beaming.

"See?" Jenn whispers. "She's fine."

We leave feeling that we've been communicating with Edie all wrong—cajoling and pushing her to do what we want instead of acting a little silly the way Sara does, using cartoon voices to convince Edie to try new things. Puppies are naturally curious, and if we act as if we are having delirious fun doing something, they will want to join in. Instead, we've been acting like overbearing mothers, demanding Edie progress through the steps we have laid out for her, and doing nothing to hide our disappointment and frustration when she doesn't pass our tests.

Back in the car, I wait until Jenn wends her way through the darkened backstreets to the freeway before summoning an apology.

"I think puppy school is good for Edie," I say, as an opener.

"She does much better in a smaller setting," Jenn says.

Edie is curled on my lap, gnawing on a teething ring shaped like a set of keys with nubby pink-and-blue bones in place of the keys. Every once in a while, she misses and chomps one of my fingers with her sharp baby teeth.

"Hey, sorry I was such a jerk," I say, prying my thumb from Edie's jaws.

Jenn reaches over and rubs my thumb.

"She draw blood?"

"Not this time," I say.

Jenn waits a beat, collecting her thoughts.

"When you get stressed out, you stress her out," Jenn says. "And me, too."

I flash back to childhood, remembering how my mother could control the dinner table, or Christmas Day, with her sour mood, willing it to equalize into everyone else until eventually nobody felt like speaking or laughing anymore. I remember the stories Jenn told me about running away into the woods to escape her stepfather's unpredictable outbursts. She'd pass the day throwing rocks at trees, practicing her aim. I don't want to become that kind of person whose emotions leak into others.

"I guess I didn't realize how deeply worried I am about Edie."

"Sara seems like a real professional," Jenn says.

I understand that I need to chill out, but I'm still concerned that Jenn's being too lackadaisical about training. I may need to bring it down a notch, but she also needs to bring it up.

"It's only going to work if we are on the same page about how to train her. We have to agree on what the hand signals are going to be," I say.

"You're worrying again," says Jenn. "Look, you're just going to have to sit your bossy-ass down and trust me to learn this, okay?"

And just like that, Jenn disarms me. She's made me see that I'm worrying about what might happen and missing the chance to celebrate that Edie had fun, didn't run out of the room, and learned some stuff. And my wife is here, with me, participating in the raising of Edie. Jenn may not be picking up the dog handling skills at my preferred pace, but I should be thankful she's here at all given the intensity of her job. It dawns on me that we are the only couple in class. The other four dog owners are coming solo.

"How about this," Jenn says. "Let's alternate being the trainer each class. One of us will give Edie commands and the other will observe?"

"Deal," I say, raising her wrist to my lips. She gets a gold star for putting up with me.

"And we need better treats," Jenn says.

"I'm sure we can find some organic, farm-to-table, artisanal, handcrafted dog treats in this town."

"Or we could just go to Westlake Joe's for steaks and save the leftovers," Jenn says, wriggling her eyebrows at me.

"I like the way you think."

Over the next few weeks, Edie continues to thrive in class. When she masters walking on a leash indoors, we try taking her on her first walk around the block outside our house. But halfway to the corner, she puts on the brakes and refuses to take another step. We swivel our heads looking for the source of her concern, but our suburban street of midcentury modern homes is quiet, the only sound the crows fussing in the trees. Edith tugs us back home, choking with the effort as if the grim reaper is on her tail. We try again a few days later, this time coaxing her to the corner with bits of leftover steak, but the first car that whooshes past sends her choking and coughing back for home with her tail between her legs.

We wait a few days between each attempt, but every outing brings a new fright—a garage door opening, a motorcycle, a skateboard, a barking dog, an airplane. One day she spots men removing a fridge from a delivery truck across the street and she halts, unwilling to move. Another time she won't walk past a fire hydrant.

Edie's fear list keeps growing. This becomes all we talk about. Instead of the hilarious puppy stories I'd envisioned us sharing over dinner, our nightly conversations turn into armchair medical consults as we try to diagnose Edie's problem. Jenn peppers me with questions about Stella's puppyhood, searching for clues, but there is no comparison. She keeps asking if Stella behaved like this, posing the question in different ways, hoping an answer will present itself. As the self-proclaimed dog expert in the relationship, I am uncharacteristically quiet, and frustrated that I don't know what's going on. I'm also starting to worry that Jenn feels misled because the puppy paradise I'd promised hasn't materialized. My wife had accepted my assurances that a puppy would enhance our relationship; now I feel helpless as our lives become more complicated as Edie gets more confusing.

Indoors, Edie is a different dog. She thinks it's funny when Lulu ambushes her, springing out from behind a corner, hissing and boxing Edie's muzzle with her paws. Lulu is just displaying her displeasure at the new housemate, yet Edie doesn't get the message and military crawls on her belly after Lulu, trying to engage the elderly cat to play. When one of us is taking a bath, Edie hops in with us, lowering herself into a Sphinx, keeping just her head above the water. I've never seen a dog that likes to just sit and soak, like she's at a spa. She seems completely at ease with the hair dryer, the vacuum, and noises coming from the stereo or TV. It's like she has a split personality, one for home and one for outside our four walls.

I tell my wife that Edie doesn't remind me of any dog I've ever known. But she does remind me of a horse that I used to ride. In my twenties I'd helped a friend exercise her two horses every week, riding them side by side along a trail through gladiola fields behind the stables. Once, there was an aluminum garbage can on the trail that hadn't been there before. My horse turned to a statue and refused to walk by it. The owner tried everything to calm the horse, but eventually we gave up and had to turn the horses around.

I hadn't thought of that horse in more than twenty years. But Edith is strikingly similar to that animal in the way she

can't seem to process new information quickly without her
circuits overloading. We give up the neighborhood walks and
decide to try secluded trails, thinking it's the movement of
street traffic that's bothering Edie. We take her to Land's End,
where there's a shaded hiking trail winding through eucalyptus and cypress groves with stunning views of the Golden
Gate Bridge. We arrive at six in the morning on a weekday,
hoping to avoid people. Edie walks farther than ever before,
until someone approaches with an umbrella. She turns and
streaks for the parking lot, pulling me for a good ten minutes all the way to my truck. She rises on her hind legs and
scratches the passenger-side door to hurry me to open it. She
leaps inside and wedges her backside into a corner of the cab.

Back inside the truck, Edie's shallow panting is fogging
up the windows, and I feel the heat of tears collecting in my
eyes. It's as if Edie's skittishness is metastasizing.

"Nothing is working," I say.

"Maybe she is slower to learn than other puppies, but she'll
grow out of it. We just need to give her more time," Jenn says.

I'm worried her fear is chronic. I've never seen a puppy
spook this easily. I'm now having second thoughts about our
upcoming trip to Montana, where Jenn's college friends Karen
and Suzette are getting married. The small ceremony will
be alongside a river within a nature preserve, and the recep-
tion will be at their two-story log cabin they've christened
"Shangri-Log." I tell Jenn that maybe I should stay home
with Edie.

"What? Meredith, no. What happened to leaving Edie with
Kendra?" Jenn asks.

Kendra, who now operates a doggie daycare and boarding business out of her home in a quiet East Bay suburb, had

agreed to take Edie for the long weekend. As someone who has always preferred the company of dogs to people, Kendra left the flagging newspaper business to follow her true passion, and now blissfully shares her two-bedroom house with up to five dogs on any given day. When her charges aren't romping around her big backyard, they're dogpiling on her sofa, or sprawling out on the various dog beds that sprout like mushrooms from the floor, as Parisian café music streaming from the TV lulls them to sleep. Her pampered pooches do double duty as her muses—Kendra creates black-and-white documentary-style photos of dogs that she sells for good money to pet owners. Kendra is a self-made artist and entrepreneur with a sixth sense for dogs. I trust her implicitly, but I don't trust Edie can cope with a change in routine. When I brought Edie to Kendra's house for a practice visit a couple weeks ago, she took one look at the dog pack and wedged herself into the space between the couch arm and the wall and refused to come out.

"I'm afraid she'll be too traumatized at Kendra's," I say.

"But how is Edie supposed to learn, if we don't expose her to new things and give her challenges to overcome?" Jenn counters. "I get that we have to take good care of her, but we can't keep her in a bubble. We can't let a puppy rule our lives."

We both have a point, which is the point—there's no easy answer. Am I overreacting? Would a few days with other dogs be good for Edie? Would she learn about self-assurance by observing them? Or am I being irresponsible? I want to do what is best for our puppy, yet I want to do what is best for our marriage. Jenn would be crushed if I backed out of the wedding, and I wouldn't blame her. My wife keeps her inner circle of friends very small, and Karen and Suzette were her best friends in college. We'd been looking forward to celebrating, hiking, and barbecuing with them in Big Sky Country. I don't know how this came down to a choice between abandoning my puppy or abandoning my wife. I look from Jenn, to Edie in the back seat, and they both have the same dejected look.

"We need to enroll her in Puppy II," I say.

Which turns out to be an excellent idea. Halfway through the second class, Edie learns to come more reliably, to stay in one spot when we walk away from her, and to go sit on her yoga mat on command. She's learning impulse control. We can put a treat before her and make her wait for permission to eat it. Long gone are the first-day jitters, and she now leaps out of the car to greet the bar regulars and to roll around with her classmate Teddy, who matriculated with her. Edie does much better if she's allowed to go at her own pace. She can acclimate to a new environment if she returns to it over and over again, for brief visits. And Jenn and I have figured out how to take turns teaching Edie in class, and I am keeping my unsolicited dog training advice to myself, so my wife can also learn at her own pace. I see now why people say dog training is really people training...with a dog. The routine is good for Edie, giving her enough time to get familiar with the building and the scents and the dog owners so she feels safe enough to interact. And it's relaxed me and Jenn, too, to know that even if our puppy is too afraid to go on walks, at least we have this one respite, this one safety zone where Edie can stretch her legs and her mind. Puppy class is a ray of hope.

I make a second practice visit to Kendra's house, and Edie does a little better this time. She still shies away from the other dogs, but she doesn't hide from them.

"She'll be fine," Kendra says, picking Edie up and cuddling her. "If she gets overwhelmed, I can separate her from the other dogs and put her in my bedroom."

Edie nuzzles her nose into Kendra's long brown hair. I decide to go to Montana.

We have an early morning flight, so I drive Edie to Kendra's the night before. As soon as we walk through the front door, the handful of day care dogs erupt into a bark-fest, excited to see a newcomer. Edie recoils, and tries to run down the hallway to escape, only to get herself cornered in Kendra's small office. While Kendra calls the dogs back, I crawl under her desk and extract Edie, and press her trembling body to my chest. She's panting hard, and her lips are pulled back in a pained grimace.

Kendra suggests taking Edie to the sanctuary of her bedroom, where she can acclimate to the sounds and smells of the house. Once we are inside the room with the door closed, I settle Edie with her own blankets inside one of the empty crates that are clustered at the foot of Kendra's bed. I shut the window and close the curtains to drown out the sound of the elevated BART commuter train, which rumbles overhead on a regular commute schedule.

Edie trots straight into the crate and sits with her back in a far corner of it, ignoring the chew bones and toys I place next to her. I stroke her fur, whispering soft encouragements until she relaxes enough to lie down. She keeps her eyes locked on me, and I get the sensation that she knows something is different this time, that I'm leaving her behind. I feel my resolve melting away, and I decide that I will stay with her until she falls asleep, no matter how long it takes. I text Jenn to tell her to go ahead and have dinner without me. I can't leave knowing Edie watched me walk away from her. I bunch up some blankets for myself and shift onto my side, keeping one hand extended into the crate so I can feel the rise and fall of her breathing. I sing softly to her, alternating between "You Are My Sunshine" and little ditties I make up about being a brave girl with golden hair.

Thirty minutes go by, then an hour. Kendra pokes her head in to check on us and see if I want any mushroom soup for dinner. The sun goes down and darkness descends. I feel Edie lick my fingers, and I keep singing. Finally, I hear faint snores, and feel Edie's breath settle into a rhythm. I slip off my shoes and tiptoe out in my socks.

Kendra is washing the dinner dishes in the sink when I re-emerge. The dog pack is pattering around her legs, hoping for a morsel to drop.

"She finally calmed down," I say. "But now I'm a nervous wreck."

"Don't worry," Kendra says, taking me into her embrace. "She'll be fine with me. And I'll call you every day to let you know how she's doing."

"Thank you, K."

The first Edie report comes when Jenn and I are settling in for the night in the "Casita," Karen and Suzette's sixteen-foot fiberglass travel trailer they keep parked next to their log cabin. Kendra calls to say Edie isn't ready to come out of the bedroom. I put her on speakerphone.

"She's okay, though. In fact she's curled up in bed with me right now."

This is significant, because Kendra allows only the smaller guest dogs, or the particularly insecure ones, into her bed. Her own dog, a wiry, white terrier mix named Loofah, has bed privileges but prefers sleeping in a dog bed on the floor. Loofah only hops into Kendra's bed each morning for a quick snuggle.

"Thank you, Kendra," Jenn says. "You're taking such good care of her."

"It just seems like Edie needed the reassurance."

It's a relief, of sorts. At least Edie is safe. But of all the countless times we left Stella with Kendra, it never crossed my mind to call for status updates. I remind myself she's in good hands.

The second day brings better news. Edie has left the bedroom, but she won't leave Kendra's side. Our puppy apparently feels better knowing she has a pair of human legs to hide behind if she needs protection from the other dogs.

"She's warming up to the other dogs, but for now, she likes to peek at them from behind me," Kendra says.

"Progress!" Jenn says.

From the airport, I call Kendra for a final Edie check-in.

"Um," says Kendra. There's a potent pause as I wait for her to find the right words. "She had a little setback today."

The day started off full of promise. Edie was finally following the two Lab mixes and Loofah around the house and into the backyard. After lunch, Kendra decided to take the pack of four on a neighborhood walk. They made it just two blocks before a dog started barking from behind a fence, startling Edie. She listened for a second, then began lunging toward every parked car on the block, trying to claw her way inside each one for safety.

"I couldn't *be-lieve* how hard she was pulling me. Her fight-or-flight is off the charts!" Kendra said. "The farther we got away from the house, the worse it got."

It's not uncommon for guest dogs to resist leaving Kendra's house because it's the last place they saw their owners, she said. But she's usually able to coax them through it with treats and encouragement.

"But not Edie. It's like she was just shutting down, entering a zone where I couldn't even reach her. At one point she laid down on the sidewalk, refusing to move."

"Oh no, Kendra. Are you okay? Is Edie okay?"

Jenn, who is hearing only my side of the conversation, places a hand on my arm and lifts her eyebrows in concern. I give her the okay hand sign, signaling it's nothing life-threatening. She exhales in relief.

"It was too hard to restrain her, so we had to turn back. When we got home, she was visibly relieved," Kendra continues. "But it's taking her a long time to recover. Most puppies snap out of it quickly. They bounce back into puppy mode. But it's like Edie can't forget. The terror stopped, but she's...disengaged."

"What's she doing?"

"She's back in her crate, resting."

Kendra has spent nearly fifty years in the company of dogs, so it means something when she says she's never seen a puppy with an escape urge as strong as ours. If Edie is off the charts in Kendra's opinion, then we are in way over our heads. I feel my words shrivel in my throat, but I manage to thank Kendra once again, and apologize for putting her in a bad situation. She tells me it's not our fault, and suggests we try noise-blocking dog earmuffs for Edie.

Which doesn't sound so outlandish in a place like San Francisco, where canine couture is elevated to a whole new level. I've seen dogs wearing mirrored goggles, bow ties, Chanel

sweater vests, gay pride rainbow hula skirts, leather motorcycle jackets, Superman capes, high-top sneakers, nail polish,
tiaras, and once I spotted a French bulldog with a GoPro
camera mounted to his chest harness. But never have I seen a
dog rocking the noise-canceling headphones. Still, this does
not deter me.

"Ordering some now," I say. "We'll come straight over from
the airport. Be there as soon as we can."

I relay the episode to Jenn, and she drops her forehead into
her hand as if she can't believe what she's hearing.

"Well, I guess this means we won't be going on any more
trips for a while," she says.

I give her a weak smile, and she frowns back.

5

Fort Funston

The canine noise-canceling headphones are pale pink, a color I chose because I thought Edie would look cute, like a DJ girl. Edie thinks they are baloney, and the second I secure them to her head with the chinstrap, she tugs them off and tries to puncture them with her fangs. I make several attempts to get her to wear them, but in the end, it's a war I'm just not going to win. I toss them into the bin we keep in the garage for things to donate to charity.

Edie and I are back at square one. I'm once again faced with the futile search for an isolated place to take Edie for a walk, one that doesn't expose her to traffic, a parking lot, people, dogs, or loud noises of any kind. Until I find such a nonexistent place, we're stuck together on house arrest.

And then a solution appears before me, materializing like a mirage right across the street. I'm at the kitchen window,

watching elementary school parents escort their children up
the stairs that lead from the sidewalk to the school's soccer
field. This is the "back way" that some intrepid parents use
to avoid the congestion at the drop-off point in front of the
school. The stairwell is a busy hub for twenty minutes every
morning and afternoon, but otherwise deserted. Maybe, just
maybe, I could get Edie to jog the stairs on-leash with me.

I wait until the morning rush is over, then convince Edie
to cross the street by tossing cookies ahead of her. She sniffs
at the bottom of the staircase, and at first she's unwilling to
go higher than the first step, but that's okay. I praise her for
trying something new and resolve to try again later. Every
day we leave the house to go look at the stairs, and we climb a
little farther each time. She eventually becomes familiar with
the routine, and within a month, she's my running partner.
We sprint to the top, over and over, and it feels like absolute
freedom, even though all we're really doing is pacing. But
we have a place to exercise, finally.

Once she's mastered the stairs, Jenn and I try opening the
gate to the soccer field in the evenings after the children
have gone home. Turns out Edie likes running off-leash on
the big, empty field of grass, especially when we throw her
toy rubber monkey with yellow rope arms for her to fetch.
But Edie has her limits. She won't leave the perimeter of the
grass, refusing to go anywhere near the playground climbing
structures looming at the far end of the soccer field. When
the wind makes the chains clang on the tetherball poles, she
wants to go home. If a siren wails or a motorcycle roars from
the street below, she calls it quits. If another dog shows up
and barks at her, she's out. But if the dog is calm, she'll play
as long as we let her.

Feeling bolstered by Edie's budding confidence, I take her to Fort Funston one morning while Jenn's at work. I make sure to park in the small area near the ranger station, out of sight of the main parking lot crammed with cars, a good percentage of them bearing the same bumper sticker, "Dog is my Copilot."

When I open the truck door for Edie, she sniffs the wind and then leaps out, eager to investigate. She surges ahead on the leash, leading me down a sandy path worn through a carpet of rubbery ice plant succulent, dotted with brilliant magenta flowers. Up ahead I can see the fluorescent triangles of the hang gliders clustered on the sea cliff, waiting their turn to launch into the offshore upswells where they can float alongside the seagulls and ravens.

Uh-oh, I think. There's no way Edie is going to walk by those.

Edie struts by my side, ignoring the hang gliders and cruising along like she owns the place. When we reach the paved path that loops through the park, she stops to greet every person and pooch. It's a complete turnaround. I should have listened to Jenn, I think; Edie just needed to absorb the newness of the world at her own pace. It may have taken her longer than Stella or Layla, but by five months old, she got there. I exhale, long and slow, feeling that everything is going to be all right.

When we are about a half mile in, Edie takes a special interest in a bulldog puppy with a grumpy-old-man scowl sauntering near a public drinking fountain encircled by several banged-up aluminum dog bowls. He catches her scent and lifts his head to spot Edie, then bounds toward her, his skin bunching into folds around his neck with each stride, as if he's wearing a coat three sizes too big. He's an exquisite creature, and I can see by the delight in Edie's eyes that she agrees. She's so eager to play with him that I decide to reward her with a few minutes of off-leash time. It's also a test for me, a way to check Edie's bravery barometer to see if she's ready for more freedom. I ask the bulldog's owner if they can play, and when I get the go-ahead I unclip Edie, vowing to grab her by the collar and say "Gotcha!" in five minutes, using the time-out command we'd practiced in puppy class.

Their instant love affair stops foot traffic. He is so ugly-cute, while she got in the beauty line twice. They are Beauty and the Beast, and I am watching our puppy, in real-time, take the practice play sessions from Sara's class and apply them to the real world. I want to take a video for Jenn, but I'm not willing to take my eyes off Edie.

Two minutes pass.

"Awwww, which one is yours?" a passerby asks.

Just as I turn to answer, the crack of gunfire pierces the air as police officers take target practice at the shooting range down the hill. In a yellow flash, Edie is gone. She has taken off like her own bullet, in a blind panic. I see my puppy flee-ing back down the path from the direction we came, aiming straight for the sea cliff.

I scream for Edie to stop, and dog walkers rubberneck as I streak by them hollering for anyone, please, somebody to catch her. We are both running as fast as our legs will go, but she's got at least one hundred yards on me, and she's gaining speed. *So this is how it happens*, I think. Every year dogs die tumbling over the cliffs at Fort Funston. The foreboding whir of Coast Guard helicopters is all too common here, signal-

ing pilots searching for lost dogs and sometimes their owners, who occasionally fall trying to rescue their beloved pets.

We are on our way to becoming a statistic, but by some
miracle, Edie banks left just before the drop-off. Now she's
completely out of my sight. I make a vain attempt to cut her
off by scrabbling over a sand dune, just as my wallet goes
flying out of my peacoat pocket like some cruel slapstick. I
have to run back to get it, and all I can think is that I have
no idea where my terrified dog is, and she's heading toward
the parking lot. My pulse sounds like a mallet on the inside
of my skull, and my windmilling legs feel like they are getting heavier and heavier, when a man on the footpath shouts
to me, "They've stopped your dog up ahead."

I want to kiss his forehead but there's no time. I come bar-
reling around the bend to see a cluster of people about fifty
feet in the distance surrounding Edie. "Hold her, she's just a
puppy!" I screech. Relief brings warmth back to my blood,
and I allow myself to slow to a jog.

"Thankyouthankyouthankyou," I chant under my breath, to
every deity there is.

I'm ten feet away when Edie shoots out from the cage of
legs and vanishes again. *How the hell can five people not contain
a fifteen-pound puppy?*

"Stop her!" I shriek. Instantly, I'm reptile cold again.

Thankfully Edie skirts the edge of the parking lot and runs
through a wide, sandy field netted with ice plant. That's when
I realize she has a destination in mind. She's aiming for my
truck. How she remembered where we'd parked, a half-mile
away, is a mystery. The blocky heels of my heavy cowboy
boots are sinking into the sand, making me lurch side to side.

I can't keep up with her, and if she doesn't stop at the truck, the only place left for her to go is the four-lane highway.

Finally, I get a lucky break. Two women getting out of a car in the parking spot next to mine hear my screams and snag Edie's collar. By the time I reach them, I'm dry-heaving and choking back sobs. I can feel the lactic acid in my muscles, and my lungs are burning with overexpansion. I drop to my knees with the leash in my hand and wheeze out, "Thank you." As I'm clipping Edie back to the leash, I hear one of the women say:

"*That* dog needs to be on a leash."

My adrenaline-soaked brain obliterates my filter and I snap, "NO SHIT, LADY!"

The woman laughs uncomfortably, backing away from me as I scoop Edie into my arms. I'm shocked by my white-hot response, that I have become a scary person. But I take umbrage at the unspoken in her unsolicited advice—that I am an idiot dog owner. I scowl at her as I get into my truck and slam the door. I sit holding Edie tight to my chest, and we tremble together like that for a good, long time. That woman got to me. She got to me because she's right.

When Edie and I are both breathing somewhat normally again, I call Jenn. She picks up on the first ring and lowers her voice, which means she's surrounded by people at work.

"Hey," she says, sotto voce.

I try to respond, but all that comes out is a squeak.

"Meredith, what's wrong?"

I begin with the bulldog puppy and relay the whole ordeal, finishing with my cussing out a Good Samaritan.

"Just a minute," she says.

I hear murmuring, then footsteps down a hall, then a door closing.

"I'm in another room now. Wow. Are you okay?"

"I will be. But something is definitely wrong with Edie. Terror hijacked her brain."

Jenn offers to get the training schedule from the shooting range so we can avoid the park when police officers are taking their weapon qualification tests. I count to ten and start over. Jenn is not listening to me. Avoiding the park is beside the point. If Jenn had been the one tearing after Edie, she wouldn't have said that.

"It's not just the shooting range," I say. "What if a car backfires? What if there's thunder? A door slams? Fireworks? What's to stop her from doing this again?"

Jenn pauses, waiting for me to answer my own question.

"This is beyond my expertise," I say. "We need help."

By the end of the call we decide to hire Sara for private sessions with Edie. I hang up and stay in the truck so long the windows fog up, just trying to sit with the heavy realization that we have bitten off more than we can chew. I wanted a puppy, not a project. When I assured Jenn that we could fit a puppy into our lives, I meant a regular, ordinary scamp. As the work-at-home half of the couple, I thought I was the lucky one because it allowed me to be with the puppy all day. But that was assuming I'd also be going outside with the puppy whenever I wanted. Now that it's becoming increasingly clear that Edie doesn't function well in the outside world, it feels more like I'm trapped indoors with a nervous rabbit. I didn't sign up for this. If Edie can't overcome her fears, I don't know if I can commit to a dozen more years of house arrest. I feel like a horrible person, but the truth is I wish I were more noble.

No one has ever accused me of being a patient person. I have always moved at warp speed and get irritable when people and circumstances slow me down. And sometimes my thoughtless forward motion comes back to bite me, like now, when this dog is here because I insisted on it, and this dog is asking me to please be a different person for her. A person with the selflessness of a mother. The irony is not lost on me that I avoided motherhood my whole life and now I am being asked to behave more like one. Do I love Edie enough to take this on? Do I even know how to rehabilitate a dog? I've always had a dog in my life to make *me* feel better; I'd never considered that the roles could someday be reversed. I don't even know where to begin.

"Oh, Edie, what are we going to do with you?" I whisper, looking down at my lap, where she's curled into a tight fist. I place my hand on her shoulder blades and she lets out a long sigh, then tucks her nose into my armpit as if trying to escape the chaos of the world. I wait for nearly an hour until Edie finally stands up, stretches, and walks over to the passenger seat. It appears the worst has passed, and she's ready to go. I put the key in the ignition and drive straight home to her safety zone.

We go early to the next puppy class to tell Sara about the gunshots and she winces—Fort Funston is too much chaos for a sensitive dog like ours, she says—too many dog walkers with large packs, too many cliffs, and unpredictable gunfire from the shooting range. It's definitely not a place for her to be off-leash, she says. Edie has likely stored the awful memory of what happened there and may panic again if we bring her back, Sara explains.

"Edie should have shorter excursions to safer places," she says. "Places where you have a better chance of managing her experience."

I'm crestfallen. Not only will our dog not take a walk outside our home, now she won't go to our local dog park, which just happens to be the most popular place for dogs in the city. I blame myself for trying to wish Edie into the dog I want her to be, for constantly testing her when she's not ready, for putting my need to have her be Stella II above her need to feel safe. I am starting to realize that I am completely achievement-oriented, inept at understanding different, at taking things slow, at admitting that perhaps I don't know the first thing about raising dogs.

Sara agrees to make a home visit and asks us to prepare a list of Edith's fears in ranking order. We write: 1. Barking dogs. 2. Traffic. Then: motorcycles, strangers, bicycles, garage doors opening, people in hats, flashing lights, umbrellas, fire hydrants, delivery boxes left on the front step. Gunfire.

When Sara walks through the front door, Edie doesn't seem to recognize her. The very same Sara she obeys like an angel in class is now out of context, and Edie keeps a wide perimeter, uncertain. She steps gingerly toward Sara, as if she's walking on thin ice.

"Edie, it's Sara," I say, trying to wave Edie closer.

"Let's do this instead," Sara says, going down on one knee and getting a treat out of her pocket. She tosses it over Edie's body, so it lands a couple feet behind her tail.

"Find it!" Sara says.

Edie turns her back to Sara and runs after the treat, then

returns for more, a little closer this time, but not all the way to Sara. We watch as Sara tosses again and again, allowing Edie to increase the distance between them before returning.

"This way, she gets to decide how close she's willing to get," Sara explains. Also, she adds, searching and exploring are pleasurable activities that can help distract Edie from her fear.

After a few more games of "Find it!", Edie finally decides she's ready to greet Sara and closes the gap, nuzzling Sara to pet her.

"I like that," Jenn says. "We can have new people do that when they come over."

Edie is now dancing in circles around Sara, apparently remembering that this is the fun lady from the classroom with all the treats in her pocket. We take Sara's coat, get her a glass of water, and settle around the dining room table to talk about the Edie fright list she'd asked us to prepare. Sara studies the list; she asks if we think Edie is most afraid of loud noises, sudden movements, or unfamiliar places and objects.

"All of them?" we say.

"If you had to pick one?" she asks.

"I'd say she doesn't like the movement or noise of traffic," Jenn says. "Every time a car comes by, she freaks out."

"She freaks out at lots of things, though," I say.

Sara asks us to elaborate on "freak out."

This takes some time to unpack. Jenn and I tell Sara that Edie walks fine on a leash indoors, but when we try to take her around the block, something inevitably terrifies her. Someone getting out of a parked car. A motorcycle roaring by. A barking dog. The backup beep of a delivery truck. We share the story about the disastrous trip to the SPCA play group. About the time we opened an umbrella in the house and Edie almost slammed into a wall trying to get away. I mention that Edie used to enjoy going with me to the nearby café, but the last two times I brought her back she'd refused to set foot inside.

Sara takes careful notes, sits back, and says she's noticed some little flags, too. She remembers Edie startled when she unfolded a plastic baby gate in the classroom. Another time, Sara was setting up some folding chairs and one of the chair legs scraped on the floor. Our puppy was the only student that jumped at the sound. And Sara did notice that Edie wouldn't come willingly into the room for the first few classes. Taken individually, those things didn't necessarily mean much to me at the time, but combined with everything else we're telling her, I'm beginning to sense they were early warning signs.

"How does Edie do when you take her to the soccer field?" Sara asks.

This is a tough one to answer, because it all depends on the degree of tranquility Edie encounters. Jenn gives it a try.

"If we go very early in the morning, or late in the evening, when it's deserted and commuter traffic is over, she seems to enjoy it. We throw her toy monkey for her and she likes to fetch it."

"You let her off-leash?" Sara asks.

I nod sheepishly. The reason we're all here around our kitchen table now is because I let Edie off-leash. In retrospect, we were playing with fire.

"It's fenced, though," I say, hoping that will make us sound less careless.

"Only on three sides," Jenn adds. She's right. The blacktop along the south side of the soccer field leads to the classrooms, and beyond the buildings is the school's front entrance on a busy two-lane street.

"Yeah, I wouldn't let her off-leash yet. She's not ready," Sara says.

Gently, Sara lets us know that our dog is not, and never will be, like Stella.

Edie has extreme anxiety and needs to be introduced to unfamiliar places and objects much more slowly. Instead of taking Edie into traffic, we could sit in the car with her so she could listen to muffled traffic noise, as long as she can tolerate it without becoming frightened, she offers.

Sara explains Edie is a much more reactive dog, and that she can get spooked by a sudden event such as a gunshot, or by more of a slow build, in what's called "trigger stacking." Each mild fright Edie encounters can add to the one before, ramping up her stress level. When something alarms her on a walk, she at first may be able to tolerate it, but the second or third scary thing begins a buildup of the cortisol stress hormone, and her body language will change. Her tail may go down, she may begin to pant, she may grimace and drool, and if we don't intervene it takes only one more stressor to push her past her threshold and Edie can have an all-out panic attack just like the one at Fort Funston.

"I feel like I can say this because you are starting to get it," Sara says. "Edie is not like any of the dogs you've had before. You're going to have to treat her differently."

Sara is trying to help us shift our expectations, yet everything in me wants to resist what I'm hearing—that Edie is wired differently, that she will require extra help to learn how to cope with everyday life. I'm so devastated for our beautiful girl, and for how this may impact our marriage, that I can only grasp every third word Sara is saying. She's explaining that there's plenty we can still do for Edie, but her voice is becoming fainter, and I'm only catching snippets: "managing her environment," "nutraceuticals," "desensitization," "counterconditioning."

I am sinking in a quicksand of buzzwords, and as my ears and eyes shut down, all I can think is: this is what I get for steamrolling over Jenn and rushing us into getting a puppy.

Sara pauses, searching our faces for signs of comprehension. Jenn and I are silent, letting reality sink in. I'd wanted a playful puppy to brighten our days. I'd convinced Jenn that a puppy would tighten our bond and bring us the family we'd both never had. All of which I now realize is entirely too much pressure to put on a puppy, and on our relationship. I never meant to bring more stress into our home. But I have inadvertently confirmed Jenn's girlhood fear about puppies—that they only bring you grief. I struggle to absorb the news through my narcissistic disappointment: I wanted a canine companion, not a canine dependent.

Desperate for an upside, I tell myself that at least it's not the fight part of Edie's brain that's overactive. She doesn't seem like the kind of dog that bites when scared. Our puppy is an uber-pacifist, hardwired to run first and ask questions later. But that's a paltry consolation to say that at least our puppy is only a danger to herself.

Sara can sense how crushed we are and asks us to look on the bright side. Most fearful dogs can be helped. My mind stops spinning and I somehow swim to the surface of consciousness.

"Will Edie ever get better, or is this just it?" I ask. It's a wounded question, and it's unfair, because there's no way Sara can predict the future. She chooses her words carefully.

"You may be able to change her emotional response to some of her fears. And with the fears you can't eliminate, you can help her learn how to manage them," she says. "It's not possible to know how much better she'll get until you start a behavior modification program."

"You mean, like, confidence building exercises?" I guess.

Sara smiles, and clears her throat in a way that indicates there's way, way, more to it than that. She outlines a mul-tipronged approach, beginning with temporarily reducing Edie's world to a small sphere of comfort. While Edie's learn-ing, we shouldn't take her to places where she's likely to get spooked, like noisy cafés or crowded Fort Funston where we can't predict what will happen. We need to manage her en-vironment, limiting her to calm locations where she has fun, doesn't stay long, and leaves on a good note before anything bad happens.

"You have to try to increase the areas in the outside world where she feels safe."

"Can we still take her to the soccer field?" Jenn asks.

"In small doses, when no one else is there, and as long as she's safe and continues to enjoy it, yes," Sara says. To help Edie build a positive association with the soccer field, we could toss cookies on the grass and play the "Find It!" game, she suggests.

Done right, the outings will boost her overall bravery. To work on changing Edie's emotional responses to her spe-cific fears, Sara suggests a bedrock method in animal train-ing called "counterconditioning." We give Edie something she likes—in her case a high-value treat—each time she encounters something she doesn't like, such as a car or a barking dog. Eventually, she'll learn to associate the scary thing with the good thing. The goal is to replace her fearful response to the stressful thing with her pleasurable response to a special cookie. Trainers use counterconditioning to help rewire the fight-or-flight parts of the primitive animal brain so anxious pets can better self-regulate their moods.

But we shouldn't leave the counterconditioning up to chance, whipping a cookie in Edie's mouth whenever she happens to get frightened in the real world. We can create the scenario ourselves, introducing Edie to her triggers in low, controlled doses to gradually desensitize her to them. Sara suggests downloading one of the various sound apps designed to desensitize puppies to the common noises that scare them. We can play audio clips of sounds she doesn't like while feeding her treats, and by gradually increasing the volume to just below her limit, her tolerance builds. But Edie has so many noise phobias I could make a mixtape of her fears, with different tracks for barking dogs, motorcycles, gunshots, children shouting, flags flapping in the wind, and delivery trucks.

"You can only desensitize her to one sound at a time," Sara warns. "It's important you go slow so she doesn't get overwhelmed."

Jenn and I want to start with barking dogs first. We'd noticed in class that Edie startled when another puppy barked at her during playtime. It would be devastating if her fear kept her from bonding with other dogs. At the very least, we want Edie to experience friendship.

"Now, I want to make sure you hear this next part," Sara says. "You must start the barking so low that it doesn't bother her, then gradually increase the volume over time. As she gets more comfortable, she'll start to anticipate the treat when she hears the sound. The sound must predict the treat. When the sound stops, the treats stop."

Pairing Edie's triggers with treats is delicate business. If we aren't careful to ease Edie into the sound of barking dogs, the whole thing could backfire. If the barking is too loud and scares her, she could wind up more terrified of barking than when we started. If we choose a treat she doesn't consider valuable enough to offset her fears, or if our timing is backward and we give her the treat before the sound, she'll learn that a certain treat predicts barking and hate that treat. If we accidentally feed Edie treats after the barking sound stops, we'll only confuse her and she won't learn to associate the treat with anything at all. It seems incredibly easy to screw this up.

"What about medicine?" Jenn asks.

"Some people also find it helpful to change the dog's brain chemistry with either natural biological substances, or pharmaceuticals," Sara continues. "You can talk to your vet about it."

Sara mentions other remedies we can use to supplement counterconditioning. She says there are swaddling vests for dogs, massage techniques, calming music composed specifically for dogs, and collars designed to give puppies a sense of security by emitting a scent that mimics a mother dog's pheromones.

It takes a while to figure out which strategies work best for your dog, she says. But we must begin with counterconditioning and desensitization, then maybe add in pharmaceuticals, then layer in whatever combination of over-the-counter calming aids work for Edie.

"In these situations, it takes creativity, and consistency, and patience," Sara says.

Patience. My favorite word. My limbs feel heavy, as if someone just plopped a mountain in front of me and told me to climb it. I imagine years of work ahead to rehabilitate Edie. I glance over at Jenn, who is staring at a fixed point on the wall. My wife has hit tilt.

"Where do we begin?" I hear myself asking.

Sara reaches into her bag and pulls out a sheaf of stapled pages and slides it across the table at us. The title, in all caps at the top reads: RELAXATION PROTOCOL. It's a fifteen-day program of behavior-modification exercises designed to help dogs learn to manage stress. The font is miniscule, and I feel overwhelmed just looking at it. The basic concept is to help Edie develop a habit of calm, relaxed behavior by rewarding her for remaining seated and undisturbed while we make potentially unsettling movements in front of her. We begin with a simple step left or right, escalating to running around her in circles while singing.

These body movements serve as low-dose, artificially controlled triggers, and allow Edie to practice remaining calm at home before we begin counterconditioning in the real world.

"You might feel a little silly doing these exercises," Sara says, "but you are teaching her to pay attention to you for the appropriateness of her behavior, and when she gets rewarded for staying calm she's learning that strange stuff can happen in front of her and she doesn't have to react to it…she doesn't have to go to one hundred first. The exercises are designed as a slow build, and it's very important you don't push her beyond her tolerance limit, or you might increase her anxiety."

If Edie wanders off during the exercises, we are to back up

the task list to an easier one she can accomplish. If she gets frightened, we stop and try another day. Doing some quick math in my head, if there are forty to fifty exercises per day, and if we must back up the ladder each time Edie can't sit still, we might be at this a lot longer than fifteen days.

Sara sits back and waits for us to say something. I don't know if she's just given us a treatment plan that will help Edie function, or a glimpse into a frustrating future of futile training. I'm glad Sara has connected us to the larger universe of veterinary scientists who have studied these things and can offer help, but it's a community I never would have wanted to join.

"I realize this is a lot all at once, and I expect you'll have questions," Sara says. "So call me anytime, or you can always talk to me in class."

"We can't thank you enough," Jenn says.

That night as I'm trying to fall asleep, I listen to Edie's light snoring and do something I never do. I pray. I ask Grandpa, who always had a way with animals, to guide me.

His answer comes in the form of a memory. When I was in first grade, Grandpa woke me up one night to show me a scrawny black kitten with matted fur and yellow eyes. It was a wild stray he'd rescued from underneath a cabin while doing some plumbing work in Big Sur. I couldn't believe my luck. I reached for it in the dark, and the frightened kitten hissed back with fanged hatred. Grandpa stepped away from the bed, lifting the kitten out of my reach.

"You can have him, but only if you tame him first."

He kept the kitten in his detached office, where at first, every time my brother and I entered the room to feed it, the kitten whirred around all four walls looking for a way to escape, sending dust and stray papers flying in its wake. The thing was absolutely terrified of humans. It took weeks of kibble offerings and just sitting still in that room before the kitten stopped panicking at the sight of us. My brother and I worked on this project every day, until finally the kitten began greeting us at the door, looking for food. But every time we tried to pet him, he scratched us.

"Let him come to you," Grandpa said.

I kept up my silent visits to the office, and kept my hands to myself as the kitten eyeballed me from the higher ground of Grandpa's bookcase. I'd sit there for hours, waiting. When the kitten finally approached me one day, I held my breath. He carefully put two paws on my leg and sniffed my knee. Still, I did not look at him. I stayed perfectly still as he lifted himself into my lap, turned around twice, and nestled down. I slowly reached out with one finger and stroked his head. It was the first time an animal had chosen me, and it gave me a unique feeling of specialness I'd never experienced in the human world. His purr was the sound of all the fear leaving his body and proved to me that love is so powerful it can turn a wild animal into your friend. Only when I had earned the kitten's trust did Grandpa allow me to name it.

"Name it after something you like," Grandpa had said.

I named him Pretzel. My first pet started out as a wild, hissing spitfire from the woods, and as a little girl, I'd managed to help him overcome his primal fear. If I could do that, there might be a chance that I could help Edie, too.

6

Bravery Lessons

From beneath the covers where I'm hiding from dawn, I can hear the soundtrack of Jenn's morning routine. The hiss of the shower, the sliding of dresser drawers, the grinding of coffee beans. When the kettle whistles, I know I have only ten minutes before she's out the door for the police academy where she's been newly reassigned, leaving me to face another nine hours with our agoraphobic dog. I feel overwhelmed by yesterday's reality check, not ready to get out of bed as the owner of a problem puppy.

Edie is up too, her toenails scrabbling over the hardwood floors, dropping squeaky toys at Jenn's feet trying to convince her to stay home and play. I know how our puppy feels. I want to chain myself to the front door in a nonviolent protest to block Jenn's departure, so she'll be forced to stay home and help me. I'm still trying to wrap my brain around Edie's bro-

ken one, and muster the wherewithal to start her rehabilitation project. If I heard Sara correctly last night, I'm about to
embark on a marathon of training to try to reprogram Edie's
brain. It sounds like it'll require the patience of a Zen master,
the dedication of an Olympian, and even then failure could
be a real possibility.

I feel it's my responsibility to fix this, but I'm having trouble mustering the energy to do it. I'm too heartbroken over
losing the road dog I thought we had, the one I had envisioned taking hiking or to the beach. I have no idea what to
do with a dog that refuses to go anywhere. What kind of life
is that, for Edie, and for us?

I feel as if the universe has cheated me out of something—
has punished me without naming my crime. I know I have a
lousy attitude and wish that I were one of those people who
stay calm in crisis, who inherently believe that things will
turn out all right. All I feel is that I want a refund, a do-over;
the one thing I can't have. I peek out from under the sheets
and see Edie peering at me over the mattress, her eyes two
black marbles following my every move. Instead of feeling
maternal, I feel shackled.

I hear Jenn rinse her coffee cup and zip up her insulated
lunch bag. She comes into the room and sits next me, unpeel-
ing the bedsheet cocoon to find me.

"You all right?"

"I'm sorry," I say. My words come out like a croak.

"Sorry? For what?"

"Edie."

"Hey, don't cry," she says, wiping away a tear I didn't want
her to find. "There's no way we could've known."

As if on cue, Edie pounces on Jenn's shoelaces, and tugs them loose. How can she look so ordinary on the outside?

"She may be a monster, but she's *our* little monster," Jenn says, prying open Edie's jaws and lifting her onto her lap. Edie finds the buttons on Jenn's shirt and tries to bite one off, so Jenn turns her onto her back and pins her down with one arm so Edie can't do any more damage. "She's lucky we aren't the kind of people who would just abandon her to a shelter. We have the time and resources to help her. We just have to figure out what she needs."

Jenn's comment makes me imagine what would have happened to Edie if she had been chosen by someone other than us. What if she had been a gift for a child? Or if she'd been taken home by a single person who works long hours, leaving Edie alone with her demons. Or someone who lives above a loud restaurant? Or in a home with aggressive dogs? What if that person couldn't afford trainers and medications for her? If they left her tied up in a backyard? What if they gave up on her, left her trembling in a shelter with barking dogs? A mama tiger awakes inside me, and suddenly I am protective, possessive. Edie may be extra work, but no one else knows Edie's neuroses as intimately as we do, and I don't trust anyone else to take proper care of her. I see what Jenn means. Looked at another way, this is our chance to rescue, rather than reject, a fragile creature.

Somehow Jenn always knows exactly what to say. But I still need to hear that she doesn't resent me for complicating our life.

"You're not mad at me?"

"This dog chose us for a reason. We just don't know what that reason is right now."

Jenn's right. I'm making this all about me and my disappointment, rather than having faith that there's a larger picture I just can't see yet. This time my pet is not here for me; I must be Edie's caretaker, protector, teacher. Edie is going to require me to finally put another's needs before my own. Perhaps, I allow, my malaise is masking my true emotion— my own fear that I'm incapable of unconditional love. I've made sure that I've never had a dependent because I never wanted to find out if I'm as unmaternal as my mother. What if I'm also terrible at caretaking?

"I don't know if I'm cut out for this," I whisper.

"I don't know if we are, either, but we have to try," Jenn says. "I think eventually, Edie can be a really good dog."

Edie is attacking Jenn's hands now to free herself, so Jenn reaches under Edie's armpits and lifts her into the air. Edie pedals her paws in protest. She may be a project, but she's also 50 percent clown. The two sometimes cancel each other out.

"C'mere, special sauce," I say, getting out of bed and taking Edie into my arms. As I nestle my nose in Edie's soft fur, Jenn kisses me on the forehead, and I'm seized by a solid feeling of family. The three of us, whether we like it or not, are in this together. I remind myself that Jenn and I are first and foremost survivors, and we've been through much, much worse.

Edie is indeed lucky, I think. We aren't the kind of pet owners who blame the dog, dismissing her as "just born that way" and absolving ourselves of any responsibility to rehabilitate her. Something's wrong with Edie, and if she could speak she would tell us what that is and what she needs. But she's doing the best that she can to alert us to her emotional storms; we just have to learn how to read her body language. It's a miracle that dogs can adapt to human environments and communicate with us at all, and Edie deserves bonus points for managing this feat when her nerves are haywire. So yes, it's on us to fix this. We took her from her pack and are forcing her to live outside her own species, so we owe it to her to try everything we can until we figure out what she needs to feel safe.

"We'll get through this," Jenn says. "Now, I'm late for work."

"Go!" I say, waving her away. "Bravery school starts today."

Inspired by my wife's pep talk, I make myself an espresso and fire up my search engine, and type in "fearful dog remedy." I get nearly four million results in half a second. I scroll through pages and pages of traditional and holistic therapies, everything from serious pharmaceuticals to acupuncture, and Reiki—healing energy touch. I find swaddling vests, pheromone sprays, and an herbal tincture of five calming floral essences marketed to help dogs mellow out before going to the vet or on an airplane. Some people add brewer's yeast to their dog's food or buy "calming beds" made of a pillowy, furry material designed to mimic the feel of being surrounded by littermates.

There's an entire industry dedicated to doggie chill pills—many of which are off-label uses of human medicines: melatonin, cannabis, the amino acid tryptophan, and prescription pharmaceuticals such as Zoloft, Valium, and Xanax. I watch instructional videos about how to give targeted massage and download soft piano music designed specifically to calm dogs. What works depends on your specific pet, how debilitating their fear is, and what you believe.

I look over the list of resources Sara left with us and decide to start with the minimalist approach, hoping we can get by without prescription pills. I decide to try an over-the-counter anxiety drug for pets called Anxitane. Its main ingredient is L-theanine, an amino acid found in tea leaves that is believed to boost dopamine and serotonin—two brain chemicals associated with pleasure and happiness.

Scrolling around the dog wellness websites, I discover a GPS dog collar made by a tech company in New York that will let us monitor Edie's location with our cell phones. If she ever runs away again, satellites will help us triangulate her position within seconds. I buy it, along with the three-year tracking plan, and shell out for overnight shipping.

I download a sound desensitization app for puppies. I choose one designed in Australia called Soundproof Puppy Training, because it has the audio clips I need for Edie: motorbikes, barking dogs, and smoke alarms. It doesn't offer gunfire, but it does have fireworks, which is a good substitute. The app's sound catalog is impressive, and there are other noises Edie has never heard but I suspect she also won't like: power saws, helicopters, crying babies, crowds.

This is retail therapy on steroids. Each hail-Mary purchase gives me hope that I'm buying back the dog I thought I bought. As the little number above my online cart symbol ticks upward, I feel more responsible, more motherly, and quite clever. I believe that I'm beating the odds by trying every remedy, because at least one of them has got to work. I'm seduced by the promise of a quick fix because it pairs nicely with my denial—if I can find a magic solution, then I won't have to do the hard work of retraining Edie myself.

Edie wakes from a nap, groaning as she stretches all four legs as far as they will go, shuddering with effort. She yawns and blinks at me, her eyes still half covered by her inner eye-lids. The first day of Project Edie is about to begin.

"Ready for school, Miss Thing?"

She perks her ears at the lilt in my voice, expectant. I turn my phone volume down to one notch above mute. I open the sound app and press the icon of a barking beagle.

The bark is barely a grunt, so quiet it could have come from a dog barking on a television upstairs behind a closed door. Edie swivels her head left and right, looking for the dog. Perplexed, she trots over to the big bay window in the living room and scans the backyard, softly growling. I didn't even get the chance to feed her a treat. Already I'm messing this up. I shut off the phone and kneel down next to Edie, to give her support as she surveils the landscape, determined to find the intruder. She looks up at me expectantly, as if I can clear up the matter of the invisible dog.

"There's nobody there, buddy," I say, pointing to the empty yard. "See?"

I hadn't asked Sara what we should do if Edie can't handle the lowest volume possible. Where do we start if we can't start? Only Edie would be too sensitive for desensitization training. Not only is she afraid of barking dogs, she quite possibly will become afraid of phantom dogs, too, if I don't get this right.

Edie is still not convinced we're out of danger. I scoop her up in my arms and take her outside so she can see for herself that there's no dog lurking in the bushes. I wonder if this is what parents feel like when they flick on the bedroom lights to show their children that in fact there are no monsters in the room. All you can do is hope that they believe you.

I set Edie down in the backyard and she runs the perimeter with her nose to the ground, inhaling for clues. Satisfied we are alone, she perks up and trots back to me, but not before peeing at the base of the deck stairs for good measure.

"Oh, Edie. Should we try again?"

Walking back into the house, I can't help but laugh that I've become a lady who has one-way conversations with her dog.

On our second attempt with the sound app, I make sure I'm more prepared. I hold a treat in one hand, and cue the sound file on my phone with the other. When Edie lifts her ears in response to the soft barking, I whip a treat in front of her mouth before she has time to run to the window. She peers around me to look for the dog while she chews, but at least she stays in place. I turn off the audio and shower her with praise. I want to repeat the exercise until she nails it, but I have to force myself to remember that this is not a contest, and Edie needs to go slow. Her definition of success is not mine, nor should it be. I decide that's enough sound exposure for one day.

Later that afternoon, I pick up Sara's Relaxation Protocol paperwork. The first task is to simply stand in front of Edie for two seconds. If she doesn't move, she gets a cookie, and I progress to the next movement, which is to take one step to the left. Skipping ahead, I see that my movements will become increasingly unusual to her. Sometimes I'll count out loud. Or leave Edie alone in the room for a minute. I'll ring the doorbell and return. By the end of the entire program, I'll be running around Edie in circles, clapping and singing. This is all designed to help Edie practice relaxing.

I'm not sure how any of this actually works, but the woman who created the Relaxation Protocol, Dr. Karen Overall, holds a doctorate in veterinary medicine, she's a diplomate of the American College of Veterinary Behavior, and she's certified by the Animal Behavior Society as an applied animal behaviorist. She's written hundreds of scholarly articles and several veterinary textbooks, including the *Manual of Clinical Behavioral Medicine for Dogs and Cats*. I'm inclined to trust her.

I turn to Day One of the fifteen-day program and find a list of forty-three things Edie is supposed to watch me do without reacting. Number one: she's to sit at my feet while I stand for two seconds. Piece of cake; she already learned this in puppy school.

"Edie, sit!" I say, finger up.

She does, and looks at me, waiting for a reward. The instructions say to reward her when she has a relaxed face. I examine her face for clues, but all she looks is perplexed. But she didn't freak out, so I'm going to say she aced it. Boom! I whip my hand out from behind my back and let her lick some organic goat cheese off my finger. Following the instructions, I have Edie sit while I stand silently for five seconds, then ten seconds. She's thrilled by this bonanza of sudden cheese for doing what she already knows how to do.

Now, something harder. She has to sit while I take one step backward and return. And as soon as I move away from her, she stands up and follows me. I can see why, because we used to reward her for following us in puppy class. I return her to her sitting spot and try again.

This time I drag out the command as I move backward, *"Siiiiiiiiiiiiiiiiit."*

She trembles, fighting the urge to get up again, but she remains in place.

"GOOD GIRL!"

I stride back over and reward her with a huge scoop of cheese.

Next I walk backward, clapping my hands softly, and Edie cocks her head and looks at me like I've lost my mind. And in a way, maybe she's right. This whole situation seems like lunacy. I'm sequestered in the house with my puppy, clapping and humming before her with soft goat cheese on my fingers hoping to untangle her brain circuitry. She's never seen me clap before and has no idea what I want from her. She gallops over and tries to climb up my leg.

We're not even a quarter of the way through the first day's assignment, but Edie is already starting to lose focus. I consider it a legitimate reason to cut the lesson short. I give in to Edie's wishes and wrestle with her on the floor, letting her lick the rest of the cheese from my fingertips. I'm supposed to be counting to five out loud while she sits, but as a compromise I let her run all over me while I giggle out, "One-twothreefourfive!"

This is what we are doing when Jenn opens the door. I'm surprised to see her, and have to check my watch to confirm it's after 5:00 p.m. I'd lost track of time, spending the whole day working with Edie.

"Uh, hi," she says. "Why are you teaching Edie to count?"

Delighted to have a second wrestling partner, Edie flings herself at Jenn and tugs on her pant legs.

"We're doing her homework."

"Her what?"

"The Relaxation Protocol. The plan Sara gave us last night?"

Jenn nods slowly, as if she's trying to remember. "Ah, right. Explain it to me over a glass of wine?"

I follow Jenn to the kitchen, Edie twirling around her feet, as I chatter at a manic pace about all the things I bought and the recovery program I've hammered out for Edie. Jenn is half-listening as she uncorks a bottle, eager to begin unwinding from her day.

"It's a Sangiovese from Doug," says Jenn, pouring a wine our friend made into a stemless glass and handing it to me.

"Thanks, but check this out," I say, spreading the Relaxation Protocol paperwork on the counter. "It's science-based."

Jenn scans the first couple pages and sets it back down.

"I'll finish it later."

I get that Jenn's workday at the police academy is already full of paperwork and teaching plans. Her job is to develop use-of-force and implicit-bias training programs for officers, following state and federal civil rights reform mandates. The last thing she wants to do when she gets home at night is to read over another syllabus, especially one in 8-point type. But why am I suddenly feeling like only one of us has been tasked with Edie's rehabilitation?

"Well, I can just summarize," I continue. "We have to do weird things in front of Edie like count out loud and give her treats if she remains relaxed."

"Why?"

"We're training her how to stay calm."

"Sounds easy enough."

"The exercises are simple, but there are a ton of them. They take about twenty minutes and we have to do them at least once a day, every day, for at least two weeks. We can't slack off. And I've started a diary to monitor her progress."

Jenn moves to the living room and pulls the foam back roller out from behind the stuffed chair. She puts it under her back and rolls from one side of the rug to the other, pushing with her feet. I hear a vertebra crack.

"Ahhhhhhhhh," she exhales.

"Long day?" I ask.

Jenn rarely tells me about what goes on at work. I don't know if it's part of the police culture to keep things close to the vest, or that she doesn't want to bring the trauma home. I'll often find out months later that she talked someone down from jumping off a building, or visited a little girl with terminal cancer in a hospital. Maybe it's because she can't feel the emotions of her experiences until she's had some distance from them. She rarely cries, but when she does it seemingly comes from nowhere, and has nothing to do with what's happening at the moment.

"Same old, same old," she says, giving her standard non-answer.

Jenn stands up from the roller and then bends forward at the waist, placing her palms on the rug in a downward dog yoga pose. I can almost see the stress hissing out of her joints as she breathes into the stretch, lifting her rear end skyward and peering at me between her legs.

"Ya know," she says, her face turning pink as the blood rushes to her head, "that's why I've always had cats. They're like succulents. They take care of themselves."

"Jenn!"

"What?" she says, standing back up to face me.

"Edie isn't a plant."

"It was just a joke."

"This is serious. I need to know that you're going to be part of this work we have to do with Edie."

Edie is wiggling her spine across the rug with her front

paws dangling limply from her wrists, giving herself a back massage. At the sound of my raised voice, she leaps to her feet and holds her body still, sensing the tension in the air. Jenn scoops Edie into her arms and kisses her forehead.

"Of course I will."

"Don't do that turtle thing you do."

"Turtle thing?"

"You know, when things get complicated, you retreat."

"I'll read those papers. Promise. Tomorrow."

Jenn keeps her word, and over the next month runs Edie through the relaxation exercises on weekends, giving me precious breaks from Edie monitoring so I can get some writing done. We find a way to bend our schedules to ensure that one of us is always home with Edie, keeping her to a familiar routine that will help her focus and learn. Counterconditioning has a better chance of success if we shrink her world to her happy place—home with us—and limit her exposure to new environments where she could have a bad experience and relapse.

It requires a ridiculous amount of organization to coordinate our separate calendars so that one of us is always home with Edie. In April, it gets even more complicated when my memoir is released and my publisher plans a book tour with stops in various states. Writing a book and meeting readers is a dream come true that we'd both been anticipating, and Jenn had planned to travel with me so we could celebrate together. But now, to avoid an interruption in Edie's recovery plan, Jenn must stay home to be with Edie. She is forced to use her hard-earned vacation time while I leave on book tour without her.

Most of the time, we're able to coordinate our schedules

around our dog, but when a Bay Area bookstore plans an event for my book midday on a Wednesday, at the exact time Jenn has a meeting with her captain, we're stuck.

"I don't want to take her with me and leave her in the car," I say. "It's too hot."

"Think she'll be all right if we leave her home?" Jenn says.

Given Edie's delicate nerves, it's a miracle that she hasn't shown any signs of separation anxiety, content to gnaw on a hollow chew toy filled with frozen banana if we need to run to the store. But I'll be gone at least four hours, by the time I get through traffic, speak, sign books, and get back home again. I don't think Edie's ready to be left alone that long, and I can't bring myself to ask Kendra to watch her again. Yet it would be career sabotage to turn down an opportunity to promote my book.

"Do you think Mag and Barbara would take her?" I ask. "Edie has met their dogs before. Maybe she'd feel safe at their house?"

We never spent this much time talking about Stella's emotional state. It never really came up. When we needed a pet sitter, all we had to do was drop Stella off at Mag and Barbara's house. They gave us a house key, and it was so convenient to just pull up, open their front door, and watch Stella race up two flights of stairs to find her friends Toby and Phoebe without a glance over her shoulder. It was such an ideal pet-sitting arrangement that no one even needed to be home; the dogs entertained themselves and had access to the fenced-in yard through a dog door. In return, whenever Mag and Barbara went on vacation, I relocated to their house with Stella to take care of their animals until they returned.

But with Edie, things aren't that simple. We'd need Mag

or Barbara to agree to stay home with Edie, to help her cope with being in a new place, and to soothe her in case she had a panic attack. And they wouldn't be able to take Edie on outings to the park or the beach with their own dogs like they would with Stella. After what happened with Kendra, I can't trust Edie to behave on a walk. Basically, we'd be asking our busy friends to agree to stay indoors with our puppy.

But they are understanding and offer to watch Edie. On my way to the bookstore, I drop Edie off without much trouble. I carry her inside and she seems to remember meeting Toby and Phoebe before. While she is distracted in a sniffing circle, I whisper thank you and kiss Barbara on the cheek, reminding her that Edie shouldn't leave the house, and slip out the front door.

I'm pulling into the parking lot of the bookstore when I notice my phone pings with an alert message from Edie's GPS collar saying she's left Barbara's street. I tap on the message and a map pops up with a red flashing dot showing me Edie's current location is Fort Funston, the park where she fled from gunshots. My stomach drops. As I'm dialing Barbara's number, Jenn calls.

"Uh, did you just get an alert about Edie?"

"Yeah. I think Barbara took her to Fort Funston," I say.

"Uh-oh. Let me call Barbara and find out what's up. Go do your book thing," Jenn says.

"Call me right back."

I don't go into the bookstore. I stay in the car waiting for Jenn's call. If Edie's in trouble, I'm not going to be able to go through with the event. I'll have to turn around and call the store from the road to explain the emergency. And that would be very bad, not only for the bookstore, but for the publisher, and for my reputation among the tight-knit group of Bay Area independent booksellers who would be disinclined to invite me to their stores for readings.

I wipe my sweating palms on my skirt, and stare at the phone, willing it to ring. When it does five minutes later, I lunge for it, knocking it to the floor mat. I scramble and manage to catch Jenn just before the call goes to voice mail.

"What happened!" I shout.

"Everyone's okay," Jenn begins, which means she's about to deliver bad news.

"The dogs were getting along so well at the house, Barbara thought she'd take them all to the park. She thought Edie could handle it if Toby and Phoebe were with her."

I squeeze my eyes shut, bracing for the rest of the story. As Barbara recounted to Jenn, everything was going fine for the first few minutes, until suddenly Edie "smelled something" and started tugging Barbara back toward the car. Edie was so determined that she pulled Barbara to her knees, and Barbara had to sit in the sand and lean back, using all her strength to keep Edie's leash from slipping out of her grip.

"Ohhhhhh, no. Did she get hurt?"

Barbara is strong, a lifelong swimmer, but she's also a former ballerina with a petite frame. I have a horrible vision of her getting dragged through the sand like a kite that won't launch.

"She's fine. She got all the dogs back in the car and she's on her way back home."

"I can't believe this."

"Have you started giving Edie those calming pills you ordered yet?"

"They're supposed to arrive any day now."

"Wait, hang on," Jenn says. "Barbara is texting."

I glance at my watch. It's only five minutes before I'm supposed to start speaking. The calm I'd cultivated on the drive over is no more. I can't think about anything but Edie and how she needs me right now and I'm not there. I chose myself over her and this is the result of my poor decision. More wishful thinking that leads to disaster.

"They're back home now," says Jenn when she comes back on the phone. "But Edie refuses to get out of the car. She's just sitting in the garage by herself, in the back of Barbara's Prius."

"What now?"

"I'm on my way to get her."

"But what about your meeting?"

"My captain has dogs, so she'll understand. Now go, I got this."

"I love you."

"Everything's going to be okay."

I know that neither of us truly believe that. Edie is making it very clear that she's too much of a handful, even for our friends who have decades of experience with dogs. Which begs the question, is Edie too much of a handful for us? I don't want to answer that just yet, because my gut tells me to keep trying, but a little voice is starting to grow inside me, and that voice is saying that maybe this is all a terrible mistake.

I do my best to hide my distraction during the book event, but it's harder than usual to smile. The moment I'm back on the road heading home, I call Barbara and ask her to tell me what happened. But that was just it. Nothing happened. They were alone, on a trail, and there was no sound. It was absolutely serene when Edie panicked.

"You'd told me that Edie is fearful, but I didn't get what you meant until now," Barbara says. "It just came out of nowhere. That's not puppy fear. That's something totally different."

7

Canine Cannabis

One by one, we're crossing off all the places we'd expected to share our life with Edie: Fort Funston, Kendra's, the beach, Mag and Barbara's, Java Beach café. Edie's world is shrinking, and ours along with it. I struggle to not let this get to me, and cling to reasons to stay positive.

On the final day of puppy school, Sara passes out graduation certificates. Right there in swirling calligraphy it attests that Edith May-Jackson has earned all the rights and privileges of a well-behaved canine citizen. Below Sara's signature is a gold seal with a black paw print in the center. I'm oddly comforted by the officialness of this simple piece of paper. Not so much for what it may say about our puppy's manners, but for what it says about Jenn and me. It's proof that we are making an effort to make Edie a priority, that we willingly gave up ten weeks of Monday nights to be together as a family. I'm proud that we trekked to San Carlos every week with hope in our hearts, and puppy school never deteriorated into a dreaded obligation.

Sara thanks everyone for their dedication and congratulates us for building a foundation for better lifelong relationships with our dogs. Dogs that begin behavior training as puppies tend to live longer and healthier lives, she says. We are each bestowed with a roll of pink dog poop bags, and Sara has us pose with our dogs for graduation photos.

Edie's four classmates sit perfectly still for their family portraits. We're up last. Sara goes down on a knee before us while Jenn and I kneel on either side of Edie. In one hand I have Edie's leash, and in the other I hold up her graduation certificate.

"Smile!" Sara says.

We do as we're told, and at the exact moment Sara presses the button, Edie leaps into the air. Sara bursts into laughter, turning her phone to show us Edie's two blurry feet in the frame—a perfect display of disobedience.

"Let's have a do-over!" Sara exclaims.

We coax Edie back into position and smile once more. Edie pauses for a microsecond, then times her exit perfectly, zipping out of the frame like a hummingbird. It's as if Edie refuses to be legally bound by what it says on the certificate. She ruins shot after shot, and by the fifth attempt, the whole room has erupted into a sitcom laugh track.

"Edie has spoken," Sara jokes. "I guess I'll just send you the least blurry one."

Edie's graduation photo turns out to be a total blooper. None of us are looking at the camera. Edie is leaping off the ground, her body stretched in a near horizontal line in front of us, paused in midflight. I'm still holding the certificate high, but I'm looking down at Edie in disbelief, as if I've just discovered someone else's dog at the end of the leash. Jenn is laughing in surprise as she tries to catch Edie in midair. Our puppy's brow is wrinkled in worry. Her ears are back, and she appears to be panting.

"It captures her personality," Jenn offers.

"There is that."

We're still holding out hope for our little troublemaker because help is on the way. Over the next few days, boxes appear on our doorstep with everything I'd purchased for Edie's emotional first-aid kit. I start giving her Anxitane tablets each day and adding drops of calming floral essence to her water. I'd read that the high levels of vitamin B in brewer's yeast may reduce canine anxiety, so I start sprinkling it on her food. I buy an "anxiety wrap," which is like a tight dog T-shirt that acts as a swaddling vest, and a "calming" dog collar that emits a scent that mimics a mother dog's natural nursing pheromones.

An internet search produces a library of books on dog fear, and I order a half dozen that promise to explain, and help, dogs like ours. The journalist in me spends the better part of the day researching scientific reports, newspaper stories, and blogs, determined to find a path to Edie's, and our, serenity.

I discover a 2018 article in *Whole Dog Journal* in which dog behavior professionals report an uptick in clients coming to them with fearful dogs. The author theorizes it may be due to an increase in rescue groups rehoming timid dogs that in the past would have been euthanized, or that more Americans are adopting extremely undersocialized street dogs from other countries. Or it could be that more people are becoming open to the idea that animals have emotions, and turning to specialists to help them with their dog's chronic fear.

It's reassuring to know that there are a lot of Edies out there, and a whole community of experts and pet owners crowdsourcing the issue. Certainly, with this much collective conversation and research, we'll find the remedy Edie so desperately needs. The deeper I dive for a possible cure, the more I feel that I am *handling* things, assembling a team of experts around Edie and enrolling myself in a self-directed course on dog behavior modification. Once I am locked on to a goal, it's hard to shake me off. I am going to conquer Edie's fear, come hell or high water.

Over the next several weeks, I continue the goat cheese– reward relaxation exercises, and Edie starts to catch on that she is supposed to sit still, no matter how goofily I behave. For as cautious as Edie is when confronted with something new, she's a quick study when it comes to figuring out what she needs to do to get food. She quickly learns that if I have a white ramekin in my hand, the cheese feast is about to commence. She gets so good at sitting still that eventually she can remain seated while I leave the room for a whole minute. She even stays put when I go outside and ring the doorbell. The Relaxation Protocol seems to be working in a controlled environment, but will it work in the wild? There's no way to tell if this is making her a calmer dog, or if she's simply trained me to give her more cheese.

I decide to test it out. It's been about a month since we've tried to take Edie on a walk in the neighborhood, and I'm hoping all this remedial education has inched her confidence up enough so she can stroll by the unfamiliar without freezing up. On a Saturday morning, when the elementary school across the street is deserted, I clip Edie into her harness and strap a fanny pack stuffed with hard-boiled eggs to my waist. I grab the door handle and summon my inner cheerleader:

"Okay, you wanna go? Outside? Go outside? For a walk? Yeah? Let's go!"

Edie is hopping up and down in agreement. She runs in a circle around my feet, tangling my legs in the leash. She springs out the front door and rejoices in the sunlight. I make her sit before we cross the empty street, and when we reach the back stairs leading up to the school's soccer field, I unclip her. She gallops up the concrete stairs, taking them two at a time, so fast I'm afraid she's going to slip and clonk herself on the head. She waits at the top for me to open the chain-link gate, and once she's on the soccer field, she races to a puddle, and slides on her belly through it. If dogs can laugh, I swear she's doing it. She looks back over her shoulder to see if I'm going to stop her. I'm just so relieved she is behaving like a regular puppy that I decide to let her get as dirty as she wants.

With a little coaxing, I'm able to get Edie to rise from her mud bath and follow me toward the other end of the soccer field. We are almost at the centerline when a little girl in a neon pink bike helmet rolls up on a tricycle on the playground. She's so far away, she looks like a little shrimp swimming in circles. But Edie sees every spoke, every glint of Mylar ribbon fluttering from the handlebars. Edie stops midstride and clamps her mouth shut, widening her eyes at the trespasser as a telltale string of stress drool slips out the side of her mouth. I reach into my fanny pack and waggle a piece of egg white in front of her nose to distract her, but it's too late. Edie twists her head away from my offering and streaks for home with her tail between her legs. As she paces before the chain-link gate waiting for me to catch up to her, all I can think is thank God I'd remembered to latch the gate.

Back home, I flop down on the couch and spiral into self-pity. Nothing seems to be working. And my own impatience isn't helping. Maybe I should give the new supplements more than a few weeks to kick in. And it was also pretty unscientific to try several therapies at once, because now there's no way to tell which one is or is not having an effect.

I wish Jenn were here to help me. I wish I could get a day off from the constant and exhausting drama that is Edie. I fantasize about switching places with Jenn. Just for one day. Then she would understand how unrelenting it is to oversee Edie. I don't think my wife really, truly gets how my life has been consumed by our puppy. I haven't been able to write in forever. I need a haircut. My friends no longer invite me for dog walks, or out to lunch, because I can't bring Edie with me, and I'm too worried to leave her home alone because I won't be there if something scares her. How did I become the harried indoor housewife, and Jenn the husband who sees his kids for a few breezy hours at the end of each day and calls it equal parenting?

I consider making myself a martini even though it's not even lunchtime, but the pathetic cliché of it stops me. Instead, I kick my way out of my funk and call Kendra. She'll know what to do.

Our conversation, as usual, is a bit truncated, with dogs yapping in the background and occasional interruptions as Kendra puts the phone down to mediate a squabble over a chew toy or to meet a client at her door. But she gets the gist of my problem: I'm at a loss with Edie.

"She needs a role model," Kendra says matter-of-factly. "A confident dog that she can emulate."

It just so happens that Kendra is boarding a female golden puppy named Ginny that has confidence to spare. Ginny is ten months old, only three months older than Edie, but because she lives with a massive French herding dog called a

Beauceron that looks like a cross between a German shepherd and a Doberman pinscher, she's fearless, already scrapping with dogs more than twice her size. Kendra's invitation is a flashlight that breaks through my own personal fogbank.

I give Edie a few days to calm down following the Pink Tricycle Incident, and then drive her to Kendra's. I'm lightheaded with hope, the same feeling I used to get in high school when classes let out for summer, and we'd all pile into a friend's Volkswagen van headed for Carmel Beach, tossing our homework papers out the windows as we went. Anything felt possible in that moment of new beginnings. When I arrive, Kendra is already waiting for us at her side gate, and I follow, carrying Edie to the backyard. When I spot Ginny tussling in the middle of the dog fray like Stella used to do, my breath catches in my throat. I can feel my puppy trembling in my arms and the contrast between the puppy I have and the puppy I was supposed to have is so painfully sharp that it feels like an actual bruise is blossoming behind my rib cage. Ginny is the smallest dog in the pack, yet she's throwing her body under, over, and around five dogs that tower over her, taking whatever they throw at her and giving it back to them with glee. She's not just confident. She's resplendent. Kendra is saying something, but her words are garbled as I spiral inward, unable to stop my envious tears. I turn away so she can't see how crushed I am.

When Sara had explained that Edie is different, I'd understood it conceptually. Intellectually, I had accepted the fact that our dog has limitations. But an abstraction is emotionally safe because it allows me to shape it into whatever I need it to be. Now, I can't turn away from the naked truth. And it's heartbreaking. I pine for ordinary Ginny so badly that I indulge myself with a wicked thought. *What if I "accidentally" took the wrong dog home?*

I come back to reality and find Kendra herding all the dogs back into the house.

"Sorry, Kendra, what'd you say?"

"Edie looks nervous," she shouts over her shoulder. "I'll put the rest of the dogs inside so she can play alone with Ginny."

I sit on a lawn chair with Edie in my lap, and when Kendra reemerges, I set Edie on the ground. Edie makes a few tentative steps toward Ginny, then loses conviction and runs back to the safety of my lap. Ginny seems to sense not to push it, and busies herself sniffing the grass. I set Edie down several times more, and Edie manages to approach and even play with Ginny, but only for about two minutes before returning to my lap. My face crumples. I was so certain this was going to work.

"Just a minute," Kendra says, jogging to the house.

She returns and holds out her palm, revealing a heart-shaped dog biscuit that looks like it's made out of bran.

"I keep these on hand for my nervous dogs. It helps them mellow out."

"What is it?"

"CBD dog cookie. There's hemp in it."

I'm leery. The few times I tried pot in high school, my friends almost took me to the emergency room because I was certain "secret agents" were spying on me, ready to haul me to jail, thus dooming my chances of ever reaching college and making it on my own. Ever since then, I've avoided cannabis in all its various forms, not counting the cream my cousin makes for muscle aches.

"Is it going to make her stoned?"

Kendra explains there's no THC in it, so dogs won't get high. "The CBD just takes the edge off."

"Maybe just half," I say, breaking the cookie in two.

"It takes about twenty minutes to kick in," Kendra says. "Some dogs can't function without a little CBD, other dogs fall asleep, and some dogs have no reaction at all."

"Where'd you get these?"

She names the holistic pet store in Berkeley a couple miles from her house, and on the way home I stop there. A cashier in dreadlocks with little crystals and amulets woven into them directs me to a shelf lined with small silver bags of treats containing organic mushroom powder and hemp oil. He recommends the pricier soft chews instead of the biscuits because they absorb faster in the body. I pick up a bag, flip it over to find the price, and wince—forty-five dollars for thirty chews. Then, with the suave timing of a car salesman, the cashier tells me that I'm lucky the silver bags are in stock—it's the store's fastest selling product. And the recipe is proprietary—I can't get them in mainstream pet stores.

"I'll take them," I say.

"Sweet," he says, reaching for a bag and turning back toward the register.

"No, I'll take all of them."

He wheels around with an incredulous smile. *"Sweeeeeeeeeet,"* he says, sweeping the shelf clear with his arm and embracing the bundle of bags like pirate's booty.

I swipe my credit card and for the first time in my marriage, consider keeping a secret from my wife. But of course, the moment I see Jenn walk through the door later that evening, I blurt out where I've been, and what I've bought. Jenn seems nonplussed, as she reaches down to lift Edie, who's scrabbling to scale her leg. I'm waiting for her to tell me I shouldn't have thrown away money, but instead she walks over to the pile of silver bags on the kitchen counter, and chuckles to herself as she reads the ingredient list.

"They're making CBD for dogs now?"

The irony is not lost on us. Jenn fled from cannabis culture, once upon a time even arrested people for carrying marijuana, and yet here we are now in 2019, and cannabis has legally boomeranged back into her life. No matter how hard we try, we can never outrun our pasts. We just learn to see them in a new light. But I'm pretty certain this is tickling her childhood PTSD, and not in the fun way.

"Turns out…yes."

"Well, human and dog brains are supposedly very similar," she says, quoting again from her Monks of New Skete book.

I sigh, relieved the confrontation I'd expected isn't coming. I'm so desperate, I will try anything, even things that make my wife uncomfortable.

"I'm actually hoping it doesn't work," I say, now having had the gift of time to reflect on my purchase. "Because if it does, Edie is going to become a lot more expensive," I say. A year's worth would be $540, and that's if she ate only one chew per day. The recommended daily dose is two a day, so basically a little over a thousand bucks a year. Why this hadn't occurred to me earlier when I was in the store is an astute observation.

As we become ever more obsessed with Edie's welfare, our friends are also getting swept up in the saga of our skittish dog. They no longer greet us with standard how-are-you conversation openers; instead everyone asks about Edie, and if she's had any setbacks or successes. We get lots of free advice, and everyone tries their best to solve the riddle of our dog. But so far, no one's come up with the solution.

One morning at the Peet's Coffee where my rowing team gathers after early morning practice, I bring up the CBD dog cookies. This causes a flurry of stoner jokes among my teammates, and everyone is poking fun except our bow seat, Barb, seventy-three, who is shaking her head.

"Hemp oil is fake CBD," she says. All heads turn. Barb's son is the CEO of Cookies, the multimillion-dollar cannabis empire with dispensaries and clothing stores around the world. When her son was getting started, she helped out by hosting Tupperware-style house parties for seniors to introduce them to the health benefits of "modern marijuana" for arthritis and other aches and pains, offering samples of all the new ways cannabis can be consumed: in teas, gummy bears, popcorn, chocolates, lozenges, and fruit roll-ups. She knows of what she speaks.

What follows is an impromptu TEDx Talk on the difference between CBD oil derived from hemp versus CBD oil derived from marijuana. While both plants are cousins in the cannabis family, Barb explains, hemp contains so little THC that you can't get high smoking it. Marijuana, which as a controlled substance is selectively bred for high CBD strains and subject to rigorous lab testing for purity, can contain as much as 30 percent THC.

"What you want is pure cannabis oil, from the marijuana plant," Barb says, "because you need some of that THC to work in concert with the CBD molecule to chill your dog out."

According to Barb, people who take CBD oil from hemp for anxiety are getting something only slightly better than a placebo. What's more, farmers historically planted hemp to rid crop soil of bacteria, then sold it to make rope. Hemp is not a controlled substance, so who knows what's lurking in it before it's turned into oil, she says.

I feel like a sucker for buying all those hemp dog chews. But as aforementioned, my cannabis education had been less than fleeting.

"Don't I need a medical marijuana card to get it?"

"Not in California anymore. You can walk into any dispensary and buy it off the shelf. My son sells a ton of it."

She raises her reusable coffee travel mug, takes a sip of her latte, and pops the lid off her glass container from home, revealing yogurt topped with granola and blueberries and digs in. I notice the café is oddly attuned to her movements and realize Barb has captivated more than just our table with her mini master class.

I wait for her to swallow before asking.

"Do you think you could…"

"Ummmmmm-hmmmmm," Barb says, stretching the word out to let me know she was anticipating my question.

And so that's how I find myself a few days later, sitting on the steps leading to Barb's pretty white Victorian in Pacific Heights, forty in cash in pocket, waiting for her to arrive with a bottle of cannabis-infused pet drops. There's plenty of street entertainment while I wait, listening to chirping birds in the sidewalk trees beatboxing with the beeping delivery trucks. Sighing Muni buses inhale and exhale passengers at the corner while bicyclists on the trendy, brakeless, fixed-gear bikes "California stop" at the stop signs. I imagine the city is a brain, and I am watching its neurons fire in all directions.

Then from out of the frenzy I spot Barb approaching in

her white compact SUV, on her lunch break from one of the old-money mansions up the hill where she works as a personal assistant. She slows to a stop in front of her house and lowers the tinted passenger window. I jog down to meet her and as I reach in to hand her my cash, I see she's wearing a matching salmon cashmere sweater set, and pearls.

"Here ya go," she says, handing me a padded white envelope with the flap torn open. Inside, there's a one-ounce brown bottle with an eye dropper top. "That oughta do the trick."

She gives me a quick parade float wave, then up goes the window and she's off again, leaving me to wonder if I'll be half as beguiling as Barb when I grow up. And while we didn't break any laws, I still can't shake the notion that I just bought drugs off the street for my dog.

According to the ant-sized type on the label, the pet drops are nonpsychoactive and made from non-GMO olive oil infused with "clean green" cannabis that contains 20:1 ratio of CBD to THC. I like that it says "handcrafted in small batches" on the label, because I'm a total sucker for that kind of David vs. Goliath marketing that makes me feel like I'm doing something about corporate hegemony. I twist open the cap and take a whiff. Black pepper, with a note of skunk. Just like the scent of the bongs that were passed around at high school parties.

The serving size for a dog Edie's weight is two dropperfuls a day. I can add the drops to Edie's kibble, put them on her paws to lick off, or try them directly under her tongue. I choose tongue, because if there's one thing Edie is not afraid to do it's to test an unfamiliar item for edibility. There are puppy bites on our succulents and vegetables, I've pulled cactus spikes from her muzzle, and stopped her from chewing rocks, deck screws, candy wrappers, cigarette butts, dirty socks, and dead mice. We've yet to see her reject anything we've hand-fed her, marveling at how she swallows the watermelon or banana or cucumber slice first before considering taste. I once even caught her gobbling her own turds.

"C'mere, Bunny."

Interest piqued, Edie walks over to sample the half-filled dropper I'm holding out for her. She lets me put the tip in her mouth but then tries to bite the glass tube, forcing me to abort mission. Instead, I squirt the oil into goat cheese and watch its color go from bright white to faint green as I mix the two together. Edie's toenails are ticking on the floor as she hops in anticipation. I set the ramekin down on the floor and in the time it takes me to stand back up, she's already licked it clean and is looking skyward for more heavenly manna.

"Oh no, sister, you gotta go easy with this stuff," I say, walking back to the living room as Edie follows at my heels. The cat is lounging in a square of sun on the carpet and Edie spots her; she sticks her nose in the cat's belly, prodding her to get up and play. Lulu declines in her usual fashion, with a swift claw swipe across Edie's nose. Edie finds this hysterical, and runs around the cat, taunting her for more and ignoring the low growl of an exasperated feline elder. At times like these, I wish very much that Edie had a sibling to play with. I wonder if things might have turned out differently if she'd had the security of a buddy. I snatch the puppy away from Lulu, and the cat takes her opening, streaking back to the bedroom to her sanctuary under the sheets.

When I return to the living room, Edie is in her bed, curled around her stuffed raccoon. Within an hour, she's fallen into a deep REM sleep, because the small whiskers that sprout above her eyes are rapidly twitching back and forth. I tickle her to see if I can get her to play, but she just flicks open her eyes and stares at me, shifts to her other side, and lets her eyelids float back down. I find this slightly alarming, so I wake her again to see if she can focus on my finger as I move it around. She can, so I relax a bit, but am still concerned by her grogginess.

I check on her every half hour, while I spend this windfall of free time on long overdue chores, dusting, vacuuming dog hair, and washing Edie's blankets and bowls. The busywork makes me feel industrious and clean, but it also feels like cheating. If Edie gets overwhelmed easily, the answer isn't to knock her out so she doesn't have to face anything at all. Sleeping through life is how my mother coped with the overwhelming prospect of starting over after divorce, so something just feels wrong about choosing a similar path of least resistance for my dog. Making Edie go to sleep is the equivalent of the frazzled mom plunking her children in front of the television to get a moment's peace. It feels like a selfish shortcut to steal a few hours of freedom from my puppy by knocking her out.

Over the next few days, I experiment with smaller doses of cannabis oil, but Edie keeps falling asleep. Maybe resting can train her muscles to remember what relaxing feels like, so it's not all a waste. But in the end, I decide the drops aren't the answer. I may not want to live with a hypervigilant puppy, but I don't want to live with a lethargic one, either. There's something fundamentally depressing about watching a puppy behave like a geriatric version of itself.

As the cannabis makes its way out of Edie's system, her lengthy slumbers recede and she returns to her regular routine of multiple daily powernaps, followed by indoor zoomies to release her pent-up energy. She always wakes refreshed and ready to pounce. Which means I'd better be wearing sturdy jeans tucked into my boots. Edie has mostly given up trying to get Lulu to play with her, so she's taken to running up behind me, reaching around the front of my calves to grab me with her paws, and sinking her sharp baby teeth into the back of my leg. I know it's a phase, and I know she's teething, but I also know that if she weren't a special snowflake she'd be working this out with other dogs in the great outdoors. But because I can't take her outdoors to burn off her energy the way I'd like to, I'm her stand-in wrestling partner. And I have the scratches raked down my legs to prove it.

I try yelping like an injured puppy as the guidebooks suggest, to show her that she's playing too rough. She backs off… sometimes. I buy her a cornucopia of "long-lasting" non-rawhide bones and dental chews to give her something else to gnaw on, but the little bugger chomps and swallows them like she's eating potato chips. When I get so frustrated that I push her off of me, she thinks it's a fun game and leaps back at me for more. Her ankle biting is increasing in direct proportion to her cabin fever.

After a particularly hard day of puppy pouncing, after Edie's drawn blood and I've screamed myself hoarse for her to stop, I march her to the bedroom and slam the door. Her plaintive whine wheedles all the way back to me downstairs, where I'm sitting on the couch shaking with frustration.

"Edie, shut up!" I bellow.

I'm so frazzled that I'm shivering as if it's snowing indoors. I'm mad at Edie for being a lousy student, for showing no discernable uptick in bravery despite all the different therapies I've tried. I'm angry at myself for my scattershot approach to helping her, for giving each new therapy not even a week to work before losing patience and moving to the next. And even though I know it's unfair, I'm mad at Jenn, for having no idea what it's like to live as a shut-in with Edie, for acting more like a hands-off stepparent when it comes to our "joint" responsibility.

Meanwhile I've become that person who wears the same yoga pants all week and can't recall what day it is, or when I last took a shower. I feel my free will, and my sanity, slipping through my fingers. Silent tears roll down my cheeks, while my puppy cries mournfully on the opposite side of the door.

When Jenn walks through the door, we're both having meltdowns. But the first thing she notices is that there's no jumping puppy to greet her.

"Hi. Where's Edie?"

"In the bedroom."

"Why?"

"She was bad." My voice sounds robotic.

"Oh, Edie, did you bite your mama again?" Jenn calls out, as she ascends the stairs. I hear their joyful reunion. Jenn descends carrying Edie, who is showing her gratitude by licking every inch of Jenn's face with her pink tongue. There goes my punishment training.

"Do any writing today?" Jenn asks.

For a trained observer, Jenn is being especially clueless right now. I shoot invisible hot daggers out my eyes at my wife.

"Ooooh! She lost another one," says Jenn, bending over to pick up one of Edie's baby teeth from the floor. She's sentimental about them, and jogs up the stairs with Edie in tow, to put the tooth with the others in her keepsake box. I hear her change out of her work clothes and chitty-chat with Edie, asking her how her day was. Jenn returns and takes a chair facing me in the living room and waits for me to say something. When I do not, I notice her expression change from relaxed to perplexed. There's no smell of dinner cooking.

"What's for dinner?"

I want to say that it's amazing how sexist lesbians can be, but I bite my tongue. Hard.

"Dinner is you going down to Westlake Joe's and bringing us back a wedge salad and fries."

"Whoa!"

Now I have Jenn's full attention. She leans forward for a closer look and asks me if I've been crying. Which melts my steely resolve, eliciting a whole new round of melodrama.

"You have no idea…"

Jenn whips over to the couch and throws an arm over my shoulder.

"What? Tell me," she whispers. I take off a boot, roll up a pant leg and show her where Edie drew blood. Jenn softly traces the red line with her finger.

"Does it hurt?"

"It's not so much that it hurts, it's that it's all day, every day," I say, pointing accusingly at Edie, who is now trying to take a bite out of my leather boot. "I need more help. I need you to co-parent Edie, not just stepparent around the edges."

Jenn is aware now that this is a serious plea, not a run-of-the-mill complaint. I'm losing it, and she is taking it seriously, but her reply is as expected. She can only do so much because she can't stay home during the week.

"Do you think you could take Edie with you to work sometime?"

"What?"

My desperate idea could either be outrageous, or accidentally brilliant. Jenn's job at the police academy is administrative; she spends her time at her desk or in meetings, managing professional development programs for officers—everything from mindfulness to cultural sensitivity. Her job is to make sure police officers are taking care of their mental health so they maintain their well-being, and their professionalism, on the streets. A puppy could fit into her stress relief strategy.

Dogs have been permitted inside the San Francisco Police Department before. Two of Jenn's colleagues brought their dogs to work. A female officer in the canine unit had dog privileges, but also Jenn's friend Pete, an investigations lieutenant who brought both his puppies to his station. When we'd mentioned our troubles with Edie, he'd said taking his puppies to work was great for their socialization and it lifted office morale.

I'd even seen dogs in Jenn's office at the police academy. Once, when I came by to take her to lunch, one of her coworkers had his two French bulldog puppies under his desk. He used a baby gate to keep Boris and Hazel in his workspace, where they tussled with each other while he worked on his computer. No one had seemed to mind, most of all Jenn, who as the boss could've said no.

"We could take her there for a practice visit to see if she can handle it?" I ask.

The police academy is run out of a former public elementary school in a quiet, residential part of the city. It's a good place for a dog because it's atop a hill, surrounded by nature parks. The building is a little run-down, with stained carpets, and chipped linoleum hallways, the kind of place where a little dog hair or scuff marks on the floor aren't going to draw attention.

Jenn's office is a former classroom, the back half of it divided by nine cubicles with chest-high dividers. The front of the room is a central gathering area with a conference table, the copy machine, coffee maker, and a row of metal filing cabinets. Jenn can park behind the building and access her office through a side door, so Edie won't need to come in contact with crowds or traffic to get inside.

Jenn's rank means she is assigned one of the roomier cubicles, with an L-shaped desk and space for a couple visitor chairs in addition to her own. More than enough space for Edie to hang out for a day. All Jenn would need is a baby gate, a dog bed, some toys, and a water bowl. And I would get one precious day back to think about anything other than Edie. To meet a friend for lunch. To go to the library and write. To row my single shell on the lake. To remember who I used to be before I became Edie's everything.

"I don't know," Jenn says, frowning.

"What about Boris and Hazel?"

"He only brought them a couple of times," Jenn says. "I'd have to get permission. I don't think we're really allowed to bring dogs to the academy."

"I thought you were the boss."

"I am, but…"

I'm frustrated that Jenn bends the rules for Boris and Hazel, but not Edie. Not for me. I'm worried that Edie's needs are starting to weigh too heavily on Jenn. And when Jenn gets overwhelmed by others, by their emotions or their demands, she withdraws and shuts down. It's a survival strategy she developed growing up in a volatile home, to fade into the background when the world around her starts to spin out of control. She's disengaging, right when I need her to dive into this mess with me. Is she saving herself, or is she passively punishing me so I can feel the full weight of what I brought into our house? Jenn wouldn't do that, would she? I mull this for a second before casting it aside. No, Jenn's not manipulative, but do her childhood emotions have a mind of their own, is her self-preservation instinct taking over? Does she have the capacity to stick with this?

For the first time, I have doubts. I know Jenn loves Edie, but I'm not sure if she's willing to bend her life this much for a dog. Sure it's a wild idea to bring Edie to work, but I wish she were more willing to try. I want her to be mildly amused by the idea, and hopeful she can make it happen. But her immediate resistance has an undertone of exasperation, as if she's already given up on Edie. If Jenn is only capable of going through the motions of caring for Edie, that could send the first fissure through our marriage. If we were to replace the word "puppy" with "baby," we'd be having a classic couple's fight over how to bring kids into a relationship. Do you really want Edie, or are you just going along with me? If Jenn is having second thoughts, would that be enough to break us? Would she eventually become weary of wishing her home life were different? Would I be able to pretend I didn't notice her spirit crumbling a bit more each day? Would I feel guilty for ruining the carefree fun life we used to have, or would I eventually resent her for walking away from puppy parenthood?

These are the deep disagreements that loosen the foundation of a relationship. The ones that until now Jenn and I have been able to avoid as urban professionals with no family responsibilities. But these core beliefs about your deserved baseline happiness lie dormant until tested by an unexpected crisis. Often, they are vital needs we didn't even know we had until our carefully guarded individuality became threatened. They rise to the surface after the fact, when we've already made a life-changing decision to bring Edie into our lives. Now we're discovering we have very different definitions of what being a parent entails.

"Please, find a way, Jenn. I've rearranged my entire life for Edie. All I'm asking is that you do it one day a week."

"I'll try," Jenn says, kissing me on the forehead. And with that, she heads out the door to fetch our restaurant takeout, leaving me with my four-legged cellmate once more.

Edie posts herself at the front door, and whimpers for Jenn. Her cries have the dual effect of softening my heart and flushing all the anger out of my system. Despite all the trouble Edie brings us, she's still bringing more love into the house. If I could just stop fixating on long-term outcomes, I could see how much she feels for us right now.

"Oh Boo-Boo, she'll be right back," I say, scooping her up in my arms. "Should we play a game?"

Edie cocks her head to the side and studies my face, unsure what I'm offering. I take the nearly empty toilet-paper roll out of the bathroom and bring it to the kitchen. I kick it for Edie and she springs into action, pouncing on the paper tube and tearing it to shreds. It never occurred to me that maybe Edie might be frustrated too. Watching her uncork her compressed fury makes my shoulders relax.

"Feel better?" I say, to both her and myself.

8

Panic Attack

We've been in the car too long, and now Edie needs to pee. The poor thing is shouting for a potty break the only way she knows how, leaning so far from the back seat that she's panting on Jenn's shoulder.

"We really should stop," Jenn says.

I check the clock on the dash. There's not enough time. We're on our way to Big Sur where I've been invited to give a talk about my grandfather, who mentored several generations of beekeepers in the area. It's a trip that should take less than three hours from San Francisco, but in May when the weather is gorgeous like this you can always count on some sort of food or art or car festival on the Monterey Peninsula to gum things up. And now it looks like we are going to be late.

"We're almost there," I say.

If Edie wasn't Edie, we could just pull to the side of the

road for a pit stop. But of all the bogeymen in her life, the biggest and baddest is the bloodthirsty automobile. What we see as a car, she sees as a snarling dragon-on-wheels that hasn't eaten in a week. Putting her within earshot of rushing traffic would be like forcing a person with a fear of heights onto the Golden Gate Bridge and then encircling them with funhouse mirrors. Terror would take over her brain, and the chances of her bolting onto the highway would be approximately one in one. Imagining this, I feel a phantom whoosh of a semitruck on my skin and the burn of Edie's leash as it tears from my grip.

"It's fine if she goes on the blanket. We can wash it," I offer, which is a terrible thing to say, and I know it. But we don't have time to search out a tranquil bathroom for Edie because we are cutting it too close. A crowd of Grandpa's relatives and friends is already gathering in the Grange Hall, waiting to see my family snapshots of the man they knew as "the Beekeeper of Big Sur."

We reach the intersection where Carmel and Carmel Valley meet at a shopping center of groceries, gas stations, banks, and a post office, then pass through a final stoplight before entering coastal Highway 1. The land of retail recedes in the rearview, and suddenly we're on a curving two-lane road, hemmed in by barn-dotted pastures on the left and isolated sea coves on the right.

Edie's plea has intensified to a high whistle, aching and full of want. It's the pitiful sound of a broken promise, the one I made to take care of her. It makes me ashamed of myself. Now is a perfect opportunity to put Edie's needs before mine, and all I can think about is being punctual.

"How about we pull over there?" I say, pointing out the

passenger window toward Monastery Beach, a curved spit
of sand directly across from a Spanish Mission–style convent
where the Carmelite nuns are cloistered. This beach, unlike
the one in Carmel, is definitely not a tourist spot and it's deserted as usual. The notoriously wicked undertow swallows at
least one person a year, prompting locals to dub it, "Mortu-
ary Beach." All we'd have to do is pull over, lift Edie over a
two-foot wooden guardrail, and she'd have the whole beach
to herself.

Jenn whips the Prius to the side of the road with the reflexes
of someone who drives police cars in San Francisco for a living. I clip Edie to a twenty-foot leash, swing open the back
door, and she pauses for a microsecond to sniff the salty air.
Satisfied, she leaps out and in four steps she's in the sandbox
of her dreams, scattered with so many new sea treasures to
smell, it's as if the waves put out a buffet just for her. She's so
enchanted by the salty ropes of giant kelp and prickly purple
seaweed fronds that she pees without stopping, running from
one delicacy to the next. She tastes everything, and I have to
sprint to keep up with her as she gallops through a seafood
feast, sampling everything on the menu. We scramble after
her and remove burned driftwood from her mouth, steer her
away from a dead seagull, and try to distract her with a tennis ball. She ignores the pedestrian plaything and charges for
what might be a rotting jellyfish.

I remember what Sara told us about dogs associating good
and bad memories with places, and what I want more than
anything is for Edie to fall in love with the land where my
grandfather raised me. Big Sur is home in my bones, and it's
where Jenn and I go to breathe in nature and exhale urban
stress. And it's tailor-made for traveling with a dog. The cen-

tral Monterey coast is one of the most pet-friendly areas in the world outside Paris. Nearly all the motels and restaurants make room for pets, many beaches are off-leash, and most shops keep a water bowl near the door and treats behind the counter. Stella used to love strolling Ocean Avenue in Carmel for handouts, then finishing her day being adored at "Yappy Hour" at Doris Day's Cypress Inn, where pooches chillax with their humans in the cocktail lounge. It's critical that Edie forms a positive emotional opinion of the Monterey Peninsula because coming here is an emotional need for us, too. It's where we hope to buy our forever home. More than anything, I want Edie to have fun on her first visit. So I let her taste things on Monastery Beach that she probably shouldn't.

We are taking a calculated risk bringing Edie out of her comfort zone and into the unpredictability of a road trip. We had many discussions about it, and in the end we decided to travel together rather than splitting up so Jenn could stay home with Edie. Jenn really wanted to meet my grandfather's peers and hear their stories about him. She had developed a special fondness for Grandpa from the moment he first hugged her, with a tightness she never forgot, as if he had a premonition that she was going to become part of our family. He became her muse, and in the few years she got to spend with him, she photographed him at work and at rest, providing not only the images inside my memoir about him, but the cover image of his honey bus, as well.

Leaving Edie with a friend was out of the question—we couldn't possibly put anyone in a situation where our dog might flee on them. We decided to take Edie with us because of her success at the police academy. Despite her reservations, Jenn made arrangements for her coworker to bring

his two French bulldog puppies to the office on the same day
she brought Edie. Puppy day was a success, for humans and
dogs both, as Boris, Hazel, and Edie made everyone laugh as
they careened around the cubicles stealing one another's toys.
When the puppies eventually tuckered themselves out, they
curled up underneath their masters' desks and snoozed. Edie
was able to get the kind of exercise and social interaction a
growing puppy needs, in a familiar place where she felt safe.
The plan worked so well that Jenn started taking Edie to work
every Friday. The new sights and smells gave Edie a chance
to practice confidence, and she thrived on the days she got
to go work with Jenn, while I became a much nicer person
with my weekly reprieve. Jenn was even able, after several
weeks of practice, to coax Edie to explore the hallways of the
building on-leash. Jenn made Edie sit whenever the police
recruits marched by in formation, but inevitably the sight of
a puppy caused a delighted disruption as the young hopefuls
fell out of step to greet Edie.

The academy proved that Edie could adapt to unfamiliar
places with the help of dog friends. So we asked Maile and
Eddy if they could bring Pancho and Pepper to Maile's family
home in Monterey that same weekend, so Edie could have a
sleepover with familiar dog friends. Maile and Eddy agreed
to meet Jenn and me at Grange Hall and dog-sit all three
puppies in the surrounding redwood grove while I gave my
talk. Then we'd caravan to Monterey and cook dinner while
the mutts could mingle in the spacious sunken living room
or romp on the golf course outside the big sliding glass doors.
Our contingency plan felt ridiculously orchestrated, yet responsible. Sara had convinced us that Edie's needs had to be
considered along with our own.

We packed her bed, her favorite stuffed toys, bags of treats, bully sticks, calming floral spray, dog towels, and a canine first-aid kit. I dug out the CBD oil and chews, in case of absolute emergency. I made a new playlist of soft piano music designed to calm dogs. By the time we had all her emergency gear gathered, Edie's travel bag was bigger than our shared one.

And so far, our decision is proving to be a good one. Edie is loving the beach so much, after ten minutes, she resists my attempts to steer her back toward the car. I want to leave before anything frightens her and ruins it, but she doesn't appear ready to go. She's fixated on something in the sand, all four legs and her core working in concert to resist my tug on the leash.

"Edie, Come!"

Nothing. Her tail is pointing almost straight up, an exclamation point fixed in space by DNA hardwired for the hunt. I give in and trek back toward her, just as she lifts her snout to reveal her prize: a dead crab, its black legs sticking out from either side of her mouth. Edie is thrilled with herself and whips her head side to side to snap its dead neck. Jenn is lunging left and right like a tennis player swinging at air as she tries to extract the crab, but Edie is faster, dodging Jenn with the wicked precision of Lucy pulling the football just as Charlie's about to kick it. It isn't funny, but it is.

"Oh, just let her have it—she's so happy about it," I say.

"You sure?" Jenn is a safety-first kind of gal, the kind who throws milk out on expiration dates while I grew up cutting mold off cheese before eating it and will still do so when she's not watching. I guess you'd say I'm more "safety-third." Jenn stares at Edie and with the patience of a trained martial artist, drops slowly into a squat so she has a better chance of snatching the crustacean. Edie eyeballs her warily. Sensing Jenn's intentions, Edie points her nose to the sky and chugs the crab down in three gulps. Satiated, Edie is ready to obey now, and trots back to the car without complaint.

"Protein, I guess," Jenn says, wrinkling her nose.

"It's just what puppies do—swallow gross shit."

Jenn gives me the long side-eye, so I tell her about the time Stella bolted on puppy legs into a horse paddock to stuff her mouth like a chipmunk with manure, forcing me to wade through the muck to stop her. The little monster didn't even have a burp of indigestion afterward.

We make it to the event with a few minutes to spare. Local beekeepers who were mentored by my grandfather are already inside the redwood cabin community hall, opening up jars of their honey and lining them up on a tasting table. Descendants of the same Ohlone tribe as Grandpa take the front row, including his sister and his niece. One of his longtime customers hands me a pint jar of his Big Sur wildflower sage honey that she'd been saving for me. Big Sur historians show up, as do dozens of Grandpa's mountain-man friends in their work boots and Carhartt jackets. As I walk onto the stage in his lime-green checkered square-dancing shirt and cowboy bolo tie, I swear I see the ghost of him in the back, smirking at all the fuss.

The crowd knows more about the photos in my slideshow than I do, and suddenly the audience is giving the presentation, explaining who Grandpa is with and what they are doing in the images. I abandon my planned speech and interview them. I learn that Grandpa once went lobster diving in Baja, that he rarely collected bills for his plumbing work, that he once put on a bonnet and performed as a baby in a play on the very same stage, and that he used to drive down the coast highway with his niece standing in the back of his pickup holding on to the contractor's rack, both of them shouting, "Whale!" whenever they spotted a spout erupt from the ocean surface.

Jenn and Eddy keep Edie entertained under the redwood trees until the event ends. When we reunite, Jenn's sitting cross-legged with her back against a tree next to our car. Edie is rolling in her lap tugging the strings of her sweatshirt hood. I sigh with relief. Our puppy seems content.

"How'd she do? Everything all right?"

"Oh Edie had herself a good ole time."

I notice all four doors of our Prius are wide-open. I detect a whiff of clam chowder.

"Agggh, what's that?"

"She yakked up the crab," Jenn says, pointing to the back seat.

"Uh-oh. Is she okay?"

"Seems to be. It didn't slow her down any. I cleaned it up, but it was pretty fragrant."

High on the list of reasons why I love my wife is that she takes all the nasty jobs without complaint. Maybe it's a police-thing, but Jenn is the steelier half of us; she's the one who catches the mouse, she tackles the mildew in the bathroom, she cuts the whole chicken into pieces for my recipe because dismemberment makes me squeamish. Crab vomit is definitely in her column.

Edie runs to me, and I lift her up and put her in the back seat. Jenn and I immediately lower all the windows. "My bad," I say.

Or was it? I'm not so sure. Investigating a crab is a huge

developmental leap for our dog, considering that she used to run away from plastic bags floating on the wind. So is it more beneficial to let Edie build confidence by wandering and exploring the beach, or should we have protected her stomach? Would we have reinforced her trepidation if we had shouted and pulled her away from the crab? Edie has upended everything I thought I knew about raising golden retrievers, so that now I armchair quarterback every decision I make. It's exhausting trying to figure out how to train an over-shy dog. Finally, I render my verdict.

"I'd rather have her barf a crab than run from a crab," I say.

"Me too," Jenn says. "But still that was stupid of us to let her eat it."

She doesn't have to take half the blame, but she does anyway because she's sorry that I feel sorry. I reach over and squeeze her hand, thanking her for understanding I feel bad, and that I also have a hard time admitting that I'm wrong, especially when it comes to dogs. I love it when we talk this way, without words.

If Edie has a stomachache, she doesn't show it. That night in Monterey, Edie gobbles her kibble and races around the living room with Pancho and Pepper until she crashes out on the carpet with a rope toy still in her mouth. Jenn and I tuck into sleeping bags on two couches next to her. Jenn falls asleep next, and when they both start snoring, I smile in the dark—content that they are content, and so relieved that our puppy has proven she can travel.

Something is booming. I open my eyes before I'm conscious to the world and wonder why I'm in a sleeping bag. Am I camping? The whole room flashes hot pink, and Jenn bolts upright with a pineapple hairdo.

"Was that lightning?" she asks.

There's another crack like a baseball bat hitting a homer, and Edie hops on all fours and stares wide-eyed at the ceiling. I can count on one hand the number of times I saw lightning growing up on the Peninsula. But sure enough, it's a big, juicy, East Coast thunderstorm.

"It's okay, Edie, come here," Jenn says, patting her lap. But Edie isn't listening. She is trembling, and her tail is between her legs as she squeezes herself behind the floor-length curtains.

"I'll get the CBD," Jenn says, running to our overnight bag. I get down on the floor and pull Edie onto my lap. She's not too nervous to reject the chews, and after a few of them, she seems somewhat calmer. The other dogs come bouncing into the living room to inspect, and Edie leaves my lap to join them, momentarily distracted from the thumping overhead.

The sky's mood passes like a tantrum and Edie rallies through it. By midmorning the sun is pouring over Monterey Bay again, making little diamonds sparkle on the water. It's time to go back to the city, and the usual dread shrouds me like a weighted blanket as Jenn steers the car north. We are heading back to meetings and appointments and parking tickets and alarm clocks. And sidewalks that Edie refuses to set foot on.

"Wanna stop for lunch in Carmel?" I say. It's three in the afternoon, but I don't let that stop me. And in that mind-reader way couples have of enabling each other, Jenn takes my suggestion and supersizes it.

"Emanuele's?" she says, raising her eyebrow.

Chef Emanuele Bartolini not only allows dogs on his patio, he's routinely voted one of the best chefs on the Monterey

Peninsula, building a new menu daily based on what local farmers and ranchers deliver to his 250-square-foot kitchen. He uses the ingredients and makes his own pasta to re-create the recipes his grandma used to make in the family restaurant in Florence. When I first came to his La Balena restaurant on assignment for the *San Francisco Chronicle*, Emanuele treated me like a long-lost cousin, whipping the menu out of my hands and insisting on bringing me plates and wine pairings himself, delivering each course with a joke or a childhood story. But it wasn't only me who got the VIP treatment. Although it drives his wife at the front of the house crazy sometimes, Emanuele embodies his grandma, flitting about the dining room to stop and talk with everyone about food and family and politics, no matter how many plates are flying out of the kitchen. He wasn't pandering to the journalist; he was just Emanuele being Emanuele.

"I don't see why not..."

It's the restaurant witching hour, so the patio is deserted. We don't see Emanuele and assume he's catching a much-needed nap before the evening rush. The table choice is obvious—the one tucked in a corner under an awning, farthest from the street. Jenn unfurls a gray yoga mat decorated with lotus blossoms under the table and instructs Edie to sit on it just like we practiced in puppy class. Edie drops down into a Sphinx and looks expectantly for a reward, my cue to whip open the fanny pack and toss a morsel her way, which I robotically do. We situate ourselves so that Edie is blocked on two sides by the walls of the restaurant, with the table over her forming a makeshift crate. Jenn and I situate our chairs to block her escape, and I put the leg of my chair through the loop-handle of Edie's leash so she's secured. I'd remembered to bring a towel from the back of the car, and I put it down next to her, so the familiar smell will soothe her. The server brings a bowl of water, and from the fanny pack I take out Edie's favorite chew, a bully stick made from dehydrated bull penis, and Edie begins gnawing on it with fervor. She loses herself in her new task, so much so that halfway through my pasta I glance down and see that she is completely sacked out, paws twitching in the middle of a dream.

"Look," I whisper, pointing my eyes downward.

"Cheers to that," Jenn says, lifting her wineglass. We toast to our little champ. Trusting us, finally. I feel like as a couple, we can get through anything.

Just then a door I hadn't noticed in the wall behind me swings open and Emanuele pops out, his arms spread wide in a T. *"Heyyyyyyyyyyy!!!!!!!!"* he croons, Fonzie-like.

His hello feels like a spotlight of love, and I instinctively jump up to embrace him. When I do, I hear a loud scraping and out of the corner of my eye I see my chair wobble, then topple, then slide on its side down the courtyard. For a split second my California brain registers earthquake, and then I realize it's Edie, fleeing from the man who'd just burst out of the wall, with my chair dragging behind her. I see a blur of her yellow coat before she reaches the sidewalk, then slips between two parked cars and into the street.

I don't remember bolting. I don't remember thinking. All I remember was suddenly finding myself running uphill against two lanes of oncoming traffic after her, fueled by the same sort of adrenaline that allows mothers to lift wrecked cars off their children. A block ahead, I spot Edie racing up the white line dividing the two lanes, the metal clip of her green leash furiously banging the pavement behind her. Cars are screeching out of the way at the last minute, slamming the brakes, and other drivers behind the action swerve and honk, unaware of what's happening. Edie is in full panic, zigzagging at the last second like a gazelle between squealing tires. I can feel engine heat on my jeans as I follow her, screaming for drivers to stop with both palms up like some sort of maniacal traffic control officer.

"Edie, come!" Jenn commands, and I look to my left, and wonder how long Jenn had been alongside me. She finds another reservoir of strength and sprints ahead of me past restaurants and chalet-style hotels, heading toward a gas station at the top of the hill that marks the edge of a dense pine tree forest. Again, I curse myself for wearing those clunky boots. I scream Edie's name again, but our puppy is lost in her own tunnel of terror, unable to hear us over the roar of engines, the roar of her own heartbeat. The distance between us and Edie is growing, and her chances of survival are plummeting with each second. I have that nightmare feeling of slipping backward the faster I run and all I can think is, *This is it. We are going to watch our dog get run over right before our eyes. Her life is going to end after only eight months.*

The horror of it sends my mind spinning though the five stages of grief in five seconds—*This can't be happening* (denial)… *I'm so pissed off at this ridiculous excuse for a dog* (anger)… *Please God spare her this one time and I'll never take her off-leash ever again* (bargaining)… *Oh what's the use of chasing her; there's no way she's going to survive* (depression)… *Snap out of it woman, and deal with this!* (acceptance).

Edie crests the hill and disappears from view. Now there's no way to know if she's dead or alive. Jenn reaches the top first, where a woman in a maroon station wagon lowers her window and calls out, "I saw where your dog went, get in!" Jenn, who never trusts strangers, leaps into the woman's car and they zoom off. Neither of us have our cell phones so now my wife has disappeared on me, too. We left everything, including my purse, at the restaurant. Things are spiraling too fast. I'm hyperventilating and feel like I'm going to pass out.

A white car stops next to me and the driver leans over to open the passenger door. "I just came from the police station and told them to look for a yellow puppy with a green leash running in the street," he says. "Can I drive you around to look?"

I get in his car without answering because I've suddenly lost the ability to form a sentence. Instead, I lean out the window and shout Edie's name repeatedly. We are only a few blocks north of Emanuele's restaurant, but here the roads get narrower and curvier, and there are miles of pine forests all around. Edie could be anywhere. She could be hiding; she could be injured; she could be dying or already dead. I scream until I'm hoarse, but the trees just stand there, silent and blaming.

This disaster is 100 percent my fault. I cannot believe I stood up from my chair. Why did I stand up? If I'd just kept seated, Edie wouldn't have been able to pull free. Or better yet, why the hell didn't I tie her leash in an actual knot? I was behaving as if I had Stella with me, the barnacle that I couldn't shake. I was seduced by my own denial, as if pretending Edie was Stella would somehow make it true.

The man driving the car is talking to me, but he sounds like a tape recording that's getting tangled, his words all warped and distended. I think he's asking me if we should go right or left. I point to the right, because I don't know what else to do. We turn a corner, and I see Jenn standing by the side of the road with two women. Edie is at their feet. "There!" I shout. I bend over and grab my chest, sucking in air as if I've just swam to the surface.

"You are a saint," I wheeze, and leap out of his car.

Edie is panting rapid-fire, and she has so much froth on her lips it looks like she dunked her mouth in milk foam. I drop to my knees and wrap my arms around her. She continues her vigil over my shoulder.

"Shhh-shhh-shhh-shhh, I got you," I whisper into her ear. I repeat this mantra over and over, not sure if I'm saying it for her or me. I'm so full of remorse, I don't know where to put it. I did this. I did this to our poor dog.

While Jenn thanks the two women who nabbed Edie, I lightly squeeze our trembling puppy all over her body, checking for injuries. I turn over her paws and find blood on the pads. She'd run so hard that she'd worn her toenails down to the nubs. When I look up, the women are gone. I hadn't even thanked them.

We are about eight blocks from the restaurant, and Edie walks on leash with us for about two of them, then sits and refuses to take another step. Maybe because we are getting closer to the restaurant, or maybe because her feet hurt too much. I squat and lift all fifty pounds of her, carrying her down the street with her arms dangling down my back. She squeezes her legs around my hips, and I can feel the terror in her body as she clings to me.

"I got you, I got you," I keep telling her. Tourists do double takes as we walk by, amused at first by our walking bear hug, then dropping their smiles once they register the shock on our faces. Everything about this is so wrong right now.

Edie is heavy, but I ignore the lactic acid burn in my shaking legs and keep pushing my feet forward. I have to get her back to the car—to familiarity, to safety.

Emanuele appears with our purse and wallet, and like a good friend, tries to make us feel better. He's had dogs run on him plenty of times before, he says.

"It's the electrical charge in the air, from the lightning and thunder," Emanuele explains. "Dogs can feel it long before it comes. That weird weather this morning probably affected her."

I don't have the heart to tell Emanuele that it's so much bigger than that. Something is malfunctioning inside Edie's brain. Something I'm not certain anyone can fix.

"Yeah, maybe so," I say, as I finally unload my cargo into the back of the Prius. I'm shaking all over, from both her weight and my stress.

"You okay to drive?" I ask Jenn. Thankfully she says yes, because even though I would take the wheel, I'm so jittery that I really don't think I should. Instead, I get into the back seat, and as soon as I sit down Edie lays her front legs across my lap and leans her head into my stomach, as if she can't get close enough. I reach around and slide one hand under her armpit, pulling her close. I massage her forehead and cheeks, pressing gently on her cheekbones, and the spot between her eyes. Edie's eyelids flutter down and she drools on my legs. I twist the top off the water bottle in Jenn's center console, pour it on a dog towel, and press it around Edie's front paws to clean up the dirt and blood. She winces and tries to draw her paws back.

"Sorry, buddy. I'm so sorry."

"Is it bad?" Jenn asks, eyeing me in the rearview mirror.

"They've stopped bleeding. I think they'll heal."

Edie presses harder into me, as if she's trying to disappear underneath my skin. Her heartbeat is racing double-time, and my pulse keeps up with her as I compulsively imagine all the horrific things that could have happened. I see a six-car pileup. I hear the wail of ambulances. I see our puppy disappear under a wheel. I imagine the sound my bones make inside my head when they break. I try on the word "widow."

From the back seat, I can see the tension in Jenn's jaw. She's lost in her own terrible what-ifs.

"Things just got real," I say to the back of her head.

She doesn't answer right away, then I hear her clear her throat.

"Both of us just ran into traffic without a second thought, Meredith," she says. "Edie is now putting *our* lives in danger."

I see Edie dragging Kendra and three dogs down the sidewalk. I flash to Barbara getting knocked into the sand. Now this. I shudder to imagine what's next. We can't keep skirting disaster; eventually our luck will run out.

Not facing one another gives the car the feel of being in a confessional, making it easier to finally say the things we've not had the nerve to utter until now. We blurt out all the things that good, compassionate, animal lovers are not supposed to say. I admit that I resent Edith. That I'm angry. I am devastated, exhausted, and riddled with anxiety because our dog has anxiety.

But Jenn's not merely upset. She's done.

"Most people wouldn't have lasted this long with a dog like this," Jenn continues. "We really tried."

I can sense where this conversation is going, but I can't bring myself to argue with Jenn even though my heart is breaking. Is Jenn only saying what I refuse to admit? That we are fooling ourselves? That Edie is a time bomb? As the more sensible one in the relationship, she's always been better at making the hard, adult decisions I'd rather avoid. But now I'm finally beaten down enough to listen to her.

I confess that I'm worn out from dealing with Edie's pent-up energy indoors, tired of worrying that her muscles are going to atrophy because I can't walk her, weary of scanning the internet for solutions only to get spun in contradiction. We've spent a small fortune on classes and behaviorists and toys and medications, and just when we think she's improving, something like this happens. Is this the best we can hope for…a screwed-up dog that we can keep alive? We go back and forth, discussing how Edie has completely upended our lives.

We let go of our egos, our expectations, and our emotions and for the first time talk honestly about Edie. How long can we keep doing this? Is this beautiful, broken creature going to bring us a decade or more of stress? What are the limits of our compassion? Could it be that this animal is simply too sensitive to function? The whole point of a pet dog is to be a companion, but what do we do if our dog won't accompany us anywhere?

Jenn reminds me how disappointed she is to miss my book tour to stay home with Edie. Our original plan, before Edie's neuroses surfaced, was to leave our puppy with Mag and Barbara. Now it's clear that Edie is a loose cannon, and we don't want to put any of our friends in a situation where they may lose our dog, or get injured trying to save her. Jenn says she's not willing to be held captive for the next ten or twelve years to stay home with a puppy that's too afraid of living. Stella

folded into our lives and made it better. Edie is doing the opposite. She's resisting everything and shutting down our lives
along with hers, Jenn says. She says she never expected she'd
have to give up the things that make her happy, in order to
make a puppy happy.

"I'm not sure this is the dog for us," Jenn says carefully.

A hush fills the car as we let that thought float between
us. I'm afraid to answer, as if saying anything would be tacit
agreement that we have to give Edie up. I don't want to let
go, yet I know my practical wife is making the hard decision so I don't have to. I squeeze Edie closer to me and cry
silently, already memorizing the way her body feels draped
across mine, anticipating losing her.

"But who would take a dog like Edie?" I sniff. It's hard to
look at Edie, feeling the betrayal bloom inside me.

"Someone who lives on a quiet farm?" Jenn says.

If only we knew someone who did. If sending Edie to
the country would make her happy, I'd do it, even though
it would kill me.

"And if we can't find such a place?" I ask.

Maybe, Jenn whispers, we have to think about putting
Edie down.

I feel something tighten in my chest. I sit in numb silence,
willing her last sentence to somehow rewind.

"Giving a dangerous dog to someone else isn't responsible
either," she continues. "That's not a solution, that's a liability."

My ears fill with the whine of a mosquito army. I'm not
ready to say Edie is unredeemable. But my wife, who grew
up having pets snatched away from her, has thicker skin. She
is taking the brunt of the awful decision away from me, and
I love her for being strong and sparing me, but I don't have

that kind of steely detachment. I love this dog too much now to go back. And I haven't lost faith yet. We don't know what we don't know. Maybe there's a confident dog in there, and we can persuade it to come out with more time.

"I don't want to give up on her," I say weakly.

"Me either, but it's an ethical dilemma," Jenn says. "Is it fair to keep a dog like Edie alive, when she might hurt someone, or injure herself, or cause a traffic accident? How long do we wait for her to change before we realize she's a danger to society?"

And there it is, my raw, ugly failure breathed into life. I've just reinforced my wife's worst fears about dogs. All they do is bring you sorrow. Jenn never asked for a puppy, and now she's being asked to spend the next ten or twelve years in an adversarial relationship with one. She's right; that's no way to live. Yet I couldn't live with myself if I didn't let Edie live, either.

We ride in silence the rest of the way, and after settling Edie into her crate, we go to bed before sundown, eager for this day to become history. We both have trouble sleeping, and sometime in the middle of the night I wake to an empty bed. Shuffling into my slippers, I walk into the living room to find Jenn sitting in the dark, with Edie curled asleep in her lap.

"Are you crying?"

"No…yes," she says.

I can count on one hand the number of times I've seen Jenn cry. I sit on the arm of the chair and pull Jenn's head toward me, cradling her as she lets the warm tears fall.

"Hey, we'll get through this," I say, although I'm not even sure I believe myself anymore.

Edie opens her eyes and registers me through heavy eyelids. Her tail thumps twice on Jenn's thigh, and then she escapes back into sleep. Normally Edie would be thrilled to get up in the middle of the night, always ready to romp at a moment's notice. But the adrenaline rush has left her spent, and it's clear she's not done recovering. Alone in the darkness like this, it feels like the three of us just awoke from the same nightmare; it's hard to believe that just eight hours ago we were running for our lives into oncoming traffic.

"Let's give her a year," Jenn says.

"What?"

"I agree we should keep trying. If Edie doesn't improve in a year, we'll have this discussion again."

"Thank you," I say, hugging Jenn so tightly she gasps for air.

9

Homecoming

Edie remains subdued for the rest of the day. She prefers to stay tucked into the safety of her crate, staring at nothing in particular, with a faraway look in her eyes. I wonder if she is replaying each awful moment in slow-motion, the way I can't seem to stop doing. She lets me wash her feet in soapy water, remaining uncharacteristically compliant while I cover her paws in tube socks to keep her from licking her wounds. I keep checking, hoping to see that she's yanked the socks off with her usual gumption, but she is resigned to them. I know she needs time to recover, but it's disturbing to see a puppy so listless, the youthful spunk replaced by a look of lost innocence. I remember Kendra's observation that Edie can't snap out of it the way most puppies do after a scare. It's like Edie was born with a glitchy reset button; she absorbs fear into her body rather than letting it pass through her.

I work on my laptop sitting on the floor next to her, keeping vigil over her even though she spends most of the day sleeping. Each time she cries in her sleep, I gently place my palm on her forehead until she settles. I want her to feel my presence, hoping that if she understands I'm going to stay by her side, she'll feel safe and that will help her recover more quickly. I leave a long, rambling message for Sara, trying to recap what happened but not finishing my thoughts before the beep cuts me off.

I'm also making amends. I almost broke the most basic pact a person makes with a pet: to keep them safe. And it's not like I hadn't been warned. I'd failed to listen to Sara's professional advice to keep Edie's needs in mind. Worse, I'd even failed to learn from all the close calls I'd already had with Edie that led to this.

Why is it so hard for me to love this dog responsibly? I can articulate the kind of dog owner I need to be with Edie, but when the moment comes for me to be that person, I don't do it. It's like I just can't let go of being the one in the relationship that needs to be loved. It's the default setting for people like me who grew up begging for comfort, a habitual victimhood that gets in the way of being an adult. My mother was a taker all her life, and no matter how much I tell myself that I'm not like her, sometimes I'm exactly the same. I don't know how many chances I'm going to get to do right by Edie, but if I don't stop giving lip service to putting her needs above mine, neither of us will evolve.

Somehow I've been given yet another reprieve. Every time my eyes drift from my computer screen to Edie, I listen to her soft exhale and tell myself—you came *this* close to never hearing that sound again. It feels like I'm riding a pendulum that swings between relief and remorse, creating a sort of emotional seasickness that drains my energy. I, too, want to crawl into bed and sleep away the day. And if we'd lost her? How could I live with the guilt of that? A little part of my happiness might never wake up again.

My thoughts keep going back to the only time I ever saw my Grandpa cry, when he lost his dachshund, Tina. A barrel-chested mountain man with enormous hands that could fell trees or pry abalone off rocks with a knife, he seemed to me like he possessed superhuman strength. But I knew something was wrong the moment he and Matthew came home several hours late from beekeeping in Big Sur one day. My brother's face was red and puffy, and he wouldn't look up from the ground. Grandpa's shoulders were slumped forward in defeat, and silent tears escaped the corners of his eyes.

"She didn't come when I whistled for her," he said.

When pets disappear without a trace in the Santa Lucia Mountains, the list of possible reasons is short: Mountain lion. Coyote. Raptor. Bear.

For two weeks he kept searching for Tina, hiking along the coastal meadows and into the canyon near his apiary, only to hear the echo of his own voice. He drove up and down Highway 1 below the speed limit, but didn't find her body. Finally, one day I noticed the sliding door on the redwood doghouse he'd built for her was closed. Grandpa, who'd had dogs all his life, never got another one after that. At the time I didn't understand, but now I can see how that kind of grief could do something to a person.

It comforts me to reach into the kennel and feel Edie's heartbeat, to assure myself the worst didn't happen. I'm relieved that Edie is still zealous about eating when I place her kibble bowl inside the crate. She crunches as if someone is timing her with a stopwatch, and is licking the crumbs that have sprayed outside the bowl when she detects the jangle of Jenn's key turning the front door lock. Edie's ears perk at the sound, and as she listens to Jenn's feet coming up the stairs, she finally emerges from the crate, tripping over her sagging socks as she makes her way to Jenn.

"How is everybody?" Jenn says, setting a bulging pet store shopping bag down on the bed.

"We're both pretty low energy," I say.

Edie points her nose at the bag, nostrils quivering. Jenn reaches in and pulls out a three-foot-long, bright green plush worm with googly eyeballs.

"Is this for Edie? Why, yes! I think it is!" Jenn says, dangling the prize above Edie's nose as our puppy rises on her hind legs to grab it with her paws. Jenn drops it to the floor and Edie drags it into her crate, where she does her best to rip its head off. Little cotton balls of stuffing flurry around her as she works to eviscerate the plastic squeaker.

"That's okay," Jenn says, pulling a frog made out of stiff canvas from the bag, "This one is supposed to be for tough chewers."

Jenn has purchased what looks like every flavor of training treat in the store. There are cubes of freeze-dried wild salmon, beef liver bites, pork somethings, and a cookie that looks like an oyster cracker claiming to include free-range chicken. Jenn opens every package and lays treats in a line on the floor, as Edie follows behind, gobbling them with vacuum speed. It's the most energy Edie's had all day.

"Presents. I should've thought of that," I say.

"Everybody likes presents," Jenn says.

Edie doesn't need all this stuff, but I think Jenn needs a place to put her own remorse. And it's Jenn's way of showing me that she's renewed her commitment to Edie, to finding the one treat Edie adores above all others, the magic "high-value" morsel that we can use to mold her into the type of dog that won't run away from us. I appreciate Jenn's effort, and by the looks of things, the way Edie is rubbing her scent all over the frog and the worm, she does, too.

"Also, I have some not-so-great news. Edie's been kicked out of the academy."

"What? What happened?"

"Someone complained."

When Jenn showed up back to work, she was called into her captain's office. Although her captain, who has three dogs of her own, initially approved the Friday puppy day idea to help boost morale, she'd been getting complaints. Someone said the office was looking unprofessional with dog toys strewn about. Another person wasn't pleased to see teeth marks on the plastic bases of the ergonomic roller chairs he'd just purchased for the staff. The captain, who didn't want her superiors to come down on her for running an underground doggie day care, had to put an end to it.

"Oh no. Are you in trouble?" I ask.

"No, it's not a big deal. But I am going to get the carpets steam cleaned."

If something seems too good to last, that means it probably is. At least Edie got two months of office visits before it ended. I regret that I put Jenn in an awkward spot at work, and when I tell her so, she waves it off.

"All we could do was try," she says.

"Now what are we going to do with this puppy?"

"Did you call Sara?"

"I already did."

When Sara returns my call the next day, I'm inside Bed Bath & Beyond feeling the towels. She wastes no time with pleasantries.

"Tell me about Carmel," she says.

I scuttle to a deserted corner, sit down, and lean back into the shelf of immaculately stacked bathroom towels where hopefully no one can hear me. Sara gasps as I give her the play-by-play.

"It was a perfect storm for a full-on panic attack," Sara says. "First the chef startled her, then she got 'chased' by the chair dragging behind her, then she flung herself into oncoming traffic."

A storm of my own making, all because I wanted lunch. Sara isn't blaming us, but I am. Jenn and I should have ended the trip on a good note, and never stopped for lunch. But we took the risk. Now, I feel about an inch high.

"You're so lucky Jenn found her."

"I know," I whisper, shivering at the memory.

Sara clears her throat and tells me that this changes things. Now that we've witnessed how all-consuming Edie's fear is, we must start making some serious life changes to accommodate our dog. Sara had tried to explain this to us earlier when she came to our house for a private consultation, and we had only been sort of listening. I'd petered out on Edie's bravery lessons, and never tried the puppy sound app again, nor did I call Sara to find out what to do when Edie couldn't stand the lowest volume. In the end we used what little progress Edie had been making as an excuse to do what we wanted anyway.

"You can't just go wherever you want with Edie anymore,"

she says, waiting a beat for her words to sink in. "You have to incorporate her needs into your planning now. You have to be her protector."

Sara is asking me to finally "see" Edie for what she is, not what I want her to be. Edie keeps trying to remind me that she can't handle things, and I keep telling myself that she can. Finally, in Edie I've met a will stronger than my own. My puppy is forcing me to accept that I can't control everything. Edie may know better than me what's best for her.

Traveling with Edie probably isn't a good idea, Sara says, because it's too overstimulating. As a hypervigilant dog, Edie gets rattled by being forced into unfamiliar environments where she has to take in too much, too quickly. She's a reactive dog that will always need assistance to feel safe. We have to carefully consider the impact of breaks in routine or new environments, and we have to weigh the pros and cons of introducing Edie to new places, and have contingency plans when we do.

"How is Edie doing now?" Sara asks.

"She's mostly been sleeping since we got home last night."

Sara lets out a long sigh. "She's exhausted, so just keep her home and quiet until she's ready to move around again. I'm concerned, though, if she was fearful of cars to begin with, something this terrifying might have made it worse."

If there were a way to physically kick myself, I would. Just then a shopper steps into my private phone booth and sees the despair on my face, then discreetly backtracks and disappears. I'm probably being watched on the security camera by now, and I wonder how long it will take for a guard to wander over. I get what Sara is saying beneath her words. Our current lifestyle and the one Edie needs are a mismatch. We

are at loggerheads, and one of us has to give. Sara says that
city living will be difficult for Edie.

"Does that mean she should live in the country?"

"Not necessarily. There are ways you can manage her city
life so that she's less exposed to her triggers. For example,
keep her away from busy parks and choose only the quieter
parks at specific times of day."

I swallow hard and tell Sara that we've begun weighing
our options, and we've put Edie on a one-year probation.
"We really don't want to give her away, but we've started
talking about what would make her happier. Maybe a quiet
farm would be better for her," I say, repeating Jenn's words.

I'm trying to keep Edie's best interests in mind, to think
about what she would want, but at the same time I want Sara
to tell me I'm wrong.

"There's still a lot more you can try with her."

"Like?"

Sara says I might want to seriously consider talking to a vet
about medication for Edie. She offers to connect me with a
certified veterinary behaviorist at UC Davis with extensive
training in animal behavior and pharmaceuticals.

This time, I don't bristle at the thought of chemical intervention. But I can't imagine Edie will be able to withstand a
half-day car ride to Davis to visit a bustling veterinary com-
plex, so I ask for the name of the Bay Area vet she has in
mind. It's Sara's own vet, Dr. Angelique Cucaro, a UC Davis
graduate who practices both Western and Eastern medicine
and is certified not only in traditional veterinary care, but
also acupuncture, acupressure, palliative end-of-life care, and
Chinese Tui-Na massage for pets.

"She's very skilled and will understand what you're going through," Sara says.

I rise from the floor, thank Sara, and abandon my bath towel errand. Back in my truck, I call Dr. Cucaro's office and discover her services are in high demand. The soonest we can see her is in a month. Until then, my plan is to keep Edie quiet and safe indoors, where she can't have another emotional set-back. We all need time to recuperate from Carmel. This next month will be a time to slow things down and start over, to build back her stamina with the bravery exercises, and get her ready for another attempt at the outside world.

In some ways, Jenn and I can understand Edie's discomfort with urban living. After working for thirty years in the San Francisco Bay Area, we find ourselves longing for the small-town simplicity of our rural childhoods. We, too, are becoming increasingly jangled by the constant car alarms and ambulances, the roar of planes overhead, the pitiful tent cities mushrooming under freeway overpasses, the neighborhood street festivals that now draw thousands, the seven-dollar lattes, the three-thousand-percent increase in car break-ins since we first arrived. San Francisco has always been a young person's city, even more so since the tech boom and advent of social media. Its pulsing creativity is what makes it famously irresistible, and that magnetism is what originally drew us to San Francisco after college. But now, after careers policing it and reporting on it, we no longer have the energy for the city in return. We feel our priorities shifting toward solitude, and birdwatching, growing vegetables, and baking sourdough bread. We fantasize about being able to count the stars at night like we used to do as girls, serenaded only by the sound of crickets. We are inevitably slowing down, fall-

ing asleep at approximately the same time we used to be putting on our party clothes.

We start talking more seriously about leaving the city, and
start casually perusing the home listings in the *Carmel Pine
Cone* newspaper, to see if there is anything we can afford in
Carmel Valley. But my hometown has gotten quite fancy since
I lived there in the '70s. There are now more than twenty-
five wine-tasting rooms in the village, replacing what used to
be the old video store, the bank, and the deli. Tourists, who
rarely ventured beyond Carmel to sightsee, now make the
thirty-minute drive east to Carmel Valley Village to winery-
hop and buy cowboy couture from the shops that cater to
visitors. The homes for sale have helipads and infinity pools
and are going for two hundred times the price of the house
I grew up in. At this rate I fear all we'll be able to afford is a
chicken coop.

But we keep searching, even though the futility of it leaves
me dejected. I keep hoping to find something that's been
swallowed by the passage of time—an affordable home on a
few isolated acres where Edie could run free among the oak
trees, where Jenn could finally have her vegetable garden,
and I could raise honeybees just like Grandpa did. I start
envisioning such a place in my dreams at night, turning it
into the fairy tale that magically solves all our problems. Not
only would it be our forever home, it could be the quiet farm
we'd talked about for Edie, where our jangled puppy could
finally feel peace. We wouldn't have to give her up, after all.
We could rescue our own dog.

The impossible search feels increasingly urgent, now that
we've given Edie a year to improve. I convince myself that
all we have to do is move to a more rural area and Edie will

blossom into the dog she'd always meant to be. I turn it into a rescue mission, and get more frantic as the list of mansions thwart me day after day.

So we enlist our friend Kathy, who grew up in Carmel Valley and now is a real estate agent in the area. She knows everybody, and everything, that's going on in town, and within a week, she finds a two-bedroom ranch-style house encircled by green meadows and oak trees on ten acres on a Carmel Valley ridgetop. It's in our price range, so that makes me highly suspicious. I'm guessing there's no foundation or it's haunted by ghosts. Maybe mushrooms are growing in the walls or there's a renter who's refusing to leave.

The sun is glinting off Kathy's Jackie O sunglasses as we drive there in her white Audi convertible with the top down. Her blond hair is blowing in the wind and I'm catching whiffs of her perfume, a Lancôme mix of jasmine and orange blossom, aptly named La Vie Est Belle. Kathy is thrilled we might become her new neighbors, and she can't stop smiling as she heads into the Cachagua mountains, the air thick with the tangled scent of sagebrush, chemise, and coyote bush.

"Isn't this beautiful?" she says, sweeping her arm out toward the towering Santa Lucia Mountains rising out of the southwest. Jenn and Edie are following behind us in the Prius as Kathy drives eighteen hundred feet up a rural road with hairpin turns so hairy that a warning sign at the bottom advises large delivery trucks against driving it. We pass meadows of swaying purple lupine and groves of ancient oaks, their outstretched arms draped in shawls of lacy Spanish moss. I spot ground squirrels and cottontail bunnies skittering into underground burrows as we drive by, and we have to brake for a family of wild turkeys as they shamble across our path, necks bobbing in startled confusion.

Climbing higher, with a steep drop-off on the passenger side, we round a bend and suddenly the valley floor comes into view, revealing a patchwork of wine vineyards and horse ranches. When a pickup truck comes in the opposite direction, Kathy nudges the car into a sliver of a pullout, and their side mirrors pass with inches to spare. I wince, bracing for impact, and when I open my eyes again I turn back to see the cowboy give a courtesy wave, and notice he has two dogs in the cab next to him. I'm instantly reminded of Grandpa, who always had a dog riding shotgun in his work truck.

We have left the land of dog spas and have entered a very different kind of dog paradise. This is the dog country of my childhood, where the roads are full of trucks driven by men like my Grandpa who work with their hands, plumbers and carpenters and gardeners and stone masons who bring their dogs to work with them. In Carmel Valley, people have dogs as family pets, but also for hunting, or to protect their properties, their chickens, their livestock. There are deer tracks to scent here, a river to splash in, and enough open space for dogs to roam. I imagine Edie being reborn in my hometown, where she'd never be forced to tremble in a city crosswalk again.

We ascend for about a mile more, until we spot a ranch gate with two tall wooden posts and a crossbar that marks the entrance to the neighborhood where the listing is. We turn in, and I count seven dogs that run up to roadside fences as we pass by, tails wagging in joy. I spot a man and woman walking their golden retriever alongside the road and can't believe our luck. There's the confident, slightly older, golden buddy people say Edie needs. What are the odds of finding such an ideal playmate in this remote neighborhood?

We pull up the driveway and arrive at a six-foot deer fence that surrounds the house. Kathy leans out and punches some numbers on a keypad. A wide gate swings open and reveals what appears to be a botanical garden of California native plants, their blooms filling the air with the scent of rosemary and white sage. We step out of the car to the springtime hum of honeybees—so many covering the landscape that it sounds like a hymn of a church choir. Hummingbirds joust underneath pittosporum trees, fighting over purple blooms bursting forth from butterfly sage and French lavender. I wheel around the yard and see blooming buckwheat, manzanita, and blue-flowering ceanothus. Fountains gurgle softly under a canopy of Valley oaks with bark that looks like jagged puzzle pieces. Fruit trees are bursting with lemons, oranges, and plums. The real thing is even better than my fairy tale.

"Did I mention that the owner loves bees, and planted drought-tolerant, pollinator plants?" Kathy asks, her eyes twinkling.

Jenn parks under the shade of a redwood carport so Edie can stay out of the sun, and finds me standing on the south-facing deck, taking in the wraparound views of the Santa Lucia Mountains. On the other side of them is Big Sur and the Pacific Ocean. One peak looks familiar, and as I trace it with my finger, I realize it's the backside of Garrapata Canyon where my grandfather kept his beehives and apprenticed me when I was a girl. Just on the other side of the ridge, twelve miles as the crow flies, is where I learned the language of honeybees in his apiary, and where he made me feel safe after my own dysfunctional family fell apart. He showed me how bees put chaos into order; how they live in a model society based on benevolence, cooperation, and caring. In 2015, my brother Matthew and I poured Grandpa's ashes into a waterfall where Garrapata Creek empties into the ocean, just on the other side of the mountain range.

Living here would mean spending the rest of my life surrounded by Grandpa's kind spirit, in the shadow of the place where he shaped my personality and worldview. It would mean I could honor his legacy by keeping bees the same way he did, in the land that meant everything to him.

"Grandpa's bees were right over that crest," I say, pointing southwest.

"Your honey is going to taste like his," Jenn says, smiling.

Even when I think I'm hiding my thoughts from Jenn, she still hears them.

"Let's go see what's beyond the fence," I say.

On either side of the house are two green meadows dotted with flame-red maple trees, pink peppercorn trees, eucalyptus, and I even spot a manuka tree—the source of New Zealand's famously medicinal manuka honey. There's a wooden swing hanging from one of the oak trees and I give it a test ride, soaring out over the canyon. I'm captivated by the lack of white noise here—save for the wind rustling through the leaves, the tap of a woodpecker on a tree, the croak of a frog. In the stillness, I imagine Edie running through the brush, chasing alligator lizards. There's so much space, there would be no need to take her off the property for walks. She could be free, and unfettered, and protected from the outside world. And so could we. As I swing out over the valley floor, I start another conversation with Grandpa. I tell him that I want to be with him, in a place where he can see me. I promise to drive slowly on the winding road. I tell him I will protect the land, and never build on it. I thank him for leading our family here. Then I put in a request for a little Grandpa-mojo to make this our home.

What Jenn saw, standing next to me, was the chance to live close to nature, but finally on her own terms. She could take what she'd loved about growing up in the wilderness—sowing a vegetable garden, birdwatching, tossing marshmallows to the raccoons at night—and leave behind what had tormented her—living without electricity, running water, and cut off from civilization by an unpaved road that became impassible in winter. As a girl, she'd felt like a captive to her parents' lifestyle, but now she could have the best of both worlds. She could have the adventure of living wild, but with the basic security of heat, a shower, and a paved road out.

In the same way we chose Edie, without consultation or discussion, Jenn and I tell Kathy in unison that we want the house. Kathy looks confused. "But you haven't even seen the inside," she says, tugging open one of the sliding glass doors. I hug her and whisper in her ear, "It's perfect. Please, Kathy, please you *have* to get us this house."

She steps back and studies my face.

"You serious?"

"Very," Jenn says.

My head is swirling. Jenn isn't planning to retire for two more years. If we buy this house, that means Jenn and I will have to live apart because it's impractical for her to commute five or six hours every day. And we can't afford two mortgages, so we'll have to sell the Bay Area house. Where is she going to live?

"We will figure it out," Jenn says. "I'll stay in one of those Extended-Stay America hotels if I have to."

"You'd do that?" I ask. "For two years?"

"When it's right, it's right, and you have to jump," Jenn says. "It's pretty obvious that none of us can stay in the city much longer."

I hear what my wife is saying. Something's got to give. A distant relationship would be a sacrifice, but not nearly as damaging to our relationship as the status quo, living in a bustling city where all three of us are feeling increasingly out of place. Relocating could release us from being trapped indoors with Edie's fear, and save not only our puppy, but our marriage.

That afternoon we put in an offer.

10

Doggie Prozac

With a dog like Edie, you can't just hop in the car and go to the vet. Hours before the appointment, I need to start assembling her disaster preparedness kit and begin the slow, deliberate process of getting both of us psychologically and emotionally prepared. Step one: I boil a half dozen eggs, let them cool, then chop them into treat-sized bits and stuff them into a fanny pack. I need a ton of high-value treats to counteract all the possible sights and sounds that will stimulate her fight-or-flight response. Edie monitors my movements from the kitchen floor, intoxicated by the savory scent and acutely aware that it has something to do with her.

"Listen, buddy," I say, talking to her as if she were a small child. "We are going to a new place today. We're going to meet a doctor who's going to help you. I need you not to freak out, *capeesh?*"

Edie raises her ears and tilts her head side to side, trying to make sense of what I'm saying.

"Can you be a good girl?"

Those last two words are in Edie's vocabulary, so she executes an angelic sit before me, demonstrating that she most definitely knows what good girls do—especially if they want something. She follows the jiggling piece of egg white with her eyes for as long as she can stand it, then hops in the air to try to snap it from my fingers.

"Edith May-Jackson!" I shout, whisking the treat behind my back.

She drops to the floor on her belly, lying down without being asked, and implores me for a second chance.

"Waiiiiiiiiiiiiit," I say, drawing out the word and slowly unfurling my fingers to reveal the prize. Edie trembles with restraint but does not lift herself from the floor. I place the morsel on the linoleum a few inches from her front paws and ask her to wait a little more. She keeps her eyes locked on my face, refusing to even look at the forbidden food. Before I can get to the second syllable of the "okay" command, she's already inhaling the egg white, not even stopping to chew. She likely tasted nothing other than the sweet flavor of being given a coveted thing.

"Funny bunny," I say, scratching her tickle spot on either side of her muzzle just below her eyes. It makes her draw back her lips and bare her teeth in a crazed grin that cracks me up every time. It's our private joke that never gets old.

I dunk a 100-milligram tablet of Anxitane into my latte foam and let her lick it off my finger, even though recent events would indicate the chill pill is having little effect. I only now read the fine print disclaimer on the back of the package and discover a possible reason why: "Not intended for use in animals with severe phobias." But right now this over-the-counter calming aid is what I have, and Edie needs every possible edge today, even if it's no more effective than a placebo.

I gather her cannabis oil, CBD chews, calming floral spray, and her swaddling vest. I add a stretchy fabric wrap that goes around her head to muffle loud noises to replace the doggie earmuffs she refuses to wear. I add a bone made from hardened Himalayan cheese that is the only chew I've found that can keep her busy gnawing for more than five minutes. I really hope I won't need to deploy any of these, but I know I'm courting danger by leaving the house without them. Edie knows which bin in the pantry is hers, and watches me rummage through it, expectant. When no treat is forthcoming, she starts performing for me. She rolls onto her back to expose her belly as she stretches to full length, spreading her toes and straightening her arms over her head. I accept her invitation, rubbing her belly and murmuring, "I'm not going to let anything hurt you. You know that, right?"

I have no idea if Edie understands what I'm saying. And I know how ridiculous it looks to try to rationalize with a dog. But dogs can sense their owners' moods, find their way back home over unimaginable distances, and even sniff out cancer in the body, so how can we say for certain they can't understand at least the intention of our words? At the very least, it calms me down to recite our game plan. I tell Edie that she will have to get out of the car and go into a room, and another person will come in and handle her.

"And I will be right next to you the whole time," I say. "If you feel like running, you run to ME, all right?" Maybe

I'm the one who needs to hear the confidence in my voice. I am trying to convince myself that I'm a capable adult; that I can manage Edie's forays into public so that she won't have another catastrophe.

Edie trots after me to her toy basket, where I dig for the blue rubber monkey with legs and arms of knotted yellow rope. It's something with a familiar scent that I can bring to the appointment to help her feel secure. Edie offers assistance, pulling out a Noah's Ark of plush animals until she spies the monkey and tugs it out of my grip, thrashing it so violently that she whips both her legs and mine with its rope appendages. She growls at her own prowess, looking for all the world like a typical, bouncy, desperate-to-please golden retriever puppy from every dog food commercial ever made. It would be hard to convince someone that this same animal can tumble down a spiral of primal fear by simply leaving the house.

It's time to go. I strap the canvas treat pouch around my waist. I open the bag of hemp oil–laced dog chews and slip Edie a couple. While she's gobbling them off the floor, I whip my arm down, ninja mom–style, and spritz the inside of both her ears with the calming spray comprised of five essential oils. I clip Edie into her double-strength harness, the one with a leash that connects at both her chest and between her shoulders, giving me enough leverage to restrain her if she tries to flee.

One last deep breath before I open the door. We are now ready for the outside world. God willing.

I park in the spot closest to the front door of the veterinary office, a walk of about ten steps. Still, that's way too far for Edie. All the hard-boiled egg in the world doesn't convince her to get out of the truck, so after ten minutes of wheedling and cajoling and attempted bribery, I end up carrying her through the front door as she digs her claws into my back. I feel her weight in my lower back and remind myself to engage my core, noting that she's considerably heavier than when I carried her a month ago in Carmel.

"Ah, this must be Edie," says the receptionist, when I bang through the door with Edie clinging to me. After considerable struggle, I get Edie to sit still for a microsecond on the scale that's embedded in the floor and confirm my suspicions— she's gained weight. At nine months, she's up to sixty pounds now. I don't know how much longer I can keep carrying her.

One unexpected perk of having a special dog is that we get special treatment, and we're ushered immediately from the lobby to the examination room where Edie won't encounter other dogs and their people. Unlike all the clinical veterinary rooms I've seen before, this one actually feels homey, with large windows, plants, and even a seating area with a side table and magazines. I sit in one of the chairs and Edie posts up between my legs, keeping a laser watch on everything. I slip her a CBD chew and stroke her head.

Dr. Cucaro's footsteps barely make a sound as she enters the room, walks to the opposite wall near the medical cabinets, sits on a stool and swivels to face me. A few unruly curls have sprung free from her ponytail, and she's wearing what looks like a cross between medical scrubs and a Hawaiian shirt bursting with red hibiscus flowers. Her whole being exudes serenity, like a yoga teacher. She pays Edie no mind and keeps excellent eye contact with me.

"So, I understand you have an anxious girl on your hands?" Dr. Cucaro has a soft, bedtime-story voice. I feel safe just listening to her.

"At first we thought it was typical puppy fear, but she's almost a year old now and it's getting worse."

As if on cue, a long drip of drool spills out the side of Edie's mouth and splats on the floor at my feet, where she is cowering between my legs. I reach into the fanny pack and give her a handful of egg.

Dr. Cucaro wants to know what brought me in. I begin by telling her we noticed something wrong when Edie ran from the other puppies at her first social, bringing her all the way up to the fiasco in Carmel, and all Edie's frights in between. I talk for twenty minutes nonstop in a cathartic torrent, surprising myself at how much I've been carrying inside just waiting for the right person to tell. Dr. Cucaro leans forward, concentrating on every word without interrupting.

By the time I'm finished, I notice she is standing now, leaning against a cabinet, a few feet closer to us.

"Dogs like this are incredibly difficult," she says. "Sadly, too many of them wind up in animal shelters. Your main job is to keep her alive, and congratulations to both of you for doing that so far."

I'm so relieved to finally be heard by someone who really, truly, gets it. Dr. Cucaro is the first person to put the impact of Edie into perspective, and it makes me feel less incompetent.

"How are *you* doing with all of this?" she asks.

Suddenly I am on a therapist's couch. No one, not even Jenn, has asked me that. I'm so touched to be given a voice, allowed to have an emotion, that my voice cracks as I try to answer.

"I'm…I'm…s-s-scared," I say, my voice wobbly. "I don't want to have to give her up."

Dr. Cucaro takes a few steps closer and sits on the floor.

Edie leans forward to inhale Dr. Cucaro's scent and then darts her head back to the safety of my leg-cave.

She asks if I know anything about Edie's mother. All I can say is that I glanced at the mother over a fence and she seemed all right. As soon as it comes out of my mouth, I realize how ignorant I sound. Of course I should have asked more questions, but I wanted a puppy so badly, I foolishly dispensed with the preliminaries.

Dr. Cucaro explains fear can be inherited; that puppies born to stressed, ill, or malnourished mothers can suffer from lifelong anxiety due to a flood of cortisol they received in utero. Or fear can be learned. During the three- to sixteen-week critical learning period, if puppies see a family member get traumatized, their own developing ability to respond to stress can be negatively affected, permanently altering their confidence.

"Really?" I had no idea that fear could start in the womb.

Dr. Cucaro asks if I've told the breeder about Edie. Again, my answer is lame. I say that I haven't bothered because what would be the point? It's too late now; I can't reverse time. Dr. Cucaro has incredible bedside manner, but I sense that she is slowing down her speech so that I can absorb what she is trying to make me grasp: that there's a chance all of the puppies in Edie's litter could have been born fearful. But even if Edie is the only one, one fearful dog is too many, Dr. Cucaro says, and the breeder should be warned to stop breeding Edie's mother.

"It's the right thing to tell the breeder," Dr. Cucaro says. "Fearful breeding lines just create more fearful dogs."

I promise her that I'll call him.

"Mind if I take a few of those?" Dr. Cucaro says, pointing to the bag of CBD chews I brought with me. I hand her the bag and she scoots closer now, just a few feet away from Edie. She breaks one treat into chocolate-chip-sized pieces and tosses a few on the ground, waiting for Edie to investigate. Edie takes a few tentative steps toward her, and then snatches the food and darts back to my legs to devour it. Dr. Cucaro tosses a couple more bits on the ground, and this time Edie walks closer to Dr. Cucaro to eat them.

Edie finishes, then circles Dr. Cucaro looking for a refill. Edie is careful to not get too close, maintaining a two-foot perimeter, so Dr. Cucaro patiently waits for Edie to come to her. Dr. Cucaro then drops a treat within inches of her shoe. She stands rock still as Edie walks with the careful steps of a gymnast on a balance beam toward the food. By the end of their dance, Edie is eating the treats out of Dr. Cucaro's hand.

"You can never push these kinds of dogs," Dr. Cucaro says. "Edie has to make her own decisions about her safety."

I'm impressed—this is the first veterinarian who didn't try to touch Edie immediately, but waited until Edie made the choice between friend or foe. I appreciate that she didn't ask if Edie was a rescue pup, or suggest puppy socialization classes, or brush off my concerns by telling me that she would grow out of it.

Dr. Cucaro is now able to examine Edie with her hands, and puts the stethoscope up to her chest. As she's listening to Edie's heart, a dog starts barking outside the door.

"Oh wow," Dr. Cucaro says. "Her heartbeat went from bump...bump...bump...to badda, badda, badda, badda. It just shot up."

Dr. Cucaro shows me how to apply pressure at two points on the back of Edie's skull below her ears to calm her down.

As I'm giving it a try, Edie wriggles from my grasp, clearly not in the mood for bodywork. Dr. Cucaro goes back to petting Edie instead, and gently suggests I consider a low 10-milligram daily dose of Prozac. I'm not sure I heard her correctly.

"You mean, Prozac, like…people Prozac?"

Turns out she's talking about the exact same antidepressant fluoxetine that humans take for depression, obsessive-compulsive disorder, bulimia, and anxiety. It works by inhibiting the brain from reabsorbing serotonin, a naturally occurring brain chemical that regulates mood. Enough serotonin, and you have a general sense of well-being. Not enough, and depression sets in. Prozac works so well, apparently, that one in ten people in the United States is on it, making it one of the most widely prescribed antidepressants on the planet. And as the study of animal emotions gains more traction, veterinarians are increasingly prescribing it for their four-legged patients.

As Dr. Cucaro is typing the prescription into the computer, she warns me that Prozac is not a cure, nor a replacement for the counterconditioning Edie will need for the rest of her life.

"Prozac is an aid. It simply alters her brain chemistry so she can pause a beat and think before reacting," Dr. Cucaro says. "It gives her a chance to assess a stimulus, so you'll hopefully have a moment to stop her before she panics."

"We'll try anything," I say.

The way I'm understanding it, Prozac won't remove Edie's triggers, but it could make her less reactive to them, and thus increase her life expectancy. If Prozac gives Edie a split second to think first, she could learn, for example, that the loud crash is just me dropping a dish on the floor. The more times she stands down when startled and learns that something is harmless, the more likely she is to reduce her first instinct to flee into traffic, toward a cliff, or into the woods. In other words, with enough practice and the right dosage, she might be able to learn to self-soothe.

"It can take up to a month before you notice any changes," she says, "so you have to stick with it."

I ask if Edie will need to be on Prozac permanently, and Dr. Cucaro says it all depends on the dog, but she suggests at least a year for starters. If Edie has another panic attack while on the low dose, she will write a stronger prescription. If Edie improves to the point she can walk calmly on a San Francisco sidewalk, we can consider weaning her off.

"You might want to consider Xanax, too, for emergencies," she says. "For when she has a panic attack or you need to travel with her."

Dr. Cucaro anticipates my question, and says Edie can have both Prozac and Xanax at the same time because they work on different parts of the brain. I guess it can't hurt to have Xanax on hand, so I say yes, but I hope I never have to use more than one medication on Edie.

"Thank you," I say, helping myself to the Kleenex on the coffee table. I feel spent, but in a good way. In Dr. Cucaro we've found Edie's advocate, finally. One by one, we are assembling a roster of female superheroes that includes Dr. Cucaro, Kendra, and Sara into Team Edie, giving me hope that our puppy stands a fighting chance. When I look back at Dr. Cucaro, she is patiently waiting for me to say something. She is smiling, and unhurried. She's been with me for an hour, and I know our meeting is ending, but I don't want to leave just yet. This is the most relief I've felt in months. So I just sit there, stalling, and then Dr. Cucaro starts to tell me a story.

"Dogs like Edie are similar to young children who get overwhelmed by changes in routine," Dr. Cucaro says.

She tells me about a young girl who was so upset about an upcoming family trip to Hawaii that the mother began preparing her child a year ahead of time. They watched documentaries about the islands and snorkeling, then went to a store together and bought a snorkel. They practiced putting on the mask inside the house. They practiced breathing through the snorkel. When the child was ready, she wore the gear in the bathtub, and eventually tried putting her head in the water. By the end of the year, the girl was able to snorkel in a swimming pool without fear. Only then could the family get on a plane and know that their trip would go smoothly.

"Taking Edie to a place she's never been before is like taking that girl to Hawaii cold turkey," Dr. Cucaro explains. "Edie needs lots of small doses of low exposure to work up to a new environment. She needs small victories over an extended period of time before she has the resolve to take on something new."

Finally, I get it. Edie isn't a slow learner—she's too smart. When confronted with an unfamiliar person, place, or thing, she overthinks it. In the blink of an eye, her brain imagines all the possible ways something could go wrong, hits overload, and she flees. She needs time to test each worst-case scenario and see it not come to fruition before she trusts. And if too much new stuff is coming at her from too many directions, and she doesn't have time to analyze each fear— she comes undone.

Careful consideration is woven into Edie's personality, and it comes out even when she's faced with ordinary decisions, such as whether to walk through a doorway. She stops at every one, as if weighing her options, trying to decide which environment, inside or out, is the wise choice. I hold the front door open for several minutes, waving her forward and encouraging her to make up her mind, but she doesn't budge until she's come to her own conclusion. I think transitions of any kind are hard for her.

Pushing Edie into a new environment before she's ready could make her regress, Dr. Cucaro warns. Our job as Edie's humans is to become expert observers of her body language so we can pull her out of situations before she starts to escalate, and to not assign judgment about how long Edie's confidence-building takes.

It dawns on me in Dr. Cucaro's office that I have comingled Edie's behavior with my own personal failure. It seems as though everyone in the Bay Area has an opinion about the best way to raise a dog, feed a dog, socialize and exercise a dog, and it's almost like dogs are the measuring sticks we use to judge one another. If your dog is well-mannered, you must be a good person. If your dog has some kind of behavioral problem, well there must be something wrong with the home environment, or you aren't training properly. Dogs are the social glue of San Francisco, and if yours can't mingle, you are pushed to the side of one of the largest subcultures in the city. I used to love all the praise that came my way via Stella, for her gentle demeanor, her ability to walk off-leash by my side, anywhere. She was such an accommodating dog that my friends once snuck her out of my bedroom while I was sleeping one night, left a ransom note, and took her to their neighborhood bar in Potrero Hill. She apparently had a very enjoyable time, judging from all the photos on my

phone the next morning, showing Stella nuzzling and flirt-
ing with complete strangers.

Maybe Edie came along to teach me that the human-canine
relationship isn't all about the human. I realize now that part
of my frustration with Edie is that her difficulties are making *me* look bad. I cringe retroactively at all the times I made
it a point to tell people that Edie is my third golden, and that
the first two were completely fine. I see now that's beside
the point. Edie is her own being, with her own unique way
of moving through the world. It's not good or bad; it just is.
And my only say in the matter is to choose whether I want
to fight it, or teach her how to snorkel.

"You're doing everything right," Dr. Cucaro says, and I
want to jump up and hug her. Finally, someone has explained
why Edie might be the way she is. That it may have nothing
to do with me. Dr. Cucaro opened my eyes to the neuro-
biology of canine fear, explaining it in plain language I can
understand.

"I feel so lucky we found you," I say. I lift Edie into my
arms to carry her back to the truck, and Dr. Cucaro smiles
knowingly.

"Just keep doing what you're doing," she says.

When I'd walked into the office carrying Edie, I'd felt
ashamed, but now as I leave with her in my arms once again,
I feel privileged to be the person Edie will let protect her.
Edie feels lighter, perhaps because my mood is lighter, too.
Dr. Cucaro's talk has allowed me to stop blaming myself so
much for Edie's mishaps and made me want to find out ev-
erything I can about the inner workings of my puppy's brain.
I don't want to guess anymore about what's happening when
Edie gets frightened; I want to understand the neuroscience

behind it, to become an expert reader of her body language so I can truly help my dog. I leave Dr. Cucaro's office feeling less helpless, and with a renewed energy to unlock the mystery of Edie. I begin by calling the breeder.

He is surprised to learn of Edie's troubles, and says it's the first he's heard anything like it. None of the nine other people who bought puppies in Edie's litter have reported any problems, he says. As far as he knows, there were no health problems with Edie's mother and nothing that frightened her when she was pregnant. He assures me that he was careful to socialize the puppies, and had neighborhood kids drop by to play with the litter. I tend to believe him. Many of his buyers, including one of Jenn's coworkers who was inspired by Edie, post pictures of their puppies on Facebook doing things Edie would never do, such as strolling on a busy beach or sitting at a sidewalk café table. He apologizes, and asks what he can do to make it right, offering to pay Edie's vet bills, take her back, or give us a new puppy. I shudder. Edie is not a defective toaster.

I explain that we aren't looking to trade Edie in, and I'm not calling to complain or blame, but rather to get to the bottom of her fear. Also, I relay Dr. Cucaro's warning not to breed Edie's mother again. Fearful dogs who give birth to fearful dogs only beget more fearful dogs, all of whom are a danger to themselves and their owners. He thanks me for letting him know, and promises he won't breed her again. Before saying goodbye, he asks me once more if there's anything he can do.

"Actually, one thing everyone keeps saying is that Edie might do better if we got a second golden." I can't believe how easily it popped out of my mouth. I haven't discussed this with Jenn. I am about to commit the same crime twice.

"I'd be happy to give you a puppy from my next litter," he says, his voice brightening.

The temptation is mighty, but I imagine Jenn's head exploding, so instead I thank him and say we're going to try Prozac first. By the time I get home, my phone pings with a text from the Costco pharmacy, letting me know Edith May-Jackson's medication is ready.

"I'm here to pick up a prescription, *for my dog*," I say, when I reach the pharmacy counter. I want to make it very clear that my first name is not Edith.

"Uh-huh," says the cashier, not even looking up from the register as she hands me the white bag with Edie's pills inside. She probably rings up Prozac prescriptions dozens of times a day, and I suddenly feel embarrassed for thinking I should be embarrassed.

That night I order a pizza, and while we wait for it to arrive I tell Jenn all about Dr. Cucaro, and how she said that Edie behaves like a dog that has suffered trauma, maybe even in the womb. I repeat the snorkeling story, Dr. Cucaro's kudos for keeping Edie alive thus far, and her suggestion we start Edie on Prozac.

"They make Prozac for dogs?"

"Indeed. And Xanax, too."

Jenn is silent a moment as she lets the idea of doggie antidepressants sink in. Her brow furrows and I can tell she's not a fan.

"I don't want to overmedicate her. We don't want to turn her into a zombie."

Nor do I. I had the same reservations and had asked Dr.

Cucaro if antidepressants would change Edie's personality, or make her hyper, or if she could get addicted to them.

"It's only supposed to take the edge off," I say, which I realize is the drug addict's swan song. "Dr. Cucaro said the only change we'll see is that Edie will stop and think when she gets scared."

I can't give Jenn the answer she wants to hear—that it's safe. That it will work. That it's the right thing to do. All we can do is give it a try and see what happens.

"It's the lowest dose, ten milligrams," I say.

"Let's Google it," Jenn says.

She tappity-taps on her iPad for the next twenty minutes and then renders her verdict. "Okay, it seems to be a thing. Let's try it. If we don't like what it does to her, we can always just quit giving it to her."

I remind Jenn that I'd stopped giving Edie pure cannabis oil, because all it did was make her sleep. I promise to make the same call if Prozac makes our dog worse.

And although I meant to keep it a secret, I let it slip that I called the breeder and he offered us a free puppy.

"He was surprised to hear we're having problems with Edie, and he wanted to compensate us somehow. He said that if we ever wanted a second puppy, he'd be happy to give us one."

Jenn stands up from the dining room table. She folds her arms and speaks slowly, her voice thick with exasperation: "We. Are. Not. Getting. Another. Puppy."

"Oh, I wasn't suggesting it. I was just saying he offered, is all."

"Mmm-hmm," she says. "Don't even start."

I know when I've lost, and drop the subject.

Over the next month, we keep a close eye on Edie to see

if the Prozac is having any effect. She seems the same, still running from shadows that cross the ceiling or the pop of Bubble Wrap.

Then, one night while I'm making dinner, I turn from the stove and almost step on her. She'd somehow gotten by the metal dining chair that we'd set on its side over the threshold to keep her out of the kitchen.

"Jenn! Jenn!"

I hear Jenn's footsteps running down the stairs.

"What happened? Are you hurt?" Her eyes are darting from me to Edie, checking for injuries.

"We're fine. I think Edie just squeezed through the chair legs."

She stares, dumbfounded. The reason the chair works as a blockade is because Edie is too afraid to crawl through it, even though there's plenty of room. Edie doesn't like wedging her body through tight spaces. She doesn't like being touched when she's not expecting it, and jumps several inches off the ground when it happens.

"Are you sure? Maybe she was already in the kitchen when you put the chair there."

"See if she'll come back out," I say.

Jenn crouches down and claps her hands. "C'mere, Edie. Come on! You can do it!"

Edie walks over to the chair, sticks her nose between the legs, then changes her mind and walks around it, squeezing herself into the narrow space between the doorframe and the chair's backrest.

We stand there, blinking in astonishment.

"I knew you could do it! What a smart girl you are!" I say, as Jenn scoops Edie into her arms and waltzes with her,

holding one tiny paw in her outstretched hand. They twirl
in the dining room, celebrating, while I hand-feed Edie bits
of chicken skin.

Such an ordinary thing for an animal, to skirt an object.
But for Edie, after avoiding that menacing chair her entire
life, it must have taken every ounce of courage to take such an
enormous risk. Which makes us wonder: Is that the Prozac,
or did she, after months of careful, slow, investigation, finally
decide the chair posed no threat and walk by it on her own?

My answer comes a few days later, when we take Edie to
the elementary school soccer field on a Saturday afternoon.
The playground is deserted, and Edie tires herself roaring after
the rubber monkey and bringing it back to us. It's looking for
all the world as if we are going to have an incident-free outing, when three boys arrive with a basketball and begin dribbling. Jenn and I immediately tense up at the sharp sound of
the ball smacking the blacktop, anticipating Edie's reaction.

She hears it, too, and stops midstride, letting the monkey
fall from her mouth to the grass as she searches for the noise-
maker. I jog toward her with the leash, hoping to stop her
before she takes off. But before I can reach her, I see her take
a few steps toward the basketball court. Her ears are up, signaling curiosity. Edie is…intrigued.

I stand there, leash in hand, stunned as she trots to the edge
of the grass and lies down at courtside, where she can watch
the boys. She's alert, ears up, absorbed in the game with the
intensity of a season-ticket holder. Jenn appears alongside me.

"Well, would you look at that," she whispers.

"Do you think it's the Prozac?"

"It has to be."

Edie is keeping her eyes on the ball. Her head swivels left

and right tracking the passes, and the shots that sail up and through the basket. It is pure loveliness. The boys are loud, their dribbling is loud, and their movements are wild, but Edie seems entranced. When the basketball bounces away from a player, Edie is on her feet. Ignoring my calls, she runs onto the court and chases the ball, trying to steal it for herself.

"Hey!" the boys yell, laughing at their disruptive fan. We catch up to Edie and clip her to her leash, apologizing and laughing along with the boys.

"That's okay," one of them says. "She can play with us. She's really cute."

If only I could tell that boy how enormous his compliment is.

"I guess we'll have to get her a basketball of her own," I say.

Back home, Jenn disappears into the garage and returns a few minutes later with a long-forgotten orange-and-white basketball and presents it to Edie. Our puppy is so delighted, she throws herself on top of it as if she never wants to let it go. She pulls the ball to her belly and clutches it as tight as she possibly can, looks skyward, then starts furiously humping it. Edie scoots around the back patio making sweet puppy love to the basketball, while we gawp at this developmental milestone we hadn't seen coming. By the time Edie has made a full circle of the yard, Jenn and I are in hysterics, laughing with our eyes closed. We had no idea progress could be this entertaining.

11

Fight or Flight

Ever since Dr. Cucaro got me thinking about where Edie's fear might have originated, I've been on a research mission to answer the age-old question: Nature or nurture? I want to know the *why* of Edie: Why did she turn out this way? But I also want to know the *what*: What exactly is going on inside her primal brain? Maybe, if I understood the biology behind her fear, I'd be more attuned to her body language, more able to suss out her emotions. I want to be able to predict her oncoming panic attacks so I have a chance to prevent them.

I discover I could fill a library with books just about dogs, and dedicate an entire wing to all their fears. There are dogs with separation anxiety, dogs who cower before dogs and strangers, dogs that can't handle going to the vet, and many—an estimated 20 percent—that have noise phobias, mostly of fireworks and thunderstorms. Then there are the specialists: dogs that don't like sunglasses, rain, balloons, or men.

But Edie's peculiarities are more nuanced, so she doesn't fit neatly into any one category. She's a definite yes on noise phobias if it's a loud staccato, such as a Harley-Davidson muffler or a nail gun, but then she can sleep right next to a whirring vacuum or the hair dryer. She doesn't like things that move too fast, such as little girls on tricycles, ceiling fans, and traffic. But a parked car is okay, because then it becomes a sanctuary from things that move. She's hypersocial with dogs, but only if she meets them in quiet, peaceful surroundings. She likes people, too, as long as they don't have odd silhouettes created by cowboy hats or umbrellas. The innovation of Edie's fear seems limitless. One day it's a garage door opening. Dandelion fluff on the wind. The beam of a flashlight. I can't even begin to isolate her fear when it's so mercurial. What I'm looking for is more elusive—what do you do when you live in San Francisco and your dog is terrified of crowded, hectic places?

Over summer, I start and stop book after book, and tumble down countless online rabbit holes, unable to find a situation quite like ours. So I'm not expecting much when I press Play on an audiobook with yet another promising title: *From Fearful to Fear Free: A Positive Program to Free Your Dog from Anxiety, Fears, and Phobias*, written by a team of veterinarians and animal behaviorists. One of the authors is "America's Veterinarian" Dr. Marty Becker, a syndicated columnist with twenty-three books to his name who was *Good Morning America*'s resident veterinary contributor for nearly two decades.

The introduction grabs me by the throat. Fear, the authors warn, is the most destructive emotion a social species can experience. It can damage the brain permanently.

Oh, no. Does Edie have PTSD?

Now it's me who's on high alert. The aperture of my vision narrows until I'm sitting in a dark tunnel with the narrator, engrossed in a one-way conversation. She speaks; I listen. She tells me that yes, animals can suffer from post-traumatic stress disorder, just like former soldiers or domestic abuse survivors. I feel her hands shaking me by my shoulders to warn me that Edie is in more serious danger than I'd realized. I binge-listen for the next nine hours, stopping frequently to rewind and jot down the pertinent bits in the leatherbound journal I keep about Edie.

The pages fill quickly with foreboding factoids about the lasting effects of chronic anxiety on pets. Abnormally fearful dogs are unhealthier and unhappier. I learn that increased levels of the "stress hormone" cortisol can lead to weakened immunity and slower wound healing. Fearful dogs are more likely than their mellower peers to have gastrointestinal and respiratory problems, and some researchers claim they also have shorter life spans. I press Pause and think about my own stress-induced trips to the gastroenterologist after I graduated from college without a job. Or all those gut flare-ups when I was in the middle of a particularly nasty feud with my mother. My own experience "swallowing my stress" has convinced me of the powerful mind-body connection. It makes sense to me that a dog's health could also suffer in the same way.

Edie is bored, and wanders toward the garage in search of things she should not put in her mouth. I know she's about to go treasure hunting in the clothes hamper next to the washing machine, and sure enough, she prances back into the room with one of my wool socks dangling from her mouth. She uses it as a lure, coming just within reach and leaping away when I try to grab it. Her eyes sparkle with devious pleasure, and she hops left and right, ducking and dodging like a boxer. Edie's recent discovery of the hamper is a great source of entertainment for her, and she is very selective about her digs inside it, nudging aside all the clothes to carefully extract just the socks. She never spills clothes on the ground during her searches or destroys the socks after she steals them. She carries them to her bed and sucks on them, or she taunts us to steal them back from her. I give in and chase her around the house, backing her into corners and then letting her escape for another go-round. I think she loves the role reversal of this; that she's the one shaping my behavior.

When I return to the audiobook, Edie keeps pestering me, so I play sock tug-of-war with one hand and scribble illegibly with the other. Aggressive dogs are often driven by fear, not anger, but the misconception that their behavior is rooted in violence is the number one reason why such dogs are abandoned, relinquished to a shelter, or euthanized. It's why more dogs die due to behavior problems than from disease, according to the American Veterinary Society for Animal Behavior. It's a shame, as the authors explain, because frightened dogs give off several body cues before they resort to attack. They lick their lips, yawn, tuck their tail, tense their muscles, widen their eyes, whine, spin in circles, wince, defecate, drool, or lower their heads. Their hair stands up and their pupils dilate. They fidget or refuse to move. I tick off the list. Edie does every single one of those things. Well, all of them except losing her bowels, thanks to small mercies.

The longer I listen, the more I realize how much Edie was trying to tell me that I just couldn't see. I wish that I could rewind time and do things differently. At first, when Edie would freeze up on sidewalks or trails and refuse to go any farther, part of me thought she was being ornery. I would raise my voice and pull on the leash, forcing her to scoot on her butt toward me, only making the situation scarier for her. The authors described what I did thusly: imagine you are terrified of snakes, and someone dumps a box of snakes on your head. When you try to run away, someone ties a rope to your neck and yanks you back to the slithering pile of snakes. *Oh, Edie, I'm so sorry, baby. I just didn't know.*

By not letting Edie go at her own pace, I was sabotaging both of us by reducing Edie's trust in me. By thrusting her into a new situation with my old-fashioned, "Suck it up, Buttercup" attitude, I was doing what dog trainers call "flooding"—overwhelming her brain circuitry so that she created fearful memories.

And guess what? Edie's limbic system—the inner core of her brain that deals with emotions and memory—was carefully storing those negative experiences in her fear file. Who knows what else she already had in that file when she came to us, but I certainly wasn't helping by adding to it. Belatedly, I learn that fear is like a muscle, the more times it's activated, the stronger it becomes. Dogs that are frightened badly enough or long enough can become hypersensitive to stress. I shudder to think I could have helped alter the neural pathways in Edie's developing brain, weakening her lifelong ability to cope with the unknown.

My crash course on the puppy brain helps me finally understand why Edie's fear is all-consuming, and inescapable. Dogs and humans have similar brain structures and share instinctual reactions to threat. Our breathing picks up. Our pulse accelerates. Our muscles tense. The hair on our arms and the back of our necks rise. In an instant, these physiological changes alert our primal brain to make us run for our lives or battle to the death.

When frightened, our bodies flood with a rush of neuro-
chemicals and hormones to help us prepare for fight or flight.
Specifically, two of these hormones: epinephrine, otherwise
known as adrenaline, and norepinephrine put the body on
high alert, speeding up our heart rates and increasing blood
flow to our muscles, releasing glucose for energy and expanding our air passages for better lung capacity. Our bloodstreams
become infused with the natural steroid cortisol, which gives
our muscles a boost. This would help explain why, in Carmel,
Edie suddenly turned into some sort of puppy bottle rocket and
flew uphill at warp speed, leaving us gassed in the distance.

Dogs and humans both have a small, almond-shaped area in
the center of our brains called the amygdala that acts as a clearing house for these body signals, and assigns emotional reactions
to them. The amygdala is like a neurological burglar alarm,
that when alerted to threat tells our hypothalamus to make us
pant and tremble. It tells our brain stem to run like hell or stay
put and kick ass. And it tells our prefrontal cortex to store the
moment as an emotional memory, so we can avoid getting ourselves in the same situation again. In other words, if something
frightening did happen to Edie as a puppy, chances are high
that she remembers it extremely well. When she's put back in
a scenario that evokes that memory, her body and mind behave
as if the terrible thing is actually happening all over again. If
we ever brought her back to Emanuele's restaurant in Carmel,
she'd be primed for another panic attack just by being there.

When this ancient brain system is functioning properly,
animals live longer because they can predict and avoid future
dangers. An animal learns to stay away from a certain thicket
because it saw a predator there once before. But when the survival instinct goes haywire, and animals fight, flee, fidget, or

freeze when no real danger exists, life can become miserable for pets and their people, the narrator says.

Finally, our family's particular, private misery is explained in simple, sympathetic terms. Living with a hypersensitive pet that can't forget what fear feels like is akin to living with a former soldier who jumps every time they hear a car backfire. There's a jittery energy in the house that makes everyone startle at the sound, because the whole family is worried about the fallout on their loved one. I now understand why Edie ran at the sound of gunshots at Fort Funston. Her biology made her do it. Whether that physiological reaction was inherited, or learned by experience, fear has wormed its way into her unconscious mind.

And it could have taken any number of paths to get there. I've finally reached the *why* portion of the audiobook, and the authors offer many possible scenarios.

It could have been simple genetics. Supposing Edie's parents were healthy, then Edie could have simply been born fearful, the same way some people are born with outgoing or reserved personalities. It could be no more than a quirk of her DNA.

Edie herself could have been malnourished, injured, or sick as a puppy. We did have to take Edie in for two worm treatments shortly after we brought her home. I wonder, did that do it? Should we have questioned the vet more when he told us worms in puppies is common?

Fear-based anxieties may be triggered by a single event, such as the start of hunting season, or a thunderstorm. Puppies who are attacked or abused or watch a member of their family suffer the same can also develop irrational fear. Puppies that aren't socialized with other dogs and people during the critical three- to sixteen-week socialization period could default to thinking all newcomers are threats.

A chaotic home life can alter a dog's ability to manage fear.

Dogs that share homes with stressed-out humans can absorb their frenetic energy. This gives me pause. I've been called a type A before, and I wonder if my stress about Edie's stress is causing her more stress. I remind myself that I'd promised to meditate more.

Dogs that experience too much inconsistency, such as being moved from home to home, cycling through shelters, or left in boarding facilities by the unpredictable work and vacation schedules of their owners, can succumb to fear of the unknown. This one doesn't worry me, seeing as though I'm with Edie 24/7 365.

Lack of companionship, with their own kind and with humankind, is also a risk factor. I circle this one, if I ever need to make a stronger case to Jenn for a second dog.

Dogs can lose their confidence if they are not allowed to be a dog. Just as fear is a self-preservation instinct, so is digging, gnawing on bones, and sniffing. Dogs who are not given places to do this, and worse, punished for doing it, can become fearful of their own urges. I pause again. All we have is a paved backyard with a tiny strip of dirt that we fenced off to keep her from digging up the plants. I make a note to talk to Jenn about giving her a designated area to destroy.

These theories are just that—theories. As I get to the end of the book, I realize that no matter how much I crave an answer, I've been asking a pointless question. I'll never be able to find that one thing that caused Edie's fear. All dogs with clinical anxiety are different, each affected by their unique genes and separate environments. But as I near the end of the book, I recognize a common thread among the origins of dog fear—some sort of physical or emotional trauma that occurred in puppyhood. Not only are canines and humans driven by similar brain structures, who we become is also influenced by the struggles we've endured.

Suddenly it makes sense why, of all the nests Edie could have fallen into, she landed in ours. Jenn and I are survivors of early trauma. We know firsthand what it means to be shaped by fear, and the lifelong effort to wrest ourselves from its grip. We can relate to Edie's need to protect herself, to her compulsion to hide, to the way she assumes the worst in people until proven otherwise. We remember the terror of being small and powerless.

I feel a softness come over me as I think of myself at age six, hiding when my mother would rage from her bed that no one had ever loved her. She'd howl with despair that her life was over by her thirties, blaming her ex-husband, her parents, her children, and the universe in general for conspiring against her. I'd climb trees, tuck into closets, fold myself into the clothes hamper, and stay there with my eyes closed until it felt safe to come out again. Jenn weathered similar emotional storms in Humboldt by running into the woods until she could no longer hear her stepfather yelling at her. Edie's life is also getting off to a rough start, but she's coping the best way she can, just like us.

Now that I am a middle-aged adult who has benefited from a lifetime of experience and a sprinkling of professional therapy, I'm mostly able to keep the emotions of my past in check. But if a dog can store bad memories, so can we. Every once in a while, one of my childhood fears resurfaces and kidnaps my brain without warning.

Just last spring, my palms started sweating in the back seat of Kathy's car on our way to visit a home for sale, when I realized she was turning onto the street where my mother used to live. The oak trees were the same, just broader. I inhaled the familiar metallic scent of the river, and while the homes hadn't changed, they were painted new colors and had different cars parked in front. I tried to settle my nerves, but the closer we got to my mother's former house, goose bumps appeared on my arms and I began shaking. I could tell myself that my mother wasn't there anymore, but my body wouldn't listen. Finally, I couldn't tolerate it anymore and I pleaded with Kathy to turn the car around. Just returning to the same neighborhood made my body react as if I was still living in constant fear of my mother's zero-to-sixty anger. I was trembling before a person who was no longer alive.

Turns out I have buried fears, just like my puppy.

And sometimes, an old fear can push me all the way to a full-out Edie panic attack. Like on Halloween 2018, when I ran screaming from a haunted house in Provincetown, Massachusetts, abandoning Jenn inside.

As someone who enjoys high-adrenaline activities such as skydiving, or scuba diving in shark territory, I'm not proud of it, but in my defense, this three-story house was set-designed by drag queens who had staged each room as a scene from a cult horror movie. The costumes, the makeup, and the acting were Hollywood-caliber, and I was thrilled by how gruesomely real it all looked…until we got to *The Exorcist* room. I watched that movie at a friend's house when I shouldn't have, when I was twelve, the same age as the possessed girl in the film. The queens had re-created the scene when two priests try to extract the devil from her body.

When Jenn and I entered the room, the girl leaped from the bed speaking in tongues, and scrabbled like a crab along the wall and reached for Jenn's neck with blackened, clawed hands. That was it. I didn't think, I didn't speak, I didn't breathe. I fled. I tore down a hallway, pushed through the first door I saw, and found myself on a second-story balcony in the dark. I found the stairs, made it to the yard, and then got tangled in rows of white sheets flapping on laundry lines. As I thrashed in the haunted house's final booby trap, looking for an opening to the street, more queens in monster-drag jumped out at me from behind the bed linens. Even they must have been impressed by my girl screams.

When Jenn found me a few minutes later, gasping for air on the street, we had a good laugh and then checked the heart monitors on our wristwatches. Mine had spiked from sixty-five to 172 beats per minute. Her adrenaline-trained cop heart had barely changed pace.

Whether it's a frightening parent, or a frightening movie, the body never forgets. If Jenn can forgive me for leaving her behind in a haunted house, certainly we can learn to forgive Edie for fleeing her own demons. My research is helping me see the whole of Edie, to have compassion for her limitations, and to realize that she can't help the way she is.

Over dinner I share my new theory with Jenn, that Edie came into our lives because our pasts have prepared us to care for a sensitive dog.

"Makes sense," she says. "Anyone could raise an easy dog like Stella."

The more I consider it, Stella wasn't just an easy dog; more like she was a one-in-a-million dog. I'd had no idea.

I ask Jenn if she's ever had childhood fears resurface unexpectedly, like sometimes happens to me. She thinks on it a bit, and then says that it's not old fear that affects her so much as daily exposure to fear within her career. Police officers run the risk of being traumatized by decades of daily exposure to potential threats, making them permanently hypervigilant, she says.

It's why my wife, without even thinking about it, never sits in a room with her back facing a door. Why I sometimes stop midsentence and ask her if she even heard what I said, because her head is on a swivel, scanning the restaurant for threats. Why she springs out of bed at the slightest sound in the middle of the night. Why she organizes early morning meditation classes at her station, for the emotional survival of her colleagues.

Both of us, through our own experiences with fear, are starting to get it now. Edie is not going to simply "grow out of it." Managing her fear will be a lifelong commitment, as it is for us. In several spots throughout the audiobook, the authors reiterate that canine fear has to be kept in check with dedicated counterconditioning. The upshot is this: as long as we keep working with Edie, there's a better chance she'll start looking to us to help her when she's anxious, rather than escalating to panic. Which is a compromise we'll gladly accept.

"She has to learn to trust us to protect her," Jenn says.

And we need to learn to trust her when she's telling us with her body language that something is too scary.

"Oh, and she needs a place to dig," I say.

Jenn sighs. She's not thrilled to dig up part of her garden to make room for Edie's claws, but she can't argue with the nation's top veterinarians. Edie may be living in a prison of her own making because she's too afraid to go for walks, but she still deserves a patch of open space, I argue. The poor thing yearns to feel dirt under her feet.

The next day, we get good news. The bank approved a loan for the Carmel Valley house. We'll be moving to the country, where Edie can dig all the holes her little heart desires.

12

Pet Psychic

Everyone wants to know if I brought Edie with me. My rowing team is gathered for a potluck brunch at a teammate's house in Marin, where there are already several well-adjusted pooches mingling among the humans on the expansive deck. A creek tinkles below us, and the morning sun filters through a towering redwood grove, sending shafts of light onto a long wooden table where the host is laying out a feast. This is exactly the kind of party Stella loved—plenty of guests to caress her and a very high potential for snacks to fall.

"Edie couldn't handle this," I say, as my teammates nod gravely. Many of them knew Stella as my constant sidekick, and commiserate with this new, solo, me.

There are more than twenty of us feasting on homemade frittatas, kale salad, and an abundance of healthy-looking dishes that all feature some type of grain—quinoa or millet or barley. Not a delicious pastry anywhere to be seen. Talk, as usual, is all about rowing technique: how to meld the lightness of ballet and the power of weight lifting into the perfect oar stroke. We can debate the physics of this endlessly, and while we are doing so the woman seated next to me leans in and whispers, "Have you ever considered a pet psychic for Edie?"

I have no idea what that is exactly, but I'm instantly fascinated.

"A pet who?"

I know it sounds crazy, she says, but her cat finally stopped peeing in the bed after a psychic used mental telepathy to communicate with her cat *over the phone*. My friend and her husband had just moved from a one-story to a three-story house, and the psychic silently spoke to the cat and reported back that the cat felt abandoned whenever the humans were on a different floor. The psychic used her powers to assure the cat that the house was like a tree, and each floor was a branch, separate but all connected by a trunk. Et voilà, the urinating stopped. Best $185 my friend said she ever spent.

"The psychic doesn't make house calls?"

My friend looks around furtively to make sure no one is listening to our conversation, then leans in a little closer.

"No," she whispers. "We just put the receiver near our cat."

I'm speechless. I can see why my teammate is sheepish; this sounds like a perfect way to light your money on fire. But she isn't an impressionable person. She's CEO of her own social innovation company, a creative entrepreneur who travels the globe helping disempowered communities design their own solutions to poverty. She's a former race-car driver who teaches human-centered business design at Stanford. So when she speaks, I listen. And what she's saying right now is mighty thought-provoking. Imagine, being able to just *ask* Edie what she's so afraid of.

We hold our phones under the table, and *ping!* the pet psychic's contact card appears on my screen.

"Oh, and one thing," my friend says. "She doesn't like the term 'pet psychic'—that sounds like a parlor trick. She calls herself an 'animal communicator.'"

"Got it."

Jenn doesn't even blink when I tell her that I want to hire someone to read Edie's mind. Although she finds the idea a little absurd, she's just curious enough to go for it. She thinks it sounds fun—like a parlor trick.

"What've we got to lose?" she says.

"One hundred and eighty-five dollars."

"I'm willing to try anything at this point," Jenn says.

According to the animal communicator's website, she will serve as a language translator between us and Edie. She says she receives information from animals in many different ways: sometimes she hears actual words and phrases, sometimes it's pictures or images, but more often it's pure emotion, or energy, that emanates from the pet.

How this energy travels through the phone is still unclear, but I'm not going to nitpick. I'm desperate for anything that will help us with Edie, so even if a pet psychic is false hope—it's still better than no hope. I reserve a one-hour appointment and follow-up with an email explaining our roller-coaster ride with Edie, cataloging her long list of fears. I end with the question we want to ask our puppy: Why are you so scared, and how can we make it better?

When the phone rings on the appointed evening, Edie is zooming around the house expending a day's worth of pent-up energy, bounding up and down the stairs and chasing her tail in furious circles. I put the phone on speaker and place it on the black-leather storage cube that serves as our coffee table, as Jenn and I settle on the couch. The woman's voice is soft and ethereal, just as I imagined it would be. She asks how to pronounce Edie's name, explaining that the vibration of the pet's name is important. Then she asks how she should refer to us when she's talking to Edie. Should she say Meredith, or Mom?

"Mom!" Jenn answers, before I can decide what Edie would call me if she could talk.

"Wait...if I'm Mom, what does she call you?"

"Jenn, I guess."

The way I see it, we're both moms and I would pause here to explore Jenn's reaction further if we weren't sharing our conversation with a stranger, so instead I let it go. But I find it telling that Jenn so quickly nominates me as the only parent. She doesn't have to be a mom if she doesn't want to; for clarity's sake Jenn could be Mama, or Ma, or Mum. Then I realize that this is a ridiculous internal conversation and I'm getting all worked up over nothing, because EDIE DOESN'T SPEAK. Not even two minutes into this, and I'm already getting sucked into magical thinking.

I return my attention to the animal communicator, who is explaining how she'll translate between Edie and us. By now Edie has stopped twirling, and is just standing a foot away, listening. The woman says she'll close her eyes to get centered, then she will be silent for about two to five minutes as she communicates with Edie. Afterward she'll tell us what Edie said and then relay our response to Edie, etcetera, etcetera.

As she's talking, Edie walks over and licks the phone in one swipe of her long, pink tongue. This strikes me, because she's never shown any interest in our phones before. Is there some sort of metaphysical energy pulling her toward the woman's voice? Or is Edie just trying to get us to stop what we're doing and pay attention to her?

"Gross," Jenn says, rubbing the slobber off with her shirt-sleeve.

The woman asks us if we're ready to begin. Suddenly I'm not.

"Before we get started, can you explain how this works, exactly?" I can't help it. It's the investigative journalist in me; I want proof. "How do you know what Edie is saying?"

The woman has a ready answer.

"It's not like I go into a trance or anything," she says. "It depends on the animal if I can hear any words, but I definitely feel the feelings they are willing to show me. It's like when you walk into a room and there's a person sitting there who's upbeat and happy, or sad and upset. Without a word being said, you can feel that energy."

Well, I think, *that's also because you can see a facial expression.* I choose not to split hairs. Instead, I murmur a noncommittal, "Mmm-hmm." I didn't get a solid answer, but I feel less of a rube because at least I asked it. Let it be entered into the record that I voiced my doubts.

Edie sits on my feet and leans against my legs, which is my cue to scratch her back. I obey, and she lifts her nose toward the ceiling, her eyelids fluttering with satisfaction. Mere seconds ago, she was a full-throttle Tasmanian devil. Now, she's a still lotus flower on a flat pond.

"Okay, are we ready to begin? Is Edie in the room?"

"She's right at my feet," I say.

"When I first connect with Edie, it might be nice to give her some compliments. Is there anything you'd like to praise her for, anything she does well?"

I've been focused for so long on Edie's drawbacks that the question takes me by surprise, and I can't come up with anything on the spot. Jenn swoops in to save me.

"She's getting better at coming when we call her," Jenn offers.

"That's good. I can use that. Okay, is everyone ready? I'm going to start. You'll hear some noises as I get myself clear."

I wriggle my eyebrows at Jenn, and she wriggles hers back. The woman lets out several long, whooshing exhales, and it sounds like a gale wind is blowing through the phone. Edie lies down on the rug, sighs, and rests her head on her paws. As we wait in silence for the woman to come back on the line, Jenn points at Edie. She's falling asleep. Or is she falling into a trance?

Jenn and I share a look that says, *We promised not to read too much into this.* Yes, Edie could be receiving telepathic messages, or she could simply have tuckered herself out.

Five minutes of silence doesn't sound like a lot, but it is when you're just sitting there. I check my watch and fidget. I pick at my nails. Jenn's right leg starts to bounce. After six minutes pass, I fold my arms and lock eyes with Jenn.

Another minute goes by. I do some quick math in my head. That's another three dollars gone.

I need a drink, Jenn mouths. She has enough time to mix up two Manhattan cocktails and return to the living room with two frosty glasses, and still not miss anything. When we're up to ten minutes, I am *this* close to calling BS, when the animal communicator finally communicates.

"Whoa! Sorry that took so long, but let me tell you what, Edie is *extremely* talkative. It's very clear she knew this call was going to happen, because she was excited and ready for me."

I don't think we told Edie directly about her upcoming phone call with a medium, but perhaps Edie overheard us talking about it. I remember making a few passing jokes here and there, like saying Edie had better have a very good answer for all the trouble she's put us through. That Edie had better not lie to the psychic, because she wouldn't get away with it.

"Edie kept saying how much she loves her people," the woman continues. "She has this happy glow about her and she's very secure in how much she's loved. If you hadn't told me about her, I'd be completely surprised she has any fear at all."

I envision our dog as Tigger from Winnie the Pooh, bouncing like a pogo stick on her tail, talking so fast she's tripping over her words. That's one facet of Edie—the indoor Edie. I wait for the "but…"

"But…" the woman says. "When I asked Edie what she doesn't love, she got really quiet, and then said, 'things that are noisy and really loud and large and unpredictable.'"

Which, if you're a puppy, is pretty much everything. And if you're a psychic, is a safe answer that encompasses pretty much everything.

"Uh-huh…" Jenn says, encouraging the woman to continue.

"Then I asked Edie if there's anything that helps lessen her fears. She said, 'Not really. The only thing I've learned to do is freeze and grit my teeth, and I try to remind myself that one of my people is with me.'"

So far, all of this is an easy rehash of the information I sent in my email. But we're just warming up. I'm still willing to go along.

"What kind of loud, noisy, unpredictable things scare her, specifically?" I ask.

Edie's answer? Moving cars.

"She said she's becoming less afraid of barking dogs but is still deeply frightened of cars on the road," the woman said. "Edie knows her traffic phobia is irrational. In fact, she admitted that she's a little embarrassed by it."

I brighten at this news. First, it confirms how we rank Edie's fears, with cars at the top of the list. And if Edie is sheepish about it, that must mean she wants to overcome it. Right?

"Is there anything you'd like to tell Edie about cars?" she asks.

I look to Jenn, but she brushes the air with her hand, *You go*.

I ask the communicator to assure Edie that cars stay on the road, they don't hunt down puppies. Also, we would never let Edie off-leash near cars. And lastly, because Edie likes being *inside* the car so much, I ask the woman to explain to Edie that those other cars are safe spaces for other dogs. If she saw these loud machines as dog chariots just like hers, maybe then she wouldn't be so afraid of them.

"I'll give it a try."

The communicator goes silent again, but for only half as long as the first time. When she returns, her voice is more somber.

"Okay, this took a little time to realize now how deeply frightened she has been of vehicles. I told her what you wanted her to know about cars being safe spaces for other dogs like hers is for her, and she said, 'Yeah, yeah, I've seen other dogs in cars. I just wish when we were outside it was just us and other dogs and people, but no cars moving.'"

I ask her to ask Edie what would make her feel safer around cars.

After another private conversation, the woman says Edie would like us to put our arm out to stop traffic when we cross the street. Our dog thinks that if we wave at drivers there's a greater chance they'll stop.

Jenn is smirking. I have to look away so I don't start laughing.

"We can put our arms out," I say, "but is there anything else we could do? What if we got her a reflective safety vest?"

"Let me ask."

No, says Edie. She doesn't want a vest. What she really wants is to learn how not to be afraid of cars.

I feel like Edie and the woman are talking in circles. We know she is afraid of cars, but we live in the city and we can't make them go away. We want to know what to do for her. I slump back into the couch cushions, frustrated with myself for letting myself believe this was going to give us any answers.

Jenn swirls the ice cubes in her glass and leans toward the phone.

"Can you ask Edie why she's afraid of cars?"

I can't believe I forgot to ask this crucial question, the one that could possibly contain the answer. Did Edie have a close encounter with a car before we got her? Did she see another dog get hit by a car? Did her mother get spooked by a car when she was pregnant? Was it something we did? Did we take her to a place with too many loud cars when she was too young to handle it?

The communicator goes silent again as she asks this question of Edie, then comes back online, sighs, and says even Edie doesn't have an answer. "Deep-seated fears in animals can go back all the way to a past life," she says.

Jenn rolls her eyes.

"Oh, one other thing. Edie kept saying, 'I like our car and I think we should keep it.' Does that mean anything?"

Suddenly Jenn and I snap to attention. This is pure, psychic realness. Just last week we replaced my twenty-year-old Toyota truck with a new one, and ever since, Edie has been reluctant to get inside it. We'd said nothing to the woman about this.

"Ah, she definitely prefers the old truck," the woman says.

Next the interpreter tells us that Edie knows about our move to Carmel Valley in two weeks, and our puppy wants to know more about the new house. Now that there might be some authentic pet mind reading going on, Jenn and I are engaged. We ask the woman to tell Edie that the new place will have ten acres of open space for her to run in, meadows, and a little creek. The house has a wall of windows where she can oversee the birds and gaze on the mountains. There's a swimming pool she can jump in, and best of all, hardly any traffic.

As the communicator is relaying this, Edie starts running in her sleep, all four paws twitching as if she is actually picturing herself bounding through the wilderness. When the woman reports that Edie is thrilled about the new house, I believe her because that's what I want to believe. She says Edie is especially curious about the pool, because she thinks it's hysterical for a bathtub to be that big.

While I can't say for sure if anything is really going on here, what I can say is this: the animal communicator is echoing what we are starting to believe. Edie is out of place. Whether you want to call it misaligned chakras or mismatched sensibilities, Edie is not a city dweller. The woman on the phone doesn't have a crystal ball, but she has a strong sense that a change of scenery will do Edie a world of good. She reminds us to keep Edie away from tourist spots such as Carmel Beach, and to stick to the unpopulated hiking trails in the national forests surrounding our neighborhood.

The last question I have for Edie is whether an older sibling would make her feel more secure. Jenn shoots me a warning look. I return it with a mea culpa expression, one that I hope conveys I'm just exploring the idea, not committing to it.

Turns out our puppy is lukewarm about a sibling. She likes the idea of a buddy to play with every day but doesn't want to share us. Edie said she'd have to think about it and give her answer after we move into the new house.

"She wants it to be *her* house," the woman says.

Jenn flashes a checkmate smile. She wins—two against one.

Before we say goodbye, the woman gives us the link to a website that sells an organic calming herbal spray, and I feign interest, just to be polite. We've already tried more than a dozen sprays, and none have had a soothing effect on Edie.

"Well, that was...interesting," Jenn says.

Jenn is teasing me—she knows I think "interesting" is a conversational safe-word, one that means everything and nothing at the same time.

"Come on, what do you really think?"

"I think life would be much more boring without Edie in it," Jenn says, lifting her glass in a toast.

It's a wonder where my wife stores these Obi-Wan insights, and how she saves them up for the one-and-only moment they were intended to be heard. I couldn't agree more. If it weren't for Edie, what shared obsession would bring us this close together?

"Cheers to that," I say.

13

Country Dog

It's move-in day. I shove so many boxes into my truck that poor Edie barely has room to turn around in the back seat. Jenn stuffs a clown-car amount of housewares into her Prius, and we caravan south on the route we've driven countless times to visit family and friends. Only this time I won't be returning with Jenn. I'll stay behind in Carmel Valley with Edie and our slumberous cat while Jenn will return to the Bay Area, and our long-distance relationship will begin.

We will live apart for the next two years, until Jenn retires from the police department. She'll live in the city during the workweek, and on weekends she'll drive three hours to be with us. Neither of us like the idea of so much time apart, but we keep reminding ourselves that time goes by faster than we think. We tell each other that we'll have plenty to keep us preoccupied when we're alone. I'll be renovating the new house, while she cleans and clears out the old one to get it ready to go on the market. After it sells, Jenn has arranged to move into a friend's spare bedroom in the San Francisco Sunset District. Jenn remains upbeat, but it seems like she is making the bigger sacrifice.

"It'll be like having a dorm room again," Jenn says, ever the glass-half-full thinker. "I'll put a Dolly Parton poster on the wall and get a mood lamp."

Jenn plans to work ten-hour days so she has three-day weekends, and she'll be home every holiday and vacation. We plan to video chat nightly, so then the question becomes existential…how "apart" are we, really? It will be an adventure, we like to say.

At least that's what we try to convince ourselves, but inwardly I suspect we're both having private apprehensions. Our temporary living arrangement will be the biggest test of our relationship, but it's not us I'm worried about. I feel such a solid love with Jenn that this test feels more like a pop quiz, and an open-book one at that. I'm more worried about how tiring it's going to be for Jenn to cram five workdays into four and make the six-hour round trip every week. I worry about her burning out—getting sick or falling asleep behind the wheel. I don't see her building any rest into her routine. She keeps saying she's willing to do it, but it sounds like an incredible slog.

As for me, I'm a little intimidated about living alone, with our tremulous dog, on a mountain in the middle of mountain lion country. We didn't just buy a home; we bought ten acres in the remote wilderness with spotty cell phone coverage. What am I going to do if Edie gets spooked and takes off into the canyons where she could be attacked by a coyote or wild boar, or bitten by a rattlesnake? Will that fancy new GPS collar even make a blip out there?

I've never thought I needed anyone's protection, but now,

the thought of not having Jenn there to help me talk things over, or to go out with the flashlight and investigate strange noises, makes me realize that I do rely on her. Her calm presence naturally makes me more resilient. And she makes me laugh at myself when I start taking things too seriously. Now if anything breaks or goes bump in the night, I'll have to handle it myself.

Not only have I never been a homeowner, I've never lived alone. Until now, my life has been one of constant cohabitation—with family, college roommates, friends, or paramours. What if a windstorm knocks a tree onto the house? If the pump at our well goes out? If I hear a scratching sound in the walls at night? If a wildfire comes? The list of what-ifs grows longer and longer, feeding on itself and pushing my heart to pump faster. I force myself to think of something more pleasant, but there's one what-if that refuses to leave me be: What if moving to the country doesn't bring Edie peace of mind?

I'd asked this question of Dr. Cucaro, who gave us a transition plan for Edie. Her advice was to gradually introduce Edie to her new surroundings, doling out bits of freedom very slowly. She said to first confine Edie to one room so she has time to absorb the new sights and smells. When Edie begs to be let out, we can expand her range to two rooms, then three, and so on, all the while letting our puppy control the pace. This could take days, or even weeks, Dr. Cucaro said. But above all, we must not give her more than she can handle, otherwise she could regress.

When we pull up to our new home in mid-August, the temperature is 103. We step out of our air-conditioned cars into heat so thick it feels like inhaling cotton. Gangs of heat flies appear, whining at our ears and tear ducts. I start swatting wildly, while Jenn just ignores them. To Edie, who has the golden retriever double-coat, this must feel like a sauna. She refuses to come out of the truck, so Jenn carries her into the house. The house has an open floor plan, with the living, dining, and kitchen area sharing one large, vaulted room. I unfold Edie's wire playpen into a large circle in the middle so she can watch us unpack, and fill it with her blankets and toys and add a bowl of ice water. When I set her down in the enclosure, she looks up at the ceiling fan with four-foot blades whirring overhead and starts stress-panting immediately. She doesn't like anything about this new sweltering place, nor being imprisoned inside it. She starts to cry, and her tone is so anguished, it pierces me. It's not a plea to be let out of her pen, but to be held. I can't prove this; I just sense it.

"Maybe I should sit with her awhile?" I say.

I high-step over Edie's wall and as soon as I sit down, she hops into my lap and hides her eyes in my armpit. I rub her back until her crying subsides to just one moan every few minutes or so. Jenn and I take turns unpacking and sitting with Edie until evening comes and the crickets come out for their nightly chorus. Their incantation seems to echo in the canyons, like one massive insect performance of "Row, Row, Row Your Boat." It's a sound I'd forgotten I used to know, part of the soundtrack of my childhood that has become fainter with time. The music draws Jenn and me onto the deck, where we stand beneath an explosion of stars and let the song pour over us.

"You can actually see the Milky Way," Jenn says. With the light pollution in San Francisco, we rarely saw it.

"When I was little, I'd assumed the sky looked like this everywhere," I say.

The air is still warm, but finally bearable, and carries the heady scent of wild sage bushes that grow as big as boulders all around the house. Everything feels new, yet familiar at the same time. I'm back in the nature of my childhood, but I feel out of practice, like I'll need to relearn everything Grandpa taught me about its rhythms. To recognize which plants are poisonous and which are medicinal. To remember how to prune fruit trees. To identify wildlife tracks, and build houses for the bluebirds. To learn again what it means to sit still, so quietly that wildlife will reveal itself to you.

Then, as if on cue, I detect movement in the dark, near the top of a massive oak tree a few feet from us. I turn and hear it before I see it—the whooshing sound of a huge wingspan pushing air. A creature emerges from the shadows and swoops down out of the dark, soaring at knee-level before arcing back up to perch in another oak a little farther away. I crane my neck and look skyward, and all I can make out is the dark outline of a barrel-shaped body, and a head with the telltale pointed tufts of a great horned owl. We hold our breath, as the majestic bird considers us. In that brief moment before it takes flight again, I feel an otherworldliness being in this wild place, unaccustomed to its particular sights and sounds. But at least I know what an owl, or a cricket is. I can only imagine how the strangeness must be magnified a million times for Edie.

Before turning in for the night, we open Edie's pen to see if she wants to explore the house. To our surprise, she does. Head down, nostrils flared, she follows the footboard trim, inhaling scents as she inspects the entire footprint of the building. When she finishes her perimeter check, we try to coax Edie outside to relieve herself. She takes a few tentative steps toward the door, and looks at us for reassurance. Jenn tosses a cookie on the floor and Edie creeps up to it and chews. Edie stands in the doorway, raises her ears and cocks her head to listen to the chirping crickets. She takes in about three seconds of it, then she streaks back into her pen, terrified.

"She's not ready for crickets," I say.

"Maybe to her it sounds like an animal is screaming," Jenn says.

I pick her up and swaddle her in my arms as Jenn blows up the air mattress. Until this moment, I've always enforced a no-dogs-on-the-bed rule, but I break it for Edie, and let her snuggle between us for the first time. Jenn spoons her and Edie falls asleep instantly, her whiskers twitching and tickling my shoulder. Edie wiggles and smacks her lips in her dreams, but Jenn blissfully snores through it. Me, I lie awake and think about Edie's reaction to the crickets. Is this the beginning of a whole new fear list? I'd agreed with the collective assumption that getting Edie out of the congested city would bring her peace. But now, alone with my thoughts in the dark, that seems desperately naive. Who's to say Edie won't just replace her city fears with country ones?

I wake the next morning to the sound of Edie's toenails clicking on the pinewood floor as she dances before the front door, begging to be let out.

"Jenn, wake up," I say, shaking her shoulder. "Look!"

"Wha? Huh?" She bolts upright from a dream, pillow imprints on her cheek.

I point toward the door. "Edie is asking to go outside."

Edie never begged to be let out of the city house.

"Wanna go out?" I say.

Edie apparently does, and leaps outside to sniff the base of a plum tree that is growing through a cutout in the wood deck. An animal must have been walking there during the night because Edie is sniffing like a bloodhound, tracking a scent in a curlicue pattern around the trunk. She finds a leafy shoot at the bottom of the tree and tugs on it. Above us, it looks like God had been up all night tagging the sky. The clouds are slashes of Xs and Hs and Ts spray-painted against the blue. Even the clouds seem more dramatic here.

"Should we put her on the leash?" Jenn asks.

"Not sure. Let's just see what she does."

She follows the scent off the deck, down a pebble path lined with bottlebrush and madrone trees, past overgrown bushes of ceanothus and lavender, leaving us behind to stare at each other in amazement. We hear rustling and follow the sound around the corner to find our cowardly dog racing around the property in a comet of pure joy. She crashes through the white sage and manzanita bushes, sending dust and leaves flying. Although we've seen Edie run many times, she's never run like *this*. There's a bounce to her stride without a trace of urgency. Her ears are up instead of flattened back; her tail is whirring like a helicopter blade. I see her spring up from behind the purple cones of a Pride of Madeira plant, and pounce on something.

"Edie?"

She hears her name and pauses, holding her left paw aloft as if checking her watch, then disappears again, kicking up a cloud of fallen oak leaves.

"What's she doing?" Jenn says, jogging toward her.

All we can see is Edie's tail, pointing straight up near a young olive tree. She's zeroed in on something of particular interest, because all the hair on her tail is fanned out like it has static electricity. When we reach her, she lifts her head to show us she's captured a sun-bleached rabbit leg with a scrap of fur still attached.

"Yuck," I say, wrinkling my nose. "I'm not touching that."

But my disgust is tempered by Edie's delight. She's absolutely thrilled, beside herself with this chance to engage her natural hunting instinct. She's momentarily fearless, and I assume her brain is so busy processing new, pleasurable information that there's no time for her usual doomsday thoughts. If I'd had enough forethought, I would have planted that bone myself to help Edie develop a good first impression of her new home.

Edie is standing stock-still, clutching her find and waiting for one of us to make the first move. Jenn reaches for the leg, but Edie is not about to give up her first kill. She whips her head away, taunting Jenn with a game of keep-away, then prances away from us clutching her trophy, checking back over her shoulder to make sure we are in pursuit.

"Edie! Cookie!" Jenn calls, sprinting after her.

The magic word. Edie stops and drops the rabbit leg in anticipation of something better. In a flash, Jenn snatches the bone and tosses it over the six-foot deer fence that encircles our yard, as Edie looks longingly at her beautiful femur flying toward the canyon. Turning back to us, Edie studies our faces to see if we will return her rightful rabbit to her. But our betrayal is apparently forgiven in a blink, as Edie bounds away again in search of more prey.

I hug Jenn tight to me and whisper in her ear, "I think she likes it here."

Edie is now heading toward the swimming pool, and before we can stop her, she leaps onto the pool cover. Her legs wobble beneath her as if she's trying to stride across a water-bed, and her eyes widen in fear as she stumbles the rest of the way across. She makes it to the other side, and looks back at the cover as if trying to figure out how solid earth just betrayed her. Apparently rattled, she runs back to the front door and whines for us to let her back in.

One step forward, two steps back.

"Remember Dr. Cucaro said to take it slow," Jenn reminds me.

When Jenn goes back to San Francisco the next day, I make an appointment at the nearest vet clinic to get Edie a rattlesnake vaccine. Again, she won't go willingly, so I carry all sixty-five pounds of her now into the waiting room, where she trembles at my feet, even though at eight in the morning we are the only ones there. Both of us are dreading the appointment, actually. Although Edie needs a new vet, I'm weary at the thought of having to explain our puppy's issues all over again to somebody new, to start over with a vet who may not have much experience with, or belief in, dogs with emotional issues. I know that withering look of a veterinarian who thinks you are a hypochondriac, so to avoid it, I consider not even mentioning Edie's anxiety. Even if I do discuss it, I could get an entirely different opinion about what to do with Edie. I don't want to get conflicting advice when we're just getting somewhere with Dr. Cucaro.

When the vet asks why I've come, I mention we live in an area with rattlesnakes. Then I take a deep breath and tell an abbreviated version of the last eleven months with Edie. When I finish, he says:

"I'm not a fan of Prozac."

I clench my jaw, and manage to say, "Oh?"

He suggests I try a different antianxiety drug called trazodone. He doesn't say why, he just says he likes it better. Based on a quick glance at Edie, he's telling me to switch medications?

"I'll research it," I say unconvincingly.

The vet kneels down to examine Edie's body with his hands, feeling her belly, her joints, her throat. He lifts up her lips and checks the color of her gums. Then he stands up, folds his arms and looks at her quizzically.

"I've never seen a golden this small. Is she the runt?"

Edie is only ten pounds lighter than Stella. She's smallish, but there's nothing wrong with her. I feel my cheeks flush with fury. What is this man implying? That Edie is a weakling? I feel suddenly defensive, and ready to leave.

"No."

He continues to check Edie's vitals, and suggests I try a calming probiotic powder for dogs sprinkled on Edie's food. It's very expensive, and sounds like the kind of lighter stepping-stone remedies we tried on our way to pharmaceuticals. He says there are special dog foods formulated for apprehensive dogs, and mentions one made by a pet food conglomerate. Either I have done a poor job conveying the severity of Edie's fear, or this is the standard prescription he gives to every owner who comes in complaining of an anxious dog. Then again, maybe he's never encountered a puppy with as strong a fight-or-flight reflex as ours, just as Kendra hadn't. Maybe he's never encountered a dog this far off the charts.

"You're such a pretty girl on the outside," he says, patting Edie's head as we're getting ready to leave. "It's just your brain on the inside."

Angry hornets swirl inside my head. Although this is the kind of thing Jenn and I say all the time about Edie in private, to hear a stranger say it feels demeaning and discriminatory. How dare he. How dare he insinuate that there's something ugly about our dog's brain. Edie is gentle and loving and sensitive. Her brain may not land in the middle of the canine bell curve, yes, but that's what makes her exceptional, not flawed. Once she's given a label, she'll forever be seen that way by society, shackled by each person's different negative interpretation of what that one word means. How can Edie ever rise to her full potential, or get the proper health care, if she can be so easily dismissed by the implications of one inaccurate word?

My fervor to stand up for Edie feels primal, as if someone has attacked me personally. But on the drive home, I realize that I should thank that veterinarian. What he helped me see is that the person I'm really angry with is me. By hearing my own judgment reflected back at me, I see that I was also sabotaging Edie with the lowered expectations of my own language. I need to rise to the challenge of this unique dog, not make excuses for why I can't. I promise to Edie in the car that I will do better. I will change how I speak about her, so that others will do the same.

Over the next few weeks, Edie begins adjusting to her new landscape. We don't dare let her outside the fence, but there's plenty to explore on the three acres within its boundaries. There are pine cones to pluck bald, sticks to chew, and so many gopher tunnels to unearth. She drinks from the fountains and teaches herself how to put her nose underwater and blow bubbles. She chases alligator lizards until she collapses in an exhausted heap on the doorstep. She's learned to recognize the sound of clucking California quail, and how much fun it is to ambush them, sending the startled flocks into clumsy flight. It's as if she came from the country and still remembers it in her bones.

She remains distrustful of the pool, and I want to teach her to swim in case she ever falls in. She gets very agitated when I swim, and runs around the pool deck following me as I swim

from one end to the other. She whines and snaps her jaws at the
water I kick up, and I can't tell if she thinks she needs to save
me or she wants to get in and play with me. Either way, she's
conflicted about the water. Which doesn't jibe at all with what
I know about the innate bodysurfing skills of golden retrievers.
Both Stella and Layla ran into the ocean when I first took them
to the beach, and no swimming instruction was ever required.

I begin Edie's swimming lessons by sitting on the top step
in the shallow end and placing Edie on my lap in an inch of
water. She's alarmed at first, tensing every muscle in her body
as I lower her into a seated position on my legs. But if I sit
very still and speak sweetly to her, she eventually relaxes, and
will stretch out onto her belly, letting her legs dangle in the
water. I do this every day for weeks, and that's as far as Edie is
willing to go. When I try to carry her into the shallow end,
she clings to me so hard that she leaves red welts on my upper
body. My sister-in-law, Suzanne, suggests a doggie flotation
vest, one that will keep Edie afloat, to help her learn that she
won't sink in the water. I choose a red one, with a handle on
the top so I can grab Edie if she needs rescue.

One morning I retract the pool cover for our daily sitting-
in-the-water lesson, and Edie spies a wide, brown toad with
yellow eyes sitting on the pool deck near the shallow end.
Before I can stop her, Edie licks it, then backs away in alarm.
White shampoo-like bubbles immediately foam out of Edie's
mouth, a response to the defensive slime that toads excrete to
make up for their inability to abscond.

I rinse her mouth with the garden hose and search the internet on my phone with my free hand, only to find out Edie
is either completely fine or a goner in five minutes. It all depends on the type of toad. The closest emergency pet hospi-

tal is a forty-minute drive away. My heart pounds as I dial, and the sweet-sounding young woman who picks up says late summer is an odd time of year to see toads.

"I think they like the pool," I say.

"Oh, that makes sense. Can you describe the toad?"

Beige. Brown spots. About five inches across. Shifty-looking.

"Just a minute."

There's no way I'm going to wait on hold while my dog could be dying. I run with Edie to my truck and start driving way too fast down the curvy mountain road with a cell phone in one hand. It couldn't have been more than a minute, but it feels like a lethal amount of time before the receptionist returns.

"She'll be fine. Just wash her mouth out with a hose."

I slam the brakes.

"Oh, God. Thank you. I already did that. Should I give her a tablespoon of hydrogen peroxide to make her throw up?"

"I don't think that's necessary. It's not a deadly toad."

"If she doesn't perk up, I'll bring her in."

"Sure, if you'd like us to take a look."

I can tell she's placating me, but I no longer care if I have become an overbearing dog mom. I'd made a vow to be Edie's advocate, so that means asking more follow-up questions and for second opinions. I've learned to book the first vet appointment of the day to avoid crowded waiting rooms, or to request veterinarians give examinations and injections in the back of our car, like Dr. Cucaro did for Edie's subsequent visits. After decades of being a people pleaser, I am finally learning from my puppy how to ask for what I need without apology.

I keep Edie indoors the rest of the day and repeatedly check her saliva level, assuring myself that she is fine. When it's clear the danger has passed, I finally see the humor in her escapade.

Edie must have been stunned to attack something that actually fought back. During our nightly call, I tell Jenn about the toad and we have a good laugh. It's a laugh of relief, yet also for me, happy laughter that I had handled an emergency on my own. I am getting a little better at this living alone thing.

Edie has learned to associate the sound of the driveway gate opening with Jenn's weekend return. Each time she hears it, she runs to the front door and shakes her rump so hard it looks like her back end might fly right off. I let her out and she whirls around Jenn in celebration—a visual manifestation of what I feel inside after the end of a long week without my best friend. Jenn gets Edie to be still by asking, "What do good puppies do?" and Edie freeze-frames herself, sitting expectantly at Jenn's feet. That's the signal for Jenn to crouch down eye-to-eye with Edie, to get in position to receive kisses. Edie leans in with her dexterous tongue and bathes Jenn's cheeks in long, bottom-to-top strokes, finishing her welcome by licking Jenn's ears and nibbling her earlobes. Being an emotional dog, Edie is demonstrative with not only her fear, but also her affection. She's the first golden I've had who loves to kiss. She licks our hands and faces to wake us up each morning, and gives kisses after we feed her meals. In the evenings when we're relaxing on the couch, she drapes herself over our legs, and gently nibbles on our toes. I love watching Jenn and Edie's greeting ritual, and don't mind being second in line for hugs. It's the trade-off for seeing Jenn finally make room for puppy love.

With each week that goes by, Jenn says she notices a slightly more confident dog. One weekend she photographs Edie staring up at a red-tailed hawk perched on a fence post; another time I show Jenn how Edie has progressed to sitting with me

on the *second* step of the swimming pool. By Edie's first birthday in late September, our conversations shift from Edie's fail-
ures, to her accomplishments. We feel our tension slip away
in increments, marveling at how this is the same puppy that
used to cower at the sight of dandelion dander on the wind.

The change of scenery is having an impact on Edie, and
giving us hope that over time, with lots of encouragement,
patience, and love from us, she just might grow into a dog
that can take a walk, or a road trip. Dogs have survived by
adapting themselves to the needs of the people they live with,
so maybe Edie's sensory overload in the city was a canine
manifestation of ours. Although we didn't buy a new house
for Edie, we certainly bought it with her in mind, and with
the year deadline we placed on her innocent head. Now that
we're in Carmel Valley, all three of us feel calmer, happier, and
safer ensconced in the coastal mountains, where the remote-
ness lets our busy minds unspool and our pulses slow down.
We finally are allowing ourselves to have hope.

My uncle Brian comes over to install a dog door for Edie.
Instead of the kind we had at the old house with a rubber
flap, I choose a new-fangled one with hard plastic saloon-
style doors that stay closed with magnets, figuring it will do
a better job keeping the cold air, and critters such as skunks
and foxes, from sneaking inside. Edie will need to push a little
harder with her nose to part the doors compared to the flap,
but it shouldn't be too difficult.

Edie is wary. She stares at us through the clear doors from
inside the house, as we encourage her with cookies from outside. Each time Edie nudges her nose against the saloon doors,
they part an inch and snap back, startling her.

"Maybe hold the doors open for her and just get her to walk through first," I say.

This poses no challenge, and Edie will gladly walk through a big hole in the wall to get fed.

"How about you go inside, and I'll stay outside, and we'll encourage her on both sides?" Jenn suggests.

Edie knows what we are asking her to do, and she really tries. She nudges the doors open wider and wider, but gives up each time she feels pressure in the hinges. Finally, she pushes her head all the way through. Jenn hands her a cookie from outside, and Edie looks like she's about to finally walk all the way through, then suddenly she panics and steps backward. The saloon doors close down on either side of her neck and she lets out a sharp cry, with her body inside and her head still outside the house. We rush to her aid and pry the doors off her neck. She's not injured, but she's added another item to her fear list: the guillotine.

After that, she won't even look at the dog door anymore. Which means we must kneel down and part the doors for her every single time she wants to go in or out. Which for an active puppy, is approximately 149 times per day. Which sort of defeats the purpose of cutting a hole in the wall to give your dog some self-sufficiency.

"This is ridiculous," Jenn says.

She's right; and with any other dog this would seem like coddling. But with Edie, life leans more toward ridiculous. Yet it's that very nonsensical part of our puppy that I'm starting to love the most. It's Edie's unpredictability that's pushing me to become a more sensible person, the kind who will finally let go of her old hurts to nurse the emotional wounds of another.

14

Chase

Edie starts each day on a high note. She welcomes every sunrise with a *yahoo!*, and celebrates in a jamboree-of-one around our bed until we give up on sleep and stumble into the kitchen for coffee. Our thirteeen-month-old puppy is a self-winder now, with so much on her to-do list that the claw marks on our legs are finally starting to heal. When Edie isn't removing and chewing the sandstones from the paved footpaths, she's running through the sprinklers, or digging holes in the decomposed granite surrounding the pool. She has taken up birdwatching and devotes a good portion of her day to monitoring the hummingbirds jousting at the hanging feeders. She no longer startles at the high-pitched screech of a hunting falcon or the ray-gun staccato of a titmouse. She's stopped cowering at the sound of crickets, and she's figured out why she should not bite the cactuses.

One weekend in October, Jenn comes home to see a few of our outdoor landscape lights are toppled over and cracked. Edie's nearing her athletic prime and expends her energy zipping on an obstacle course of her own design, perfuming herself as she races through the rosemary and French lavender on the west side of the house, loops back up the brick path and crashes through the butterfly sage on the north side, then finishes her circuit with a few crazy eights around the Valley oaks at the top of the driveway. When I won't play with her, she improvises by picking up the lemons and oranges that have fallen from the fruit trees and letting them roll down the slopes so she can chase after them. When she's really in a mood, she'll bite off the skinny black rubber emitters from the landscape sprinkler system.

"Collateral damage," I say.

"Or maybe she's ready for a walk," Jenn says.

"You sure?"

"Only one way to find out."

This will be the ultimate test of Edie's true progress. And part of me doesn't want to know the answer. Edie's been adjusting so well during these past two months of confinement on the property, and I don't want to ruin it. I'm starting to believe that she was a country dog trapped in a city dog's body, and I want to keep believing it because it's such a simple solution. I don't want to be reminded of what she can't do. I don't want to let go of this new Edie I see before me.

We clip Edie into her harness, attach the leash, and swing open the front gate. This time Edie doesn't hesitate, lunging out ahead so she's the one walking me. She pulls me past the row of buckwheat bushes lining our driveway like she's late for an appointment. Each tug on the leash feels like providence.

This is going to be the day, I can feel it, that our housebound hound finally finds her way.

"So far, so good," Jenn says under her breath, as if being careful not to break the spell.

At the end of our driveway, we turn right onto our neighborhood's only street, a private country road so quiet that a passing car is an event, cause for residents to put down what they're doing and stare. The mountain community is tranquil by design, with thirty-plus homes hidden from view behind pine and oak tree groves, inhabited by people with a penchant for solitude. There should be nothing here to send Edie into sensory overload. No crowded sidewalks. No traffic jams. No loud music. The only sounds this morning are the chortling of chickens, the distant whinny of a horse, and the hiss-hiss-hiss of a water sprinkler.

Our destination is a quarter mile ahead, where the pavement ends at a barbed-wire fence marking the boundary of a vineyard. The fallen leaves crunch underfoot and up ahead on the right, I can see the pond has retracted to a puddle. The earth is begging for rain, but the sky has not yet shown any mercy.

Edie soldiers on for about a minute, and then I feel her stride become more tentative. Her pace slows and she falls back by my side, then drops behind me. We make it as far as the first neighbor's house when the leash goes taut, filling me with that all-too-familiar dread. I look behind me and see that Edie's stopped. She's run out of oomph. She's sitting atop the crest of a small hill, surveying the landscape unfolding below her. The dry pond is on her right, and there's a weedy field behind a weathered and listing cattle fence to her left. There is a silver-domed observatory rising from behind our astronomer neighbor's oak trees. Everything is still, yet in her doggie opinion, something evil is lurking.

"Oh, Edie." I sigh, feeling all the air seep out of me. How can *this* be too challenging?

Jenn tosses a cookie onto the road a few feet ahead of Edie. "Find it!" she chirps.

Edie breaks her protest to sniff out the biscuit. She walks a few more paces and gobbles it, then abruptly sits again. Jenn attempts the cookie trick once more, but Edie won't be fooled twice. She leaves the bribe on the pavement and U-turns for home, lunging on the leash exactly like she used to do in the city. I'm clopping like a horse behind her, trying to slow her to a walk, when I see an SUV coming our way. I will it to please, please, pass us, but as luck would have it, it's a neighbor and as is also custom in our community, she pulls over and rolls down her window to chat. The rumbling engine sends Edie into an even higher gear, and she's so much stronger now. As we tear off together like a dog sled without the sled, I hear the driver introduce herself as Betsy to Jenn. She says the fluffy golden retriever wriggling in the back seat is named Chase.

"She's afraid of cars!" I shout over my shoulder, leaving Jenn behind to smooth things over.

Back on home base, I can feel Edie's muscles relax as I remove her harness.

"Breathe, Edie-pie, breathe," I huff, as I'm trying to catch my own breath. "You're safe."

I can't believe we're doing this...again. My panting puppy stares up at me, and I can't tell if she feels thankful to be back on familiar territory or betrayed because I took her away from it. And what about Edie? Can she tell what I'm thinking?

Can she read the disappointment on my face? If Edie can't walk here, she can't walk anywhere. So here we are, right back where we started, with the humming electricity of our jittery nerves passing in the air between us. The ache in my chest must be sympathy pain, a reaction to feeling powerless to help this creature I love from getting repeatedly traumatized. It was so easy to be lulled into the fantasy that all Edie's problems would vanish with a change of scenery.

Edie jogs over to a tall, urn-shaped fountain, rises on her hind legs to rest her paws on the lip, and drinks. *When did she learn to do that?* Edie ignores the honeybees perched on the rim drinking water, sending them to buzz angrily around her head. She won't walk on an empty street, but she will poke her nose into a cloud of stinging insects? I stare in disbelief at the perpetual contradiction that is Edie. Thirst slaked, she peers through the horizontal wooden slats of the fence, waiting for Jenn to return. I realize I'm standing there waiting for Jenn, too. I need her to make sense of Edie's relapse, to render her glass-half-full verdict that always keeps me from sinking into my dark place.

"Well, we tried," I say, as Jenn lets herself in the gate.

She smiles weakly and crosses her arms, considering things. Then she kicks an acorn, and Edie, apparently feeling much better now, scampers into the coyote bushes after it.

"Our dog needs a therapy dog," Jenn announces.

And just like that, the gloom clouds part and we're doubled over laughing at what really is a first-world problem. So what if Edie won't go for a walk. At least she adores the new house, and she has plenty of space to run now. We can make it work. We can throw the ball into the canyon for her instead of walking her. Once again, my wife has used verbal judo to pry me out of my melodramatic rut. Our life with Edie is an accommodation, not a disaster.

"By 'therapy dog,' do you mean you're ready to get another…"

"*Mare…ah…dith…*" She draws out each syllable, as if scolding a mischievous child. "No. It means Betsy and her partner, Ron, and their dog, Chase, are coming over tomorrow morning."

One of the things I love about my wife is that she doesn't rest until she's solved, or at least tried her best to solve, something that's upsetting me. It's woven into her savior personality, this superpower she employs to get people to put down their weapons, or to pull me out of a bad mood, with just a few well-chosen words. She came up with a plan B for Edie on the spot and made a playdate with the neighbors.

"Thank you," I say, kissing her forehead. She did make it better. She gave me something to look forward to, so there's less reason to fixate on today.

"Edie went as far as she could go today," Jenn says. "Maybe she'll go farther next time."

Jenn's right, as usual. There's a context I'm overlooking. I can celebrate all the steps Edie took today. Or I can bemoan all the ones she didn't take. The choice is mine, and I decide that this first outing was a practice, not a final failure. Edie is still a baby, and she may get there, in baby steps. Or she may not. Either way, she can still be happy. Meanwhile, she's about to make her first friend. Chase could be a wonderful bravery coach for Edie. He could be her therapy dog.

Of all the unsolicited Edie advice we've received, the one suggestion that keeps coming up is to get Edie a slightly older, confident, golden retriever she could emulate. Many of the books I read back this up, and when I'd asked Dr. Cucaro about it, she'd said a buddy wasn't a bad idea. But the reality of us throwing another dog into the hurly-burly of our long-distance life is just not practical. Plus Jenn would never go for it, after letting me take the lead on Edie. And if I'm really being honest with myself, I'm too afraid I'll repeat my mistake and choose another needy dog. Thankfully, nearly every home in our new neighborhood has a pickup parked out front and a dog in the house.

When Betsy and Ron arrive the next morning, they seem just as eager as we are to introduce our dogs.

Three-year-old Chase is a nutmeg-colored, big-hearted, lug of a boy from golden retriever central casting. He springs out the back seat of Betsy's Land Rover and lopes in giddy circles around it, as if expecting to find his own surprise party. My first impression of Chase is that he expects nothing but benevolent kindness from the world, that he's a staunch follower of the Stella School of Philosophy. Chase seems fearless, eager to please, and so mellow he could snooze next to a jackhammer while children pull on his ears. Edie watches this gallant gentleman from behind the clear panels of her dog door, prancing and whimpering for us to let her out.

"Use your dog door!" Jenn commands.

Edie's plea rises a couple octaves, to a high whistle. She nudges the plastic doors open a crack with her snout, then wavers and retreats.

Jenn gives in, parts the saloon doors, and Edie explodes through to get to Chase.

Tails whipping back and forth, they sniff each other head to toe, turning in a circle together. Olfactory introductions complete, they stand in a face-off, wriggling and waiting for the other to make the first move. Chase goes first. He offers a play bow, then springs back to his feet. Edie takes this as an invitation to execute her signature move...the backward-walking body check. She looks over her shoulder and backs up casually toward Chase, then when she's inches away and he least suspects it, she T-bones him in the hip with her booty.

That's all it takes to seal their friendship. Edie peels off down the canyon with Chase in hot pursuit, as Ron claps in delight. "Hey, hey! Look-it 'em gooooooo!" he says.

Edie takes Chase on a high-speed tour of the premises, running through the meadows, showing him how to do crazy eights around the fruit trees. They pinball through the sagebrush, running with their sides pressed together as one, eight-legged beast. Chase is the taller of the two, with a broad chest, longer coat feathers, and paws twice the size of Edie's, but she's able to keep up, matching him stride for stride. Watching them fall in love is proof that all that matters is this, what's happening right before us, here and now. Edie is the sidecar to Chase's motorcycle, as they rip the earth in tandem, headed for adventure. Yesterday evaporates from my pores, and my disappointment disappears into the past.

When the dogs finally lie down to catch their breath, Chase rolls onto his back and lets Edie climb all over him. She tugs on his ears and covers his face in kisses until the gentle giant has had enough, and escapes by hopping into the basin of a nearby fountain.

"Chase! No! Get out of there!" Ron hollers, as Chase splashes in ecstatic circles in the murky water. Our new neighbors don't know us well enough to know that Jenn and I couldn't care less, in fact we think Chase's antics are absolutely hilarious.

"Let's see if Edie will get in with him," I say.

Edie is spellbound by Chase's new trick. She tentatively puts her paws on the ledge of the basin, biting at the water Chase is kicking up as he whirs around and around, showing off for her. She won't go all the way in the water, but she cheerleads from the sides. Then he leaps out and shakes his coat, sending a shower over the four of us.

"Chase!" Betsy squeals, jumping out of the spray.

Edie is smitten. She waits for him to finish drying off, and then pounces on his head, wrapping her forearms tight around his waist. Then she vigorously tries to make a baby with him. Chase, ever the gentleman, remains still, politely waiting for Edie's lusty mood to pass.

Betsy looks astonished. "He's never allowed a dog to do that," she says. "I can't believe he's not growling at her."

Jenn steps in and pulls Edie off Chase. "I don't think it's a domination thing," she says. "I think she's just really excited."

"Yeah, she used to do that to a basketball," I say.

"I'd say they're getting along swimmingly," Ron says.

Perhaps there's some truth to the theory that dogs have more of an affinity for their own breed. Edie is beside herself to meet Chase, more than any other dog she's met, so it does make me wonder. Does she recognize something in him? Does he remind her of her father, or a brother?

We invite our new neighbors inside for coffee, and while it's brewing, Edie pulls all her toys from her basket near the dining room table and delivers each one to Chase, dropping them at his feet. It's like Edie wants to be a good host, too. She's certainly pulling out all the stops, suddenly interested in toys she hasn't touched in months. They tussle with rubber balls that light up when they roll, knotted ropes, and a plush quail. I tell Betsy and Ron that the playdate is going even better than we could have imagined, and they agree, saying they've never seen Chase take to another dog so quickly. After nearly an hour of nonstop play, including more attempted lovemaking from Edie, they finally tucker out and fall asleep under the dining table, their paws touching.

I sense that not only will Chase be good for Edie, the four of us will be friends, too. Ron and Betsy are also from San Francisco, and moved to the street just a year before we did. As the newest residents on the mountain, the four of us share the same learning curve about rural living. We quickly discover that we enjoy talking about the same things: fertilizing fruit trees, eradicating gophers, salt versus potassium water softener systems, wind forecasts, bobcat sightings. I offer to mentor Ron and Betsy with their first beehive. They say they'll show us the stars through their telescope. Next thing I know, Jenn and Betsy are making plans to take an online bird sketching class together.

"We've been thinking about getting a second dog for Edie," I say, ignoring the sidelong glance from Jenn.

"Well, now you don't have to!" Betsy says, which was exactly what I was hoping she would say. Ron also works in San Francisco during the week, which means Betsy and I are in similar situations, working from home, alone, with bouncy puppies that need daily exercise. We could be a great help to one another. On their way out the door, Betsy takes me up on my offer to harvest olives from our trees. "Friday?" she says. "And I'll bring Chase?"

We fall into an easy routine after that, bringing our dogs together several times a week. For Chase and Edie, every reunion is a replay of their first encounter, as they twirl around each other in a Groundhog Day delirium of adoration. I wish humans were this good at expressing their true feelings.

The first time I take Edie to visit Chase, I drive her there, a distance of approximately one-sixteenth of a mile, because walking is out of the question. When we pull into Ron and Betsy's driveway, Chase is by himself, tethered to a post on the front porch, sitting with perfect posture as if he is expecting a prom date. Edie must be able to smell him from inside the truck because she is making that high-pitched squeak again that she reserves for Chase. Betsy appears at the front door and releases Chase, who bounds over, puts his paws up on the cab and peers at Edie through the tinted windows. They press their noses to the window together, two lovers separated by prison glass.

I let Edie out and they roll together on the ground, play biting and snapping at the air—which looks a lot like the canine equivalent of Hollywood air kisses. Edie is so focused on the object of her affections that she doesn't realize she's in an unfamiliar place. She ignores the new scenery, until they pause their canoodling for Chase to take a drink from his water bowl on the porch. Edie watches him go, and then leaps to her feet, suddenly taking in the two-story blue house with white trim. She hears the neighbor's two dogs that are barking through the fence because they want to play, too, and she whips her head around to locate them. That's all it takes for Edie to hit tilt. In a flash, she darts back into the truck, abandoning Chase.

"What just happened?" Betsy asks.

"She has anxiety. She's on Prozac," I say.

It's the most direct way I know to explain it. One of the hardest things about being Edie's owner is that people don't believe me when I say she's fearful. They either dismiss her behavior as normal puppy cautiousness, or they assume I'm overreacting and feel compelled to step in and "fix" Edie themselves. They insist on petting her even though she's backing away, and when they can't win her over, they take it personally. They try harder. They keep reaching for Edie with outstretched hands as if they alone have the special magic touch, not realizing that most dogs, including mine, don't like things coming at their heads. I know they are just trying to help, but they've probably never met a dog with clinical fear, and don't realize that they're making things worse. But I totally get it. Until I met Edie, I was just as naive, and would have done the exact same thing. It's hard to accept that a puppy doesn't see your kind heart.

So now, to stop people in their tracks, I blurt out that she's on Prozac. It usually does the trick. When it doesn't, I force a smile and ask them to please step away from my puppy. If I have to ask again, I drop the smile.

Thankfully Betsy does not feel the need to show me how to train my own dog, or talk me out of the diagnosis. She gives Edie a wide berth and doesn't try to coax her from the truck. Chase seems to sense that Edie needs her privacy, too, and returns to the porch to stretch out and rest on the cool pavestone.

"She might come out again, but if not, we'll just have to try again another time," I say. There's no judgment or apology in my voice. I've gotten to the point where I don't feel ashamed of Edie or myself anymore. I just explain to other people that my dog is different, and sometimes needs to do things her own way.

"Edie doesn't do well with novelty," I say. "I'll have to introduce her to your house a little bit at a time."

Betsy asks me if Edie is a rescue dog, which is what everyone assumes. I almost wish we had saved Edie from a shelter because then we'd at least have a plausible explanation for her neuroses. I've answered this question countless times, but still I feel the need to defend myself every time it comes up. I roll out my dog résumé for Betsy just in case she thinks I'm a golden retriever novice, and then tick off the laundry list of remedies we've tried, even exaggerating Edie's role in our move to Carmel Valley to convince her we've gone above and beyond for our pup.

"Have you ever heard of DOGTV?" she asks.

The word tinkles like a little silver bell in my ear. Could there be something out there that I'd missed?

I listen, rapt, as she describes a channel created specifically for dogs, with nonstop streaming videos of other dogs. There are videos designed to calm dogs, or stimulate them, or to introduce them to unfamiliar sights such as swimming pools, crowds, or horses. People turn it on to keep their dogs company when they leave them home alone, or to expose their dogs to potentially scary things in safe, controlled doses.

"Chase loves it."

Ten minutes later, I'm calling up the DOGTV website. The creators claim their programming is informed by scientific studies of the way dogs see and hear. The colors are more saturated, and the ambient chill soundtrack is chosen for its healing sound frequencies. The camera angles are shot from a dog's point of view, focused on things in constant motion, because dogs like to watch movement. I'm not ready to commit to a monthly television subscription *for our dog*, but the wise people at DOGTV have already guessed this about me and offer a free two-week trial.

"Hey Edie, c'mere, sister!" I call from the couch where I'm holding the remote. She curls up next to me, and I choose a video from DOGTV's relaxation series and press Play. A big black Labrador's face fills the forty-five-inch television screen. He's stretched out on a Persian rug, his big pink tongue dangling out one side of his mouth, his eyelids heavy with sleep as classical piano music plays.

Edie hops into a sitting position, transfixed. Hackles raised, she emits a low, rumbling growl. I have to agree with Edie; this creature is looming down on us, even though all he's doing is falling asleep. It's informative to see the world through Edie's eyes. With the camera eye-to-eye with the Lab, I feel like he could devour me in one bite if he wanted to. Things do look scary from this vantage point.

"Okay, not that one."

I switch to a video of a woman throwing a Frisbee for two mutts in the surf. Edie is on all fours now, standing on the couch, leaning toward the screen. She's following the arc of the Frisbee with her eyes, fixated on this new toy she's never seen before.

"Get it, Edie!" I say.

The woman tosses the Frisbee to her left, and it sails outside the camera frame. Edie thinks the woman threw it into the room and leaps off the couch to catch it. She turns in circles a few times, sniffing the air, certain it's here somewhere. Then Edie looks to me, assuming I must have it.

"Oh, buddy, almost," I say, patting the space next to me on the couch. Edie hops back up and sits pressed against me, glued to the TV once more, waiting for the next throw.

I'm shocked she's into it. As a control test, I switch to regular TV to see if she keeps watching. Nope. Once the dogs are replaced by talking humans, she's completely bored. She looks away, rests her head on my lap, and sighs. I wait a few minutes, until she's almost asleep, and turn DOGTV back on to two terriers pulling on either end of a rope toy. There's a cartoon soundtrack punctuated by a child's voice saying, "Good boy!" Edie's ears perk up and she lifts her head toward the screen. She sees the dogs and sits back up, engrossed once more.

I put down the remote and buy a subscription.

Edie learns a new word. *TV.* All I have to do is say it, and she runs to the couch and stares at the television, waiting for me to turn it on. We watch ten to fifteen minutes of DOGTV every morning while I drink my coffee. We watch videos of dogs swimming in lakes. Urban dogs playing in fenced dog parks with traffic whirring nearby. Puppies chasing colored balls. Dogs running agility courses. Some videos show flying birds, or underwater shots of coral reefs, or trippy geometric patterns. I start to look forward to TV time with Edie. I like the morning ritual of it, and I must admit I find it a little soothing too, especially the abstract videos that look like spilled ink blossoming into Rorschach patterns, or the drone flyover shots of tropical islands. I bet people who don't even have pets watch this. I imagine they're the same kind of people who also like groovy laser shows.

Edie watches all of it, and I wonder if she's learning by watching dogs do the things she's too afraid to do. I text photos of Edie watching TV to Betsy, and she pings me back with shots of Chase and her cat, Valentina, watching the same show. We crack ourselves up with our cleverness.

Ron and Betsy take a keen interest in Edie's progress, and

bring her a plush toy each time they visit, something plucked from Chase's monthly Bark Box delivery of dog treats and toys. I begin doubling my batch of dog cookies I make from leftover sourdough starter for Chase. The four of us dote on our dogs unapologetically, and we can spend an inordinate amount of time discussing our pets' idiosyncrasies. Ron and Betsy are also grateful Chase has a playmate to relieve his boredom. Since meeting Edie, they say his habit of clacking his teeth when he's bored is going away.

After the third visit to see Chase, Edie warms up to Betsy and Ron's house and stops hiding in my truck. We chuck balls into the large sloping hill behind their house, and the two dogs roar off competing to fetch them. Chase is having such a positive influence on Edie that it gives me the idea to enlist him to get her to take a walk. The four of us hatch a plan to walk Chase and Edie toward each other on the road. If Edie sees Chase in the distance, maybe she'll push through her fear to get to him. She just might do it for love.

This time Jenn takes the reins. Again, Edie lopes up the driveway, full of chutzpah. This time we turn left instead of right.

"If she can't do it, that's just information. That's all it is," Jenn says, preparing me for disappointment. "Don't put a value on it."

"Right. It is what it is." I sound phony, even to myself.

Before Edie has a chance to falter, Jenn tosses biscuits ahead of her on the asphalt, and Edie scurries to eat each one. We make it halfway to Chase's house using this Hansel and Gretel technique. I realize I'm holding my breath. Edie has never gone this far. If she stops now, I'd consider this a win.

Then, she sees him. Edie halts, only this time her tail is curved up, and it's wagging.

"Ooooh! Is that Chase? Do you wanna go see Chase?" Jenn squeals.

Before I realize what's happening, Jenn has unclipped Edie from the leash.

Edie surges forward, muscles rippling in the morning light, pulled by the magnetic force of attraction. She sprints past three more houses as we jump up and down, fist-pumping like sports fans whose losing team just clinched the championship. Edie doesn't stop until she's nose to nose with Chase.

Our little underdog is soaring.

15

Leap of Faith

Once Edie figured out that the prize at the end of the road is Chase, she's willing to join us on neighborhood walks. She demands it, in fact. If she hears one of us say Chase's name, she'll run to the front gate and post there until we take her down the road to see him. We visit her boyfriend multiple times a week, sometimes twice in the same day.

Cars are still a problem, though. So we came up with a counterconditioning plan to train Edie to withstand them. We can hear a vehicle coming long before we see it, giving us time to move Edie away from the road and cue her to sit. I straddle Edie's body with my legs and pet her to give her a sense of protection and feed her a treat as the vehicle approaches. Once we can see it, I let loose an avalanche of cookies. It helps distract Edie from her fear, but, more importantly, rewires her brain to link cars with treats. Now, when she hears a car engine, she takes herself to the roadside and sits, getting herself in position for a delicious bonanza. Her bogeyman is now her sugar daddy.

Being able to walk Edie after thinking we never could makes me float on air. It makes me happier than Christmas, happier than winning a race with my crew team, happier than ice cream. To do such an ordinary thing with our most uncommon dog is such a surprising achievement that every step feels like a miracle. If there's one thing Edie has done for us, it's to teach us how to appreciate the little things, and appreciate them full tilt. I watch her trot alongside me, stopping to sniff the grass and inspect storm drains and I revel in her every move as if she's leaving a trail of gold dust behind her. Walking outside with Edie, the colors seem brighter, the birdsong more melodious, the air sweeter. Walking with Stella was always easy, but it was never this *blissful*.

I remember there were times with Layla and Stella when I skipped their daily walk because it was too cold outside, or I was pressed at work, or I was feeling lazy. I didn't know how fortunate I was to even have such a choice to make. I never appreciated how I could take those dogs anywhere without a second thought. Depending on my mood, we'd trek the forests or the beach or walk to the Castro to people-watch. I never had to consider how many people might be there, whether it might spook my dog, and never had to lug a bag of emergency gear in case they had a bad reaction. I was free and didn't even realize it.

It may be that our road is the only place Edie will feel safe to walk, and that would be 100 percent okay with me. I will never shortchange her and say I'm "too busy" because this one success with Edie will never stop making me smile. Taking the same path every day with Edie isn't about how much we won't see, but about slowing down to appreciate the complexity of sameness. Our street can be our case study—we'll learn to spot the seasons creeping up on the trees, the changing colors of the sky, and the flight patterns of the birds. I won't ever tire of taking this walk with Edie.

We are deepening our connection to the land, and to our new community. Walking a dog is a great way to meet the neighbors. We discover there's a mechanic and a veterinarian on our street, as well as a couple that hosts outdoor movie nights in their driveway. We meet an old-timer who knew my grandfather, who tells us about the pigs he plans to raise on his property. Another neighbor offers eggs from her chickens. The two men who were the first to build a home in the neighborhood a half century ago, now octogenarians, invite us over for canasta. We find the street's master gardener, who gives us succulents from her garden. A Latin jazz musician invites us to a concert on his back porch. A naturalist enlists us to help him rescue steelhead trout from the drying Cachagua Creek in summer.

And everyone has a dog. Edie befriends a spicy Queensland heeler named Stormy who loves nothing better than to herd Edie, roaring after her at top speed and nipping her ankles. The first time I witnessed this, I worried Stormy was scaring the daylights out of Edie, but after a few minutes they stopped and Stormy took a turn as the sheep, with Edie mimicking a working cattle dog, dirt and spit flying.

At the end of the street, Edie befriended a white terrier mix with Cleopatra eyeliner named Kita that was orphaned after a 6.4 magnitude earthquake rocked Puerto Rico. We watched Edie temper her play for this little bit-bit, lowering herself to her belly so Kita could get a fair shot. Kita, all fifteen pounds of her, whirred in circles around Edie, then came in for the attack, boxing Edie's face with her two miniature paws. Edie indulged Kita for a few seconds, then opened her jaws wide and engulfed Kita's head, holding her there with a soft mouth. When Edie let go, the wiry hair on Kita's head was slobbered into a mini-mohawk. Kita shook it off and went right back for more.

When Jenn comes home for the long winter holiday, I catch her up on Edie's expanding network of dog friends. When we walk Edie, I point to the houses and tell her who lives there, what their profession is, and the names of their dogs. Most of the time, the dogs come running out to play with Edie, and our walks turn into long, progressive playdates. Their owners come out, too. It's not that we wouldn't have met our neighbors on our own, it's just that with a dog, these relationships happen faster. When you love a dog, and you see how much someone else also loves their dog, you immediately have a good feeling about them.

When Christmas morning comes, it actually snows. Only for fifteen minutes, and the flakes melt the instant they touch the ground, but it counts as a Carmel Valley miracle. We run outside and stick out our tongues, trying to catch a flake. Edie bounds out the door with us, and skids to a stop on the slippery deck. She looks up at the white stuff falling out of the sky and tries to taste it, too. She snaps at the snowflakes, completely confused why a solid in the air doesn't translate to a solid in her mouth. Thinking she missed the catch, she whips around in circles, searching the deck, looking for the snowflakes that have already melted. Edie looks up at us for an explanation, her ears aloft and head tilted, stunned by this momentary suspension of the laws of physics—how a thing can fall but not hit the ground.

"Stay right there!" Jenn says, running inside to get her camera.

Our puppy is curious; she is confused, but she is not scared. It's Edie's Christmas gift to me and Jenn, watching her investigate snow instead of run from it.

Back inside the house, I open a present from Jenn. It's an oversize photobook she made, titled *Edith Is Scared*. It's Edie's emotional journey in pictures, beginning with the day we brought her home. Even as a tiny puppy, she had an expression that we've since come to recognize as wariness. It's a furrowing of the brows and a clenched frown signaling uncertainty. Page after page, Edie has that same look. It's there when she's cowering between my legs to get away from a puppy. And again at the surf's edge, or when she's refusing to get out of a car, or looking down a hiking trail at someone approaching in the distance. If only we could have read her body language back then, we wouldn't have taken her all the places we did. We can see now what we couldn't see then.

The photographs allow me to see Edie through Jenn's camera lens, and what I notice is that my wife also feels a growing tenderness toward Edie. Jenn diligently curated hundreds of photos to document our journey with our one-of-a-kind dog. Reflecting on these frozen moments in time, I can pause from the constant work of rehabilitating Edie to appreciate how far our puppy, and we, have come. Jenn is showing me what she sees when she looks at Edie. My wife sees the fear and confusion inside our puppy, but she also sees the promise.

Toward the end of the book, Edie's tense expression changes. The muscles in her face are more relaxed, and she has an open-mouthed smile. She has evolved from a puppy that prefers to observe the world to one that wants to explore it. Jenn captures her bringing us sticks from the dry creek bed, trying to tug a eucalyptus branch out of my hands, and standing at the base of a fence post, staring back up at that red-tailed hawk as it hunts for ground squirrels.

My favorite picture is of me kissing Edie's ear at Monastery Beach. Edie is looking over my shoulder, smiling with her eyelids half-mast in contentment. Beneath it, Jenn wrote a caption: "Edith can tolerate the world in little bits."

That's how I know that Jenn loves Edie for who she is. My wife has never been one to talk about her feelings. I've learned to know what she's thinking by watching what she does. And right now she is showing me, rather than telling me, that she has accepted Edie as part of the definition of us. Her photobook is a celebration of our puppy's strengths, and indirectly, ours. Jenn's resolve strengthens mine. It's the only Christmas gift I want, to be grateful for how far all three of us have come.

Later that week, when Edie and I turn onto Ron and Betsy's driveway, we see that Ron has built an obstacle course for Chase out of PVC pipe. There's an agility jump, with two vertical posts about three feet apart that hold a removable horizontal crossbar that can be placed in four different positions: twelve, sixteen, twenty, or twenty-four inches off the ground. He's also built something that looks somewhat like a bicycle rack, with a row of waist-high PVC poles staked evenly apart. The space in between each pole is about the width of Chase. These contraptions draw Edie's attention, too, and she sits quietly by my side, eyeing them suspiciously.

"Check this out," he says.

Ron calls Chase to sit at his feet near one end of the row of upright PVC poles. He pulls a Ziploc baggie from his jeans pocket and lets Chase see the piece of dehydrated turkey frank he hides in his fist. Chase laser-locks his gaze on Ron's hand, salivating with anticipation.

"Weave!" Ron commands, moving his fist in an S-curve between the poles, just in front of Chase's snout. Chase follows, fishtailing through poles, alternating left and right around each one, intent on the promise of the morsel of turkey meat. He weaves through all the spaces without touching the poles.

"Bravo!" I clap, as Chase inhales his treat. Edie leaves my side and races up to Ron for some turkey frank. The dogs have figured out that whatever one of them gets, the other will get, too.

"Edie, weave!" Ron says, trying to lead her to repeat Chase's performance through the row of poles. Edie jumps in the air to try to reach the meat in his hand.

"Ah, good enough," he says, dropping the treat in her mouth.

Ron explains that Chase is practicing for an upcoming obedience rally, which, I learn, is an obstacle course that owners walk with their dogs in heeling position, scoring points when their dog completes an obedience task at each station. Dogs demonstrate U-turns, circle their owners, step left or right or walk over obstacles. Ribbons are awarded. Chase has a corkboard full of them.

Ron and Betsy also take Chase to scent-work classes, where dogs learn to sniff out items the trainer hides in an open field. It's something fun to do with your dog, but also it helps satisfy dogs' natural seeking instinct. I wish so badly that I could take Edie to these kind of enrichment classes, but I fight back my disappointment. I pull my mind back to what Edie can do. She can take a walk to see all her friends. She's thriving within her small radius, and I need to keep reminding myself to stay in that happy place with her.

"Can Chase do the jump?" I ask.

Betsy puts the bar on the lowest rung, and makes Chase sit about five feet away from the jump, then walks to the other side. "Chase, jump!" she calls. He gets a running start and pushes himself up with his back legs, and clears the bar with the panache of a blue-ribbon winner. I can see why Betsy and Ron like this. It's dazzling to be able to communicate with your pet, to ask for an action and have the dog understand and give it so enthusiastically. The reward goes both ways.

"Good boy!" Betsy says, rubbing his neck.

"Should we give Edie a try?" Ron asks.

The quick answer is no. The long answer is I want to be gracious, but I also know my dog and she does not like to be forced into things. She will never just take a flying leap, literally. Ron has Chase demonstrate a few more times for Edie, and then it's her turn. I get her to sit while I walk to the other side of the jump, and then I hold out a cookie. I notice she's grimacing, which by now I recognize is one of her early signs that she's starting to get scared.

"Edie, jump!"

She approaches the crossbar, then walks around the left side of the jump and sits before me, drawing much praise and applause from all of us, because in Edie's world, that was success. She gets a prize for being willing to get close to the strange thing. We continue a few more times, with Chase executing the jump, and Edie jogging behind him, all the way to the bar, and then cutting left at the last second and running around it.

"What if we remove the bar? Maybe Edie will walk through the two poles," I say.

Which is exactly what she does, running through the empty space and into my arms, making me so proud.

"You are such a smart dog!" I say, giving Edie her favorite reward, a full-body rubdown. She rolls on her back and exposes her belly to make sure I don't miss any spots. Her eyes close in bliss and her tongue lolls out one side of her mouth. The grimace is gone, and in its place, I could swear, is one huge, goofy grin.

Two days later, we are back for another playdate. Jenn and I are standing in the driveway, next to the agility jump, and no one is around. Ron is still watering his new fruit trees in the backyard, and Betsy and Chase are still indoors.

"Hey Edie, sit here," I say. I unclip her leash and walk to the other side of the jump, crouch down and hold out a cookie.

"Edie, jump!"

She runs. And as my jaw falls open, she leaps with all four paws, sailing over the bar like a show horse, and sticks the landing at my feet. It's like she'd been doing it her whole life. I don't know whether to laugh or cry, so I do both.

"Edie, you did it!" I squeal. The exhilaration feels like I just walked through a secret VIP door I'd never seen before and arrived at the best party of my life. I ask Edie to do it again. And again. And again. She clears the hurdle, back and forth, back and forth, springing into the air with a flourish.

"She really *is* a smart dog," Jenn whispers, more to herself than to me.

"That bar is on the second rung!" shouts Betsy. I look up to see she and Chase are watching from the porch.

"Can you believe this?" I shout.

I realize that I'd grossly underestimated Edie. I'd short-changed her, and myself, by assuming she didn't have it in her. Meanwhile, Edie saw the jump, thought about it for forty-eight hours, then decided she was ready. In my research, I'd read that agility tricks are confidence boosters for dogs, and sometimes used to help fearful dogs overcome their anxiety. For dogs like Edie, this jump isn't just a morale builder, it's medicine. It's teaching her that it feels good to be brave.

Alerted by our shouting, Ron comes jogging up the hill and into the driveway.

"What's going on?"

"Edie's jumping," I say.

"Hey, hey! Way to go, Edie!" Ron cheers.

I don't let Ron and Betsy see, but I'm crying behind my sunglasses as I set Edie into position to demonstrate for Ron. She did something brave, and because of it, her self-assurance will inch up a micromillimeter. I'm not happy because she performed a trick and made me look good. I used to feel that way with Stella, showing everyone how I taught her to do a handshake. This time, I'm happy for *Edie*. And that's the thing about troubled dogs; while they cause so much stress, on the rare occasions they bring joy, the overwhelming flood of gratitude is so intense that it more than makes up for all the difficulty they've caused. Their lows are lower, yet their highs are astronomically higher.

"Hey, I have an idea," said Ron. He puts Edie and Chase side by side, then makes them stay in position as he walks to the other side of the jump. Jenn gets ready to take a photo with her phone.

"Chase, Edie! Jump!" Ron shouts.

The dogs take off with their sides pressed against one another, and leap in tandem over the bar. Jenn snaps the photo.

"Oh, you gotta see this," she says, handing me her phone.

Edie and Chase are cheek to cheek, hovering above the jump, with Edie's left ear flopped onto Chase's forehead, and she looks like she is laughing hysterically. It takes my breath away to see them together like this, literally supporting one another in mid-air.

16

Thunder

I'm coveting Kevin's retro tool belt. It's ergonomically correct, with leather suspenders that cross in an X between his shoulder blades, with thick, tan suede pockets encircling his hips holding a tidy selection of Allen wrenches, wire strippers, and assorted electrician's whatnot. His getup conveys confidence, making me trust that he can rewire our circuit breaker so we can run our home off a generator if the lights go out. Winter storms are a little extra in these parts, according to our neighbors, who were a tad concerned we city mice hadn't thought about getting a source of backup power when we moved in.

So when 2020 rolled around, we bumped the bathroom remodel down the list and invested in a 250-pound, gas-powered Honda 6500 on wheels, which now that it's here, I have to admit makes me feel a little pioneer-badass. It's about three feet wide and comes up to my knee, and with its gleaming red paint and chrome it looks as though it's also capable of mowing the meadow and making me an espresso afterward. Kevin's ready to show me the sequence of steps to fire it up.

"Wait until I say 'action!'" I say with a touch of big sister bossiness, as I press the video button on my phone. "Okay, action!"

Kevin gamely narrates as he uncoils a long black electrical cord coming from the transfer station he'd installed on the east side of our house. He plugs it into the 240-volt outlet on the generator. Next, he pulls the Frankenstein lever sticking out of the transfer station to switch our home from utility to generator power. He puts the key into the ignition on the Honda and turns it. The generator hops an inch off the ground, waking with a shuddering roar. Our house lights click back on and the refrigerator hums back to life.

"IT'S ALIVE!" I shout, then wonder if Kevin, whose hair has yet to turn gray, even gets my Gene Wilder reference. His expression is blank and then I see his mouth moving, but the words are swallowed by the rat-a-tat-tat.

"WHAT'D YOU SAY?" I holler back.

Just then I spot Edie rounding the corner. I instinctively lunge for the kill switch on the generator before she has a heart attack. But before I reach it, I notice her body lacks any telltale signs of stress. Her tail is relaxed, her head is up and mouth closed, and she's simply taking slow, curious steps toward the generator. I decide to sit this one out and see what happens. She circles the generator, her nose just inches from it, sniffing. I'm astounded. Canine hearing is four times stronger than ours, so I imagine the sound enters her ears like a whistling freight train. Even a typical dog would be a little more cautious than this, or look back at me for reassurance, yet here's my timid dog, practically waltzing around it.

"Wow," says Kevin, watching her. He must have seen many a dog meet many a generator, but even he seems impressed. I press the video recorder on my phone again. Jenn is never going to believe this.

Satisfied the beast is inanimate, Edie saunters over to me and lays down on the cool bricks by my feet. It feels like someone just gave me a gold star for all the work Edie and I have put in together. A pinwheel of pride spins inside me.

My hands are shaking as I text the video to Jenn with the message "I *swear* this is our dog." I wait for the three flickering dots to show up, but Jenn must be deep in the middle of some police business. It is two in the afternoon, after all, but to me this breakthrough feels interruption worthy, as important as fighting crime. I wait a few beats longer, and when she doesn't respond immediately, I know it's because she can't. We'll have to celebrate this achievement later, but I know it will lose something in the retelling. Like a parent who tells the other parent what it was like when the baby took their first steps, it's just not the same as bearing witness to it.

Edie is sixteen months old now. These days it feels like she's on the precipice of something. Occasionally, I'll notice a new way she carries her body or ignores one of her triggers that takes me by surprise. These behavior changes are so slight they're almost imperceptible; they're mundane things most dogs do like walking by a garbage can or scrabbling over a pile of woodchips, but because our dog is starting to do them, they take on monumental meaning. They're precious glimmers of reassurance that we are doing something right to help Edie cope.

Most of these hidden triumphs come when Edie and I are alone during the week, so I save them up so Edie can demonstrate them to Jenn on weekends. Jenn comes home every five days to a slightly braver dog, one who can walk by the snarling dog behind the neighbor's wooden fence without running back home, or who can thrust her body headfirst into the bushes to retrieve her ball, rather than whimpering for us to get it for her. But sometimes Jenn sees our puppy changing, too. One morning we woke to the telltale thump of the dog doors opening and closing. We both bolted upright, talking at once.

"Was that?"

"Did she?"

We tossed off the covers and ran to the kitchen window to find Edie wandering around the yard sniffing. After five months of cowering before the saloon dog door, Edie had chosen her own private moment to conquer it. I slid open the kitchen window and called her back. She looked over her shoulder, turned, and ran through the dog door into the kitchen like it was nothing.

"Go figure," Jenn had said.

When Ron and Betsy hear about our new generator, they come over to check it out. When one of us gets something new for the home, say a Weedwacker or a rainwater catch system, it's not long before an identical one will appear at the other's house. The four of us have a healthy sense of me-tooism that allows us to be country novices together, and to look out for one another. Whenever one of us makes the twenty-minute drive down the mountain on the narrow, switchback road to Jerome's Market in the village, we text to see if we can pick up groceries for the other.

Edie can smell Chase outside her dog door before she sees him. She springs up from the kitchen floor and arrows through the dog door with so much gusto I worry she'll take out Betsy or Ron at the knees. The two dogs roar off in a whirlwind of fur, headed for the canyon as the three of us jog to keep up with them. I catch a glimpse of Edie as she bounds after Chase into the tall sagebrush, where he waits to ambush her. They go back and forth like that, taking turns as the hunter and the prey, playing a canine version of hide-and-seek on a looping racetrack they've worn into the hillside.

"I love how much they love each other," Ron says, clapping his hands and adding his delighted encouragement. "Hey-hey-hey-yeah, that's it!"

Just then the honeyed light of the waning sun takes on a purplish hue, and we hear what sounds like a massive delivery truck downshifting into low gear at the bottom of the canyon. A second later we hear a loud ripping sound overhead, and a twig of white lightning blinks above the ridgetop. And just as my brain grasps that this is a thunderstorm, Edie comes whizzing out of the bushes straight for me, muscles rippling, claws digging for speed in her signature panic run. I haven't seen her do this since we moved in seven months ago.

I thank the Almighty that she's coming toward me instead of disappearing down the mountain. Recently our neighborhood phone tree lit up because a pair of mountain lions were mating below our neighbor's home across the street. A few doors down, another neighbor suspects they were the same pair that killed his miniature horse a few weeks ago. Edie stops before me and I wrap my arms around her, but then the sky booms so loudly that I can feel it in both our chests. Edie's eyes widen into what trainers call "whale eye," where I can see her whites all around her pupil, and she peels off, streaking for the house as Chase comes sauntering out of the thicket wondering what happened to his girlfriend.

"She's scared of the thunder," I call over my shoulder as I hustle after my dog, leaving Ron and Betsy in the meadow as the first drops of rain start to fall. I find Edie panting and shaking, immobilized before the very same dog door she just barreled through just minutes ago. I reach down and push the saloon doors aside to let her in and she beelines to my walk-in closet and curls herself into a tight ball. I drape a fuzzy blanket over her and tuck the corners under her body.

"Oh bunny, you're okay. I know, that was scary. Hang on, Mama's got you." I kiss her on her forehead between her ears and tell her to wait just a second as I go back out to apologize to Ron and Betsy for the canceled play session. As Edie's makeshift auntie and uncle, they are fully aware of her idiosyncrasies and generously wave it off as they pull out of the driveway, saying there's always tomorrow.

I shut the door knowing that despite whatever I had on my to-do list, the next couple of hours will be dedicated to calming Edie down. But rather than being frustrated or disappointed, I walk to the pantry where I keep Edie's things and begin collecting her therapy gear. I reach for the dog pheromone spray and spritz a few pumps into the air inside my closet, where Edie is still panting, rapid-fire. Next, I slip a gray cotton compression shirt over Edie's head and Velcro its two flaps tight around her torso to swaddle her. I give her two heart-shaped CBD dog cookies, and then toss my pink cotton nightgown on the ground so she can nuzzle in my scent. She looks up at me from the floor, following my every move. I don't know how I can prove this, but I can tell she doesn't want me to go.

"Be right back," I tell her, going to the living room to get the wireless speaker. On my phone, I scroll through my playlists of calming music designed for dogs and choose a song called "At Home Safe." I press Play and my closet fills with the sounds of lapping waves, pan flutes, and Tibetan bowls. Her body uncurls ever so slightly.

I set her water bowl next to her and she gulps at it, splashing water all over my shoes. Thirst quenched, her breathing slows a tiny bit. The thunder has stopped now, and rain is coming down in long, hard lines that sound like pebbles on the skylight. I turn up the dog relaxation music and go back to the living room to find her a toy. I choose her current favorite, a plush maroon octopus, and she pulls it toward her chest with her paws, wriggling to squish it beneath her weight. Maybe it comforts her to know that she is protecting something, too.

I sit on the floor next to my trembling dog and massage her ears, her forearms, her back. I cluck at her and make quiet kissy noises in her ear. She stress-yawns and shakes her head like she's trying to fling off water, sending gossamer strings of drool around her muzzle. I wipe them off with my shirtsleeve.

"Shhh-shhh, Edie. You're okay. I'm right here. I'm going to stay right here until you feel better. Just you and me."

Sitting on the fuzzy blanket with Edie pressed up against my leg, I realize I don't mind this. It's nice to just be quiet in a cozy place and listen to the rain. It reminds me of how much time I used to have as a child, to sit and just observe things— a ladybug on a stalk of grass, or a cat taking a bath in the sun. I used to have so much more time to just sit and think. I look up at my clothes and each shirt, dress, hat, brings up a memory. There's the faux pink sheepskin and fur "Macy Gray" coat I got for ten dollars at a neighbor's garage sale, my grandpa's lime-green checkered square-dancing shirt, the linen dress I bought on Etsy to wear to my brother's wedding in Italy. Edie feels secure in my closet because it contains my scent; I feel secure here because it contains my history. I've always loved the organization, and security, of closets. I used to hide in them too when I was a young girl. I would retreat to my closet whenever my life got to be too much—when I missed my dad or when my mentally ill mother became too scary. I can relate to Edie's chosen location for self-imposed time-outs.

We sit like this for nearly an hour. Edie has relaxed enough to roll onto her side, but she keeps one paw on me. I check my watch and see that it's past her dinnertime. Maybe feeding her will help. I'm certain she'll leap from the closet once she hears her kibble hit her bowl, but this is the one time her Pavlovian response fails to kick in. I know she heard the clatter of her kibble; she can hear us even thinking about feeding her. I wait a few more seconds and then return to the closet and place her bowl before her. She gobbles the meal while remaining on her belly.

She looks up and finally, finally, she stops panting.

I break into a smile, even though no one is there to receive it. *I was able to do this*, I think. I brought my dog a little peace. I am grateful that I can keep her safe, and in a counterintuitive way, Edie's fragility gives me a profound sense of purpose. I feel like a good…mother.

Which is something I never thought I wanted to be. I avoided motherhood because I never knew what it was supposed to look like. Deep down I always worried that I had inherited my mother's belief that to give birth is to die yourself, to forfeit your individual happiness for the drudgery and subservience of parenthood. Knowing how lonely it feels to spend a childhood trying to get your parents to pay attention to you made me terrified that I might put my own child through the same thing, even without realizing it. I'm sure everyone worries about being a good parent, but I didn't trust that I could overcome the double whammy of my DNA and my broken childhood to even know what nurturing looks like.

But Edie, in her slow, deliberate, neurotic way, is proving me wrong. As a vulnerable creature, she will need a lifetime of protection from the overstimulation of the outside world—a marathon of caretaking to ensure she doesn't get hurt or killed when fear hijacks her brain. Knowing that I can be Edie's protector and that she can trust me to be her sanctuary, shows me that nurturing doesn't have to be experienced to be learned. Unselfish love is a natural instinct, one that I may not be so bad at after all. Belatedly, I am becoming a mother of sorts. With Edie, I didn't get the dog I wanted; I got the dog I needed.

It took a sensitive dog to show me that my thinking about pet dogs was insensitive. In the beginning, my only concern was how to fix Edie so she'd become the dog I'd been somehow cheated out of. I gave myself arbitrary goals to make myself feel better. She'll probably be fine in eight months, I'd say. When she wasn't, I revised. All she needs is a little more time; certainly a year should do it. I kept giving myself assignments and deadlines, trying to force the confusion of Edie into a work plan as if that would somehow enable me to wrestle this problem to the ground. Now none of that matters. I don't expect, want, or need her to change. I just enjoy watching over her every day and being there for her when she gets scared.

If I were still ruminating about all the hikes and road trips and sidewalk strolls that I'd had to give up with Edie, I'd be missing all the chances she's giving me to evolve. I'd miss

the point of Edie, which is to push me, kicking and screaming, to grow into a person capable of unconditional love. It's
easy to love a dog like Stella; it's the difficult ones that truly
challenge us to dig deep within ourselves to find out how
far we are willing to go, how much we are willing to give
up, to bond with another complicated soul. Unlike all my
other dogs that seamlessly molded themselves into my routine, Edie demands that I become a different person for her.
Once I learned to stop fighting that, I discovered that there's
something perfect about pairing her imperfection with my
perfectionism. They cancel each other out, just like algebra.

Sitting with her now in the closet as the sun breaks through
the rain clouds, she falls into a light snore and her paws twitch
in a dream. The spa music is calming me, as well, and I rest
my head against the wall and close my eyes. It's been only
sixteen months with Edie, but she and I are completely different beings now, each having been altered by the other.
Together, we can help one another scale the rockiness of life.
I can teach her that the world is not out to get her, and she
can teach me the pointlessness of trying to get the world to
bend to my will. I have stopped pushing her to go faster, and
she has showed me how much more of the world I can see if
I slow down to stop the blur.

I tiptoe from the closet and return with a tennis ball.

She lifts her head to consider my offer.

"Wanna go outside?" I ask, holding her prize aloft.

She bounds out of the closet in big galumphing leaps, toenails scrabbling on the wooden floor after the ball that I throw
into the living room. She pounces, seizes the ball, and tosses
it into the air for herself so she can keep chasing it.

Edie is back.

EPILOGUE

2020

As she neared her second birthday, Edie fell obsessively in love with one of her toys. It's a blue-and-orange squeaky ball that fits in the cup of the long-handled ball launcher called a Chuckit! She carries that rubber ball in her mouth all day long, on the off chance someone will throw it for her. If no one is available, she'll walk to higher ground, watch it roll away for a bit, then tear after it, entertaining herself until she stretches out on her belly like a frog with her legs behind her, gasping for air with that dang ball wedged in one side of her mouth. She cuddles her ball when she sleeps, and I've even seen her get up in the middle of the night, walk into the kitchen, and drop it into her water bowl while she drinks, then carry it dripping back to bed.

Jenn calls it her "binky."

I think this simple plaything gives Edie a sense of accomplishment that boosts the serotonin in her brain. It's just a theory, but when we lob it into the canyon, she runs after it at NASCAR speed, sometimes leaping to snatch it out of the air. She dive-bombs into chamise bushes to extract it, and I get the distinct sense that the hunt makes her feel more alive. It's a bravery feedback loop she'd discovered on her own, and Edie deserves credit for participating in her own recovery, for teaching us how to teach her to feel better. We even tried giving her the same ball in a different color. She wasn't interested. It must be blue-and-orange. And we must never walk out the door without it.

Jenn has a lot more time to throw it for her. In June, she joined me and Edie full-time, deciding to retire a year early rather than risk her health working in a crowded city during an out-of-control coronavirus pandemic. Lockdown suited her. Jenn started a victory garden of vegetable seedlings, bought some colored pencils, and enrolled in online bird drawing courses.

We were only two months into our newfound domesticity, when in mid-August we were awoken by an unprecedented dry electrical storm that lit the California skies royal purple. The ominous spectacle went on for hours, and shockingly, Edie slept through it. We turned on our police scanner and reports of wildfires were already rolling in. The calls didn't stop.

By morning, the air was choked with smoke. There were 367 new fires raging in California, which was already suffering its worst fire season since the 1800s. There were so many fires burning across the state that there weren't enough firefighters to get to all of them. Our home was in the potential path of the River Fire burning to our north in Salinas, and the Dolan Fire to our south in Big Sur. But then the unthinkable happened. The Carmel Fire erupted, less than two miles from our house.

I had ten minutes to evacuate. It was just enough time to call Jenn, who was shopping at Costco, to retract the pool cover, gather the fire extinguishers and put them outside the front door, load the pets into the truck, grab a laptop, the police scanner, and flee through billowing smoke. Edie evacuated with that blue-and-orange ball in her mouth.

Our mountain road was blocked by firetrucks, forcing me to drive a half hour out of the way on the back roads to escape. Ash rained down, and I could hear distant explosions, which I guessed were propane tanks. Several times I had to pull over for sheriff's convoys that came roaring by with lights and sirens blaring, on their way to evacuate my neighbors. I had no cell phone service. By the time I'd reached the valley floor, I could see orange flames on the ridgetop where our house is.

It's hard to describe what it feels like to face the prospect of losing everything you've worked your whole life to build. Caught between unthinkable devastation and euphoric relief that my family was safe, I was trapped in a sort of emotional dead zone. I didn't know what to feel. I was numb and sounds were muted, as if my head was in a pillow. As Edie clung to her ball behind my headrest and Lulu mewled in the passenger seat, I just kept petting our rickety cat and repeating a mantra:

"You're okay. We're all okay. Everyone's okay."

We relocated to a friend's guesthouse in a nearby nature preserve, a quiet idyll with a private lake where both we, and Edie, could try to remain calm. There was nothing to do but wait it out as the winds kept changing direction and sending the Carmel Fire roaring back day after day to swallow more homes on our street.

So that's how we found ourselves under an apocalyptic orange sky, in the middle of a deadly pandemic and potentially homeless, standing at the lake's edge with Edie and her beloved ball. Jenn and I looked like some sort of dystopian refugees in our grubby clothes, fire goggles, and surgical masks. Our host, Cheryl, brought us to the lake to get our minds off things.

Edie splashed along the lake's edge, dropping her ball into an inch or so of water and fishing it back out. She was careful to wade in no higher than her ankles.

Goldens are supposed to be water dogs, bred to swim out and retrieve waterfowl shot down by their owners, and both Layla and Stella lived up to their heritage. They swam in oceans, lakes, estuaries, and every mud puddle they could find. I'd hoped Edie would take to water so she'd have another way to exercise at home, since she was such a homebody. But like so many of my misguided expectations, I'd learned to let that one go.

Jenn threw the ball a foot out, and Edie carefully walked out to her elbows, craned her neck forward as far as it could go, and fetched it from a standing position. All three of us cheered, and I presented her with a cookie when she returned.

"Do it again!" I said.

This time Cheryl grabbed the ball and tossed it out. Way out. Edie would have to swim to get it.

"Oops," she said.

Edie wailed for her binky from the shore, running up and down the water's edge in near hysterics.

"No big deal," I assured Cheryl. "We'll just get her another one."

Edie walked into the lake, crying out for her ball. She

waded all the way to her shoulders this time and stopped, too afraid to take that last step into weightlessness. She looked back to us for help, and Jenn rolled up her pant legs and started out into the lake to rescue Edie's ball.

But once Jenn reached Edie's side, suddenly, our puppy went for it. Our fraidy-cat lifted her paws from the lake bottom and swam. Snorting with exertion, she dog-paddled all the way to her ball, snatched it in her jaws, turned herself around, and swam to shore. We cheered every one of her strokes while we danced in the sand. It was the highpoint in an unrelenting year of uncertainty.

In our darkest hour, when the flames were threatening to take everything from us, when the world was on lockdown with no end in sight, Edie put everything on pause and reminded us that the most precious things can't burn. Watching her paddling into the unknown where her feet couldn't touch the ground, buoyed only by the trust she finally had in us, was her way of showing us that we already had all we needed. We'd been stripped of everything but the bare essentials, yet hadn't realized that none of it was as essential as having all our patient love for Edie come back to us, a millionfold.

We'd made Edie feel safe enough to try.

Edie emerged from the water and dropped her slobbery ball by my feet. I sank to my knees in the slime at the water's edge and threw my arms around her. And in that moment there was no fire, there was no virus, there was just this incredible reminder that we have the power to help one another get through another day.

Edie splashed back into the water and looked back at us over her shoulder, waiting for the next throw. And for the next half hour as she practiced her new skill, we found ourselves smiling for the first time in a very, very long time. Edie picked her moment well. Watching her head bop up and down with each swimming stroke, I realized that as long as we had each other, we still had the capacity to be happy. Whatever happened with the fire, the three of us were going to be okay.

Three weeks later, we were among the lucky ones who still had a home to return to. So were Betsy and Ron. Of the thirty-five homes on our street, seventeen burned to the ground. Of our ten acres, approximately seven were scorched, except for the highest spot where our home is. Flames burned our fence posts on the east side, came into our yard and destroyed part of our orchard, and then stopped within feet of my beehives. Miraculously, the bees stayed put.

Everyone asks us why we think we were spared, and while Jenn mowed a two hundred–foot firebreak around our house, others who did the same still lost their homes. In the end I say fire does what it wants, and we just have to help each other pick up the pieces.

The fire has made us more determined than ever to stay in this fragile place with our sensitive dog. Even though the landscape comes with risks, overall we feel more saved than threatened by living here. Here is where I feel my grandfather watching me. Here is where Jenn and I can discover who we want to be in the second half of our lives. Here is where we can watch Edie forge a new path to bravery, knowing that we saved a gentle soul from getting swallowed by her own fears.

When you get right down to it, Edie never asked for much from us other than time to absorb life more slowly. Gradually, as we learned to accept Edie for the dog she is, we came to appreciate her odd sensitivity and that she will never be an adventurous road dog like Layla or Stella. Edie is a ranch dog, perfectly content to stay in one place for the rest of her days, exploring its endless possibilities. It just took time for us to recognize that our cautious dog is not a failure; she's an individual.

And I had to learn that just because Edie is not the dog I had in mind, our lives with her can be just as rich if I change my idea of what it means to share a life with a dog. Jenn and I were an alternative family to begin with…what's a little more alternative added on? Edie is tearing my to-do list to shreds and forcing me to put her needs first, which is making me grow out of a selfish, untethered adult into a compassionate parent of sorts.

Don't get me wrong; going anywhere new with Edie will always be a royal pain in the ass, requiring contingency plans, and plan Bs, cautious expectations, and backup bottles of Xanax. But just because she isn't the dog we'd hoped for, it doesn't mean that she doesn't deserve our love, or that the way she wants to live is less-than. In the end, we got what we wanted anyway, which was to become closer as a couple, not because our puppy made us laugh, but because she made us cry. And just like most families, ours isn't perfect, but it's ours.

Loving an unusual dog like Edie reminds us that the unexpected is just part of life. Caring for her trains us every day how to embrace unpredictability with a steady grace. Edith, our lovably quirky oddball, has indeed lived up to her namesakes.

And she's rubbing off on us. Edie has turned us into the kind of people who, when a wildfire is bearing down on our house, decide it's a lovely time to go for a swim.

★ ★ ★ ★ ★

ACKNOWLEDGMENTS

First, I'd like to thank Kendra Luck for brokering the rescue of my first golden retriever, Layla. That was in the late '90s, and from that moment forward, my life has been enriched by the constant companionship of dogs.

The title of this book comes from my editor, Erika Imranyi, at Park Row Books, without whom I would be wandering in the dark forest of disjointed paragraphs. Thank you for helping me see that while I thought I was writing a book about our dog, I was really writing about relationships; specifically the intensely personal and life-changing ones we have with our pets. To the dream teams at Park Row Books, Harlequin, and HarperCollins who believed Edie had a larger story to tell, thank you for championing this book.

Group hug with my agents Heather Karpas and Zoe Sandler at ICM Partners; none of this would have been possible without you two dynamos. Thank you, Ken Conner, for reading early drafts and rescuing me on more occasions than I care to admit.

There would be no story, and no book, if Edie's caretakers hadn't stepped in. Huge bow of gratitude to Dr. Angelique Cucaro and Naomi Sims, and the incredibly important work you do to teach pet owners how to communicate with and care for their extraordinary dogs. And I'm indebted to neuroscientist Ari Berman, who used a Zoom link and a pull-apart model of the human brain to help me "see" what fear looks like.

To the friends who volunteered for Team Edie—Mag Donaldson; Barbara Byrnes; Betsy Vobach; Ron Hanik; Tina and Fernando Pennes; Maile and Kathy Smith; Eddy Joaquim; Tracy Bugni; Joe Schwan; Donald and Rachel Sherman; Thomas Heinemann; Debra Gluskin; The Roddas: Dar, Natalie, Jason & JT; Britt and Enrique Rios-Ellis; and Cheryl Thiele—thank you for cheering her on.

For cheering me on with your writing wisdom, I want to thank my very first friend, Elvina Scott. Ever since we got kicked out of Mr. Pomeroy's fourth-grade class for giggling too much, I knew we'd chosen each other.

Every sunset over the Santa Lucia Mountains I dedicate to Kathy Baker and Sal Rombi, who brought us home. There will never be enough words to thank you for giving us this backdrop to the rest of our lives, and for giving Edie enough space to become the dog she always wanted to be.

And to my mountain-mama-in-law, Mary Sanborn, thanks for your memories, which greatly strengthened this story. Your daughter learned courage from you.

To my wife, Jenn, thank you for always saying yes, even to things that make you a little squeamish, like me writing about you. For your love and understanding, I owe you one. So here it is, preserved in ink: *You get to choose our next dog.*

And thank you to all the people who rescue, foster, rehabilitate, and give dogs the love they deserve. Keep on keepin' on.

And I think it's only right that the last word goes to Edie, who, if she could speak, would thank the following friends for showing her that there's nothing to fear:

Artist: Mag Donaldson

FURTHER READING

Animals in Translation: Using Autism to Decode Animal Behavior, Temple Grandin, 2013

Animals Make Us Human, Temple Grandin, 2009

The Archaeology of Mind: Neuroevolutionary Origins of Human Emotions, Jaak Panksepp and Lucy Biven, 2012

Are We Smart Enough To Know How Smart Animals Are? Frans de Waal, 2017

The Cautious Canine: How to Help Dogs Conquer Their Fears, Patricia B. McConnell, 2005

Come Back, Como: Winning the Heart of a Reluctant Dog, Steven Wynn, 2009

Dog Is My Co-Pilot: Great Writers on the World's Oldest Friendship, from the editors of the *Bark* magazine, 2003

Dog Medicine: How My Dog Saved Me From Myself, Julie Barton, 2015

The Education of Will: Healing a Dog, Facing My Fears, Reclaiming My Life, Patricia B. McConnell, 2018

For the Love of a Dog: Understanding Emotion in You and Your Best Friend, Patricia B. McConnell, 2007

Free Days With George: Learning Life's Little Lessons from One Very Big Dog, Colin Campbell, 2015

From Fearful to Fear Free: A Positive Program to Free Your Dog from Anxiety, Fears, and Phobias, Marty Becker, Mikkel Becker, Lisa Radosta, Wailani Sung, 2018

Gizelle's Bucket List: My Life with a Very Large Dog, Lauren Fern Watt, 2017

How Dogs Love Us: A Neuroscientist and His Adopted Dog Decode the Canine Brain, Gregory Berns, 2013

Lily and the Octopus, Steven Rowley, 2017

Mama's Last Hug: Animal Emotions and What They Tell Us about Ourselves, Frans de Waal, 2020

Rin Tin Tin: The Life and the Legend, Susan Orlean, 2011